THE WORLD ON THE EVE OF WORLD WAR I ...

The murder of a wealthy, Jewish, Wall Street banker brings the world's most famous consulting detective face to face with death on the ill-fated liner TITANIC.

When an outspokenly anti-Zionist Jew, a convert to Mormonism is found dying in a Brooklyn gutter, a victim of ritual slashing in the same Masonic style as the JACK-THE-RIPPER case, SAM HARPER, the oldest friend of ARTHUR CONAN DOYLE and the man who served as the prototype for SHERLOCK HOLMES, is hurled by mysterious circumstances into the case. Harper, living in exile in New York City, corresponds with Doyle in London.

Sharply critical of the licentious Prince of Wales prior to his ascent to the throne, Harper uncovers a Royal scandal behind the Ripper slayings involving the mysterious death of the Duke of Clarence (the Heir Presumptive) and the Masonic brethren of his father, the Prince of Wales. Exiled to America to silence his criticism of the men who come to power when Edward VII ascends the throne, Harper is an idealist-turned-cynic over his appalling discoveries in the Royal household.

Doyle, one of many famous British figures practicing spiritualism and the occult, invites Harper to join him in solving mankind's greatest mystery — the secret of what lies beyond the grave. This joint venture of two fine minds takes an unexpected turn when Isaac Fenster is found dying with his throat ritually slashed. Before expiring Fenster alerts Harper to the danger to the former Prime Minister when he warns: "Balfour will die if he is not warned."

Harper seeks the assistance of JACQUES FUTRELLE, the only author of scientific crime detection stories to rival those of Doyle, as well as that of NELLIE BLY, feminist and the world's most famous woman reporter, of "RED EMMA" GOLDMAN, Russian radical charged by many with complicity in the assassination of President McKinley, and, finally, that of TEDDY ROOSEVELT.

But the final secret of the case is only revealed when Harper seeks the aid of and becomes emotionally involved with Cornelia St. James, the gorgeous secretary to the victim.

How Doyle and Harper then discover the attempt to murder ARTHUR BALFOUR, ex-Prime Minister and the driving force behind the BALFOUR DECLARATION, the British policy to create a Jewish homeland in Palestine is narrated, and how each finds his own solution to their original spiritual odyssey is told as the book reaches its climax in the sinking of the luxurious passenger liner TITANIC.

Detailed discussion of the Spiritualism and Occultism of Doyle and the Mormonism of the victim. Authentic background of the circumstances leading up to World War I both in the U.S. and abroad; the British-German economic rivalry, the Red Scare in the U.S., the Bolshevik agitation in Russia, and how two courageous men strove in vain to avert the unspeakable tragedy of World War.

How, on the eve of the first total global conflict, in which over 20 millions would die leaving a legacy of hatred still alive in our time, a world went into moral bankruptcy. Epitomized by the sinking on its maiden voyage of the largest, most luxurious ocean liner ever built. An event which shook the world and took over 1500 people to their deaths, as the WEALTHY claimed seats in the too-few lifeboats, leaving hundreds, including HARPER and FUTRELLE to perish in the freezing water of the NORTH ATLANTIC.

One of them survived. WHICH OF THEM PERISHED AND WHY???

THE SECRET CONAN DOYLE CORRESPONDENCE

Edited by

Leslie Vernet Harper

Inscription in the journal of Samuel Harper dated 27 October 1921 (his 62nd birthday).

"Time is the great discoverer, and, Truth is the daughter of Time, not of authority . . ."

THE IDEA OF PROGRESS
By John Bagnell Bury

1   2   3   4   5   6   7   8   9   10

ISBN: 0-935927-77-8 (paperback)
Library of Congress Catalog Card Number: 85-45779

First published in the U.S.A. by
Hascom Publishers Inc., P.O. Box 1396, Provo, UT 84603

Hascom books are also available at discounts in bulk quantity for industrial or sales-promotional use. For details write to:

    Hascom Publishers Inc.
    Premium Marketing Div.
    P.O. Box 1396
    Provo, UT 84603

Library of Congress Cataloguing-in-Publication Data

    Harper, Leslie Vernet, 1904-1984
        The secret Conan Doyle correspondence
        1.   Doyle, Arthur Conan, Sir, 1859-1930, in fiction, drama,
        poetry, etc. I. Title.
        PS 3558 .A624793S4   1986   813'.54   85-27060

Editor's Note

Wherever possible the intention has been followed in preparing this manuscript to quote verbatim from materials written or dictated by the principals. This is not to say that huge amounts of correspondence regarded as irrevelant to the main thrust of the story line have not been excluded. But the wishes expressed by my father before his death were that a work be prepared which would describe the essentials of how Samuel Harper and, at the time, the world's most famous author, Arthur Conan Doyle, decided to pool their efforts in solving mankind's most impenetrable and most important mystery, that of what exists beyond the grave, and of the dangerous secrets unearthed by them in their search. Secrets which even now, as you read this, threaten world peace. Secrets over which men in power will quite readily commit murder. Harper was, if you will forgive a daughter's irresistable temptation to express what father would have been too modest to state, the most highly respected consulting detective to the central constabularies of five countries, and the prototype followed by Doyle in creating the character of Sherlock Holmes. To the extent that it has been necessary for the editor's presence to be felt, it is regretted and every attempt has been made to minimize interruptions of this kind. But it must be borne in mind that the materials as they came from the hands of their authors were not originally intended to be integrated into a story possessing all the necessary elements to give a presentation the compelling qualities literature must possess to hold a reader's attention. If, therefore, in the process of employing actual materials it has also been necessary for the editor to supply continuity from time to time, or to elucidate what are frequently 19th Century references with which the average reader might be too young to be familiar, this is lamentable but unavoidable. The materials used represent the true voices of these extraordinary men and nothing has been fictionalized, although dialogue in a number of cases has been reconstructed after the fact by Samuel Harper employing shorthand notes taken at the time to refresh his recollection. While most of the material has been made available by the principals or their heirs, gracious and generous individuals too numerous (or for reasons of international diplomacy, impossible) to mention have also contributed invaluable assistance of many kinds. What emerges is a picture of the world as the slow-moving Victorian ways were giving way to the fast-paced change of the science-dominated modern era, as the nations were about to be sucked into the vortex of World War I, and of the forces building to a climax, forces still at work in the modern world which must be recognized and accommodated if the world is ever to know true peace. Insofar as it has been necessary for any presence to be felt other than that of Samuel Harper and Arthur Conan Doyle and those other individuals they themselves saw fit to mention, the reader is requested to accept the apologies of the Editor, and the indulgence of all who accord the viewpoints of these great men a hearing is necessarily requested.

Leslie Vernet Harper, Editor
April 15, 1934 (The 22nd anniversary of the sinking of the Titanic)

Foreword

(Written at the Editor's request by Samuel Harper as his introduction to the present work which he reviewed and approved just before his death.)

I would be lying if I said I had even the slightest premonition of what was to come. Jacques Futrelle and I were engaged in a rollicking banter with Doyle; the latter charging me with having kept the best of my cases for Futrelle. Jacques alternately agreeing with Doyle to join in the friendly joshing the huge Celt was administering to me, and then again complaining that I was but a burnt-out shell by the time Doyle 'turned me loose on the colonies.' And a bottle of vintage champagne for Doyle, vichy water for me (on the wagon) and for Jacques who is allergic to alcohol, caviar and a number of Havana cigars (Doyle) were consumed in celebration of the departure of Jacques and me on the spanking new White Star monster liner Titanic. Words are inadequate to convey the awesome impact of that enormous floating palace — the epitome in every respect of the biggest and most lavish the western world had to offer in material luxury. In an era idolatrously committed to the proposition that science unquestionably could overcome every obstacle standing between mankind and Utopia, the Titanic was living, dynamic proof of this utopian ideal. Perhaps that is why the grisly outcome of her maiden voyage changed us all, as well as the entire world, in unfathomably deep ways. Rarely, in my experience, does a single event, however stupendous, symbolize in a meaningful way, the most significant developments in an entire culture. Without doubt, however, the sinking of the Titanic was such a pregnant event. And the disgraceful way the lifeboats, in some cases only half full of first class passengers, abandoned second and steerage class to their watery fate only heightened the world's perception of the moral bankruptcy of the upper classes. The death of the Titanic tipped the scales in favor of those who, like historian Oswald Spengler, looked for the 'going under of the West.' And it fatally shook the confidence of the optimists, those who thought it possible to resolve mankind's dilemmas through science without any moral improvement in man himself. These really had little else left once science failed. It was this post-Christian belief in science that sustained the West's momentum after the abandonment of its commitment to evangelize the world, the laying down of the 'white man's burden' as my good friend Ruddy Kipling termed it when he urged the U.S. to carry on where Britons were leaving off in his (promptly rejected) advice to Americans. Now, the sinking of the 'unsinkable' Titanic having demonstrated the inadequacy of the science alternative, there remained only what a majority viewed as unworkable — the need for mankind to live the Christian ideal. The post-Christian collapse of Western Civilization was thus concluded by many to be inevitable. But not a shadow of fear passed our minds at the time. Interestingly though, I was moved, and why I shall never guess, to tell both Futrelle and Doyle that neither had yet been made privy to the facts of my most extraordinary case. Futrelle, the first chronicler of my exploits from the time I was forced to exile myself from my beloved homeland to America. And Doyle whose tales of the adventure of Sherlock

Holmes were, up to the time of my departure in 1908 in a belated aftershock of the Ripper slayings, in many instances based on my cases. This revelation occasioned additional badinage at my expense and I now recall, a strange, almost eerie reaction from Doyle, who, as many of you know, was always prone to seek a mystical portent in anything he deemed to be out of the ordinary. I believe, as I view matters now in retrospect, that Doyle's strange reaction to my disclosure that I had concealed from him, that unparalleled lover of the bizarre and exotic, my most unusual adventure, was the only untoward occurrence associated with the departure on April 10, 1912 of the Titanic from Southampton on her maiden voyage. It was somewhat later that Doyle, modern Manichean that he was, admitted to me that as he departed the ship as it prepared to put to sea, he was full of misgiving for her fate and mine, convinced in the depths of his Celtic mysticism that she was meant to sink to deny him some great secret essential to his salvation. And for once, in a long lifetime of metaphysical speculation, he was absolutely right. For with the death of Titanic, the great man-made fish, was born the modern world, a world of hellish wars in which the souls of men would be tried, a world which would ultimately have to choose between the fish, the symbol of Christ's message in the ancient world and Titanic, the failed, science-driven Utopian ideal.

Letter to Arthur Conan Doyle
from Samuel Harper

June 30, 1908 (New York City)

Dear Arthur:

The green patina gracing the copper roof of this fine hotel beckoned familiarly to us as we drove up Fifth Avenue. Across the street General Sherman riding the same valiant steed still comports himself in ungentlemanly fashion in making the lady Victory walk.

Your letter awaited me when Tony, Leslie and I checked in at the Plaza on June 1st. It has taken me the intervening time between then and now to formulate an answer. Indeed, even the decision whether to respond at all was most difficult. I would be lying to say that there isn't a rich measure of resentment over what has transpired. But you've asked me how I feel about it all, and I shall attempt an answer as much for the therapeutic value it may have to talk about it as to enter my side in the record which I suppose to be the purpose which prompts your request.

I will respond now, close after my exile, but I reserve the right to revise all my observations and conclusions if time and deeper reflection lead me to make any significant modifications. First, I must say that if the phlegmatic nature of the British working classes is all that has kept our nation from being torn apart by class hatreds as has happened on the Continent, no credit is due whatever to the aristocracy. Every form of perversion be it sexual, economic or social has quite readily been inflicted on the poor by those whose titles and privileges are theoretically and historically derived from mother Church. If any fault is to be found with the poor it can only be that they sold themselves quite readily to the rapacity and lust of their betters. Preferably that than to starve, I'm sure they feel. But there are at least 80,000 prostitutes plying their trade in London as I write. In a city of 6.6 million, that means one young girl in ten is selling herself. Instead of our wealth, we have tithed the flower of our womanhood. What single statistic could tell us more about the morals and economic justice of a professedly Christian nation?

Many a Saxon have I heard vociferate that the low morals of the British aristocracy derive from the Norman Conquest which saddled us with the feudal class system of France, replacing the more democratic Saxon system. A convenient rationalization for, in truth, both Saxon and Norman profess Christianity and neither has hesitated to grind the faces of the poor.

An apologist such as Adam Smith can rationalize the vicious excesses of the Industrial Revolution. But give me one Robert Owen for a thousand Smith's. Sad that he failed, for Owen alone saw that looking out for those he employed was not only Christian and humane, but made good business sense also, Arthur, old friend.

Be that as it may, the most appalling aspect of the entire Duke of Clarence affair was that these moral bankrupts were not the poor or even aristocrats,

1

but members of the Royal family itself.

There were those that rejoiced over the fact that Victoria and Albert were as morally straight as George IV was libertine. Indeed, the crown, at least, was redeemed of the charge of immorality due to the Queen's circumspect nature, but the nobility as a whole was not one whit better under her reign than they had been.

And the heir apparent was as indiscreet (to use a polite word) as any before him. But the Duke of Clarence not only disgraced the Royal Family by involving himself in the male brothel fiasco called "the Cleveland Street affair" but then, under the licentious influence of Walter Sickert, a promising artist but moral profligate, in whose care Princess Alexandra placed the Prince to give him relief from the brutal treatment accorded him by his father, the Prince of Wales, contracted a marriage to a Roman Catholic, an ignorant commoner, without (obviously) the knowledge or consent of the Queen. Indeed, I wonder if the current popularity of Sickert's paintings amongst the intelligentsia of the art world is not largely a result of the rumors amongst the nobility of his involvement in the murders.

It may seem like a digression, but as I worked on the Ripper case, I was increasingly reminded of a case I worked on in Italy a number of years ago. You may recall it. A British nobleman resident in Verona, was charged with the murder of a beautiful Italian peasant girl who worked in his kitchen. I was able to prove that the true murderer was a young parish priest to whom the young girl quite readily gave herself though all the blandishments of the British nobleman could not woo her into his bed.

The point is that to the religious person even sexual consortium can be granted to a priest without the sinner feeling sinful in his heart. And that is precisely how the British lower classes have given themselves body and soul to the nobility. They have accorded the nobility the same sacred standing that Italian peasant girl gave to the parish priest.

And in a nation that only recently, and in a very real sense has never entirely abandoned, the idea of divine right of kings, there is more than a slight similarity in the two circumstances.

The British common folk have truly accorded the nobility a religious obeisance. And in a case involving, as the Ripper case did, the order of Freemasons, a group who regard themselves as a holy priesthood, is it the least source of wonder I should be reminded of the one case as I worked on the other?

Doyle, old boy, the poor trollops who knew of the Duke of Clarence's wedding and of the issue of that union, a little daughter, and as a consequence met their fate under the scalpel of the Prince of Wales' Physician in Netley's hansom, believed they merely were holding a trump card to pry loose enough blackmail to end their days in comfort. I doubt they dreamed that they were shaking the very throne, and with it the privileged positions of all the Prince of Wales' Masonic brethren. How little the ordinary people of the world dream to what degree this mysterious organization controls the destiny of mankind. Or what crimes have been committed by those invoking the Masonic name spuriously.

2

Henry James once observed that " . . . an aristocracy is bad manners organized." He was too kind by half.

How, I've asked myself ten thousand times, could the worthless types who run our nation, collar the lower classes as they have? On the whole, the British working classes are fair-minded and hard-working, moral and upright. That being so, how could they tolerate a ruling group so morally depraved? Even more, accord them incredible privilege in the face of their obvious unworthiness? It is not an easy question to answer.

What does all the pomp and circumstance, to which the British above all other nations are devoted, mean to the poor bloke to whom, from one point of view, it represents but increased taxes on his all-too-meager wage? I have only been able to conclude that at the deepest level of the British consciousness, and quite apart from the worthiness or unworthiness of individual members of the nobility, the British masses pay obeisance to a sacred order of things, to a holy priesthood that the nobility hold in a British tradition so old its origins are lost in the mists of antiquity.

In this light, the masses hold on to a concept of a sacred order of things in British life which once was righteous and which, perhaps (in their deepest wishes and prayers) will once again be restored to its holy state.

This accords well with the thinking of the two million or so Englishmen in the British-Israel group who with total conviction, though considerably less proof, assure themselves the British are the Lost Ten Tribes of Israel. One need only consult, among many other sources, the Epistle of Gildas or the Venerable Bede or (more recently) the Archbishop of York whom I heard address the Palestine Exploration Fund a few years back in terms which unmistakably indicated his conviction like that of so many before him that the British are Israel. Be it true or false, it would, if true, at least offer a plausible explanation for this otherwise unexplained and perhaps unexplainable phenomenon. One is practically forced to postulate something of such magnitude to account for the incredible commitment of the British populace to the preservation of the institutions of the crown and the royal retinue. Were it not a sacred structure would it not long since have been swept away?

But enough! Let us just say that deeply as I love my native land, the Ripper case was the last straw. I've seen too much of the depravity, the seamy underside of British life, especially at the highest levels of power to be surprised that I've now been exiled as a direct consequence of the murderous propensities of those nearest to the throne. I almost don't care.

Save for the inconvenience (and perhaps I lie to myself as I say it), I don't care a fig that my countrymen must 'struggle on without me.' Yes, I dearly love home, all of it, even the London slums. And I wouldn't hesitate to stay no matter how many high-born scoundrels swore my demise if I remained.

But in the last analysis, I have left because I too, like the lowliest toiler in the London muck, believe the crown to represent something much more than any incumbent on the throne, however unworthy he might be.

New York receives me well. There are demands here for my services that long preceded my recent departure from Fair Albion. It just isn't home.

Tony is not at all well. Her illness deepens and I know that she is aware her condition is terminal. How am I to comfort Leslie when she goes?

Yours,

Sam

P.S. I enclose a copy of the dossier on General Benson and the Stone of Scone case to refresh your recollection of our past encounters with British-Israelism. Recently made the acquaintance of Nellie Bly in connection with an important assignment. Hopefully will be able to tell you the circumstances of our meeting some day soon.

Dossier
Brigadier General Richard A. Benson

Born: Bombay 1825
Graduated: Sandhurst 1847
Father: General John E. Benson, Sandhurst 1822, retired as Major General 1852.
Description and excerpts from Service background: Benson is tall and lean. Appears to be in good condition, but has a history of malaria and cholera contracted during service in Africa and India. Appearance may therefore be deceiving. Carries an enormous scar on his left cheek from a Zulu spear acquired in disastrous Battle of Isandhlwana (1879), which was the worst defeat ever administered to Her Majesty's forces by a native army and which resulted in defeat of Disraeli's government. Was left for dead by the Zulus, was found in tall grass by a young Zulu shepherd who nursed him back to health from his many wounds. Returned to Blighty, was awarded VC, promoted to Brigadier and mustered out. His father was awarded posthumous VC for valor in Bengal Mutiny.
Date of interrogation: June 1, 1896
Place: Wellington Barracks, at request of Elliott Townsend of Home office after arrest of Benson as instigator of the affair which culminated in the theft of the Stone of Scone (or Jacob's Pillar Stone) from Coronation Seat at Westminster Abbey.
TRANSCRIBED BY: David Skaggs, Court Stenographer
Samuel Harper: General Benson, I've reviewed your military record and I'm aware of the great distinction with which you've served and the look of utmost resignation tinged with fatigue upon your countenance tells me how thoroughly you have been interrogated since your capture —
General Benson: Indeed, Mr. Harper, you are the ninth or tenth person to have at it. But pay no mind, I was resigned to all that before this was undertaken.
Samuel Harper: I dare say — it is quite apparent to even the most amateur sleuth that no serious effort was made to conceal your trail. Thus, one concludes the objective was more a display of some purpose rather than the theft of the relic. Let's see if I can tell you what your purpose was using simple deduction.
General Benson: Please do. I may thereby be comforted to know that at least one party in the nation did not miss our point.
Samuel Harper: Rest assured there are many, if I am not mistaken.
General Benson: Scarcely enough. The faithful we had already. It's converts we're after.
Samuel Harper: Precisely.
General Benson: But few of these —
Samuel Harper: There are sure to be a few. You began with two million or so by my estimates. But hardly enough in a nation of thirty million.

5

General Benson: You know our organization?
Samuel Harper: Every well informed person does. British-Israelism is by no means new. The rather more militant approach British-Israelism has adopted since mid-century is — not only new, but to many — the vast majority — it is, if not disturbing, then merely an anachronistic bother.
General Benson: All prophecied by the Scriptures you surely know.
Samuel Harper: One possible interpretation, of course, and by stealing the Stone of Scone, anciently known as Jacob's Pillow or Jacob's Pillar Stone you thought to bring about the awakening of the English to their Israel identity and thus to a recommitment to Israel's Holy Priesthood role among the nations.
General Benson: Precisely — or at the very least to keep alive this awareness until God, in his own time, brings us to our knees.
Samuel Harper: I understand, but regrettably you've stated nothing new and to the unbelievers it all sounds like the same old theme of Aryan elitism, privilege, etc.
General Benson: Do I take it you agree with our basic premise?
Samuel Harper: Only as a possible hypothesis and surely not capable of complete verification as your people believe it to be.
General Benson: Then you don't really believe it.
Samuel Harper: I've seen a hundred men hanged on less evidence than we possess that the British had Hebrew origins, but that's irrelevant. Were your proof perfect you might, emphasize might, get a hearing.
General Benson: Wasn't it David Hume who said, "A wise man proportions his belief to the evidence"? Why should a people demand perfect proof of the greatest honor —
Samuel Harper: Perhaps an honor to some, but merely a burden to most.
General Benson: Honor or burden, facts don't cease to exist because you ignore them. You can't change reality.
Samuel Harper: It is a reality that exists only in your imagination.
General Benson: The belief that the Anglo-Saxon is Israel was already old in the time of Charlemagne.
Samuel Harper: Is it not strange that the Germans have lost all recollection?
General Benson: Not at all, the course of history did not see develop in their favor the characteristics set forth in Scripture as signifying Israel. The German Higher Critics attack the Scriptures as the source of British power.
Samuel Harper: In other words — no Empire — no Israel.
General Benson: Something like that.
Samuel Harper: How strange that until the unification of Germany and the threat to British hegemony the British-Israelism experts didn't exclude the Germans from the ranks of modern Israel.
General Benson: I miss your point.
Samuel Harper: Simply this — your British-Israelism thinkers seem to adapt their doctrines pretty well to the needs of the Empire. With German unification and the challenge to British power they suddenly were excluded from the elite group your people call Israel.
General Benson: Prophesies clearly indicate Israel will be known by her Empire.

Samuel Harper: Not an impossible construction I dare say, and the Germans seem dead set on building their own empire, but if the Scriptures identify Israel in the modern world, why any need for the pseudoscientific business, the strained etymology that attempts to establish a perfect trail of evidence from ancient Israel to modern Britain?

General Benson: Because the Scriptures are not acceptable evidence to most of the world.

Samuel Harper: Neither is the pseudoscientific speculation you offer to cater to the non-believer.

General Benson: I can't contest you there, if the evidences of Britain's role as a royal priesthood were any clearer they'd bite you.

Samuel Harper: There is none so blind as him who will not see. All British heraldry accords with the hypothesis of an Israelitish origin as well as hundreds of other indicia. Why do the symbols associated with the Twelve Tribes as set forth in Genesis 49:3-24 recur and recur in the heraldry of the Royal Houses of Europe?

General Benson: I've often thought it might be a case of racial amnesia.

Samuel Harper: An interesting observation. But amnesia is usually associated with trauma. If Israel's destiny is so glorious —

General Benson: Very simple. Israel's covenant at Sinai involved both responsibilities and rewards. And penalties for non-compliance. The British have received fully the blessings and to a certain extent have accepted the duties, but for generations now they have been abandoning the responsibilities. Now, Britain is Christian in name only. I think the outward evidence of Britain's apostasy came when Lord Rothschild was sworn into Parliament without having to take the Christian oath.

Samuel Harper: I regret to say British-Israelism appears to me to be a veritable hotbed of anti-Jewish feelings as well as all those who simply 'know' the white man is superior to the colored races.

General Benson: In every movement there will be an element of the alienated, the ne'er-do-well who need a scapegoat. And is not the whole world conscious of race as of nothing else?

Samuel Harper: Yes, but it represents an interesting reversal, in a sense, for British-Israelism to be anti-semitic. I see British-Israelism as a natural outgrowth of Puritanism. I'm sure you're well aware that far from being anti-semitic, the Puritans urged Cromwell to readmit the Jews to Britain as a pre-requisite condition to their conversion which had to precede, in their understanding, the Second Coming.

General Benson: You're quite right, but that was a long time ago. Our people are aware now that the Jew wasn't to be converted, at least, not now, and that many claiming the title of Jew are not of the blood of Israel.

Samuel Harper: You refer, of course, to the Khazars.

General Benson: I am amazed at your familiarity with such esoteric matters.

Samuel Harper: A dear friend specializes in that sort of thing, General Benson, but your act in stealing the Stone of Scone is simply one of a thousand concrete reflections of the anguish of the British race and of the entire Western world. The Hebrew tradition, precursor to Christianity is, and always has been a source of great difficulty. Who wants to believe the Creator could choose a single people for his purposes? No one in the world objects to the idea of a Chosen People — if they're the ones chosen, and at one time or another just about every race has laid claim to this distinction. But in an age of democracy, where all men are supposed to be equal, it takes a brave man indeed to assert the idea of a Chosen People. The clergy of the established churches were the first to withdraw from the battle. Their flocks weren't slow to follow. No sir — it will take a lot more than the theft of a stone to reawaken this people to so onerous a duty.

General Benson: Life runs in cycles Mr. Harper. And the British people oscillate between Hebrew asceticism and Babylonian licentiousness. We're in the latter now. Just as the rapaciousness of Charles I gave way to the Puritanism of Cromwell's regime which in turn gave way to the Restoration; just as the voluptuary regime of George IV gave way to the Victorian era, so will that upright monarch's influence give way to the Prince of Wales' license.

Samuel Harper: All deeply interesting General, and I am sincere in my conviction that the British are an Israel people even though I could never prove it with Euclidean precision. But I am just as sincerely of the belief that many other Israelites are to be found leavening the loaf, as it were, in every nation on earth. I see no organized group, other than yours, and the Jews who state Israel's identity to have any relevance in the modern world. And British-Israelism is not a true movement in the organizationally effective sense. So that even if one believes, there is but frustration at the lack of a means to make one's belief count in a serious way. You have no church and your members are dispersed among many churches. So there is no functioning entity or group to whom the believer can repair for organizational strength and direction. And no excommunication for defectors.

General Benson: There is such a group, but they seem to attach no greater importance to Israel identity than they do to their own concept of the priesthood, surely not as much. And any concept of an elite is rejected as is the tendency to conspire with the anti-Jewishness so strong among many British-Israel people. Indeed, there seems to be a great deal of sympathy amongst these peoples for the Jews because of the dreadful persecutions they've both endured.

Samuel Harper: How interesting. What group would that be?

General Benson: The Mormons. In fact one of their Articles of Faith declares their belief in the restoration of the Ten Tribes.

Samuel Harper: The Mormons — oh yes, I've heard of them and I've seen their missionaries in the streets of London. An interesting fact that they recognize Israel's covenant but make no fetish of it, no basis for a claim of superiority and elitism as has so plagued the British.

General Benson: They've carried their appeal to many of the British. But they find few converts in the ranks of British-Israelism.

Samuel Harper: Is that true? How very interesting. But I must get to the primary purpose of my visit.

General Benson: Please do Mr. Harper. What would that be?

Samuel Harper: General Benson, were you assigned to the British legation in Vienna in 1877?

General Benson: I was indeed. I served there immediately before the duty in Africa which preceded my discharge from the service. In fact, events which transpired during my tenure there were decisive in bringing me to the conviction of the ongoing fulfillment of prophecy and that once out of service I must devote myself to the task of awakening Britons to the perilous path our nation treads.

Samuel Harper: Which events? — If I may ask.

General Benson: You may Mr. Harper, but I am not free to discuss them with you as they involve state secrets to which I was privy.

Samuel Harper: I possess here a directive from Her Majesty the Queen, from Lord Beaconsfield, former Prime Minister and from the present Prime Minister, Mr. Gladstone, releasing you to discuss those matters. You will note Her Majesty's seal upon the envelope.

General Benson: (Having inspected letter and read its contents) What is it you desire to know Mr. Harper?

Samuel Harper: Her Majesty's government is deeply concerned that the continued deterioration of the Ottoman Empire will, sooner or later, force our nation to establish one or more bases in the Levant to defend British interests from Russian and German encroachment as Turkish power declines.

General Benson: Quite — but you've simply restated primary British policy regarding the Eastern Question for the last century.

Samuel Harper: True enough, but you were witness to a unique event in Vienna were you not?

General Benson: Unique? In what sense?

Samuel Harper: Did you not substantially implement the steps directed by Prime Minister Disraeli in his efforts to determine the political impact in Europe of any attempt Britain might make to establish a Jewish homeland in Palestine?

General Benson: (After a considerable pause) Why does Her Majesty's government —

Samuel Harper: Did you not select the printer for and those individuals who should disseminate a document recommending such a move just before the Congress of Berlin that was to divide the spoils after the Russian war against Turkey?

General Benson: Your facts are not precisely straight, but none of this can come as any great surprise to those who sent you.

Samuel Harper: True enough, General Benson. But in spite of the uproar that document caused, and the Prime Minister's denial of any knowledge of its source, there remains a small but influential group in the seats of power who would associate any British move toward creating a base of influence in the Eastern Mediterranean with a broader policy of creating a Jewish homeland in Palestine.

General Benson: I had hoped they had learned their lesson —

Samuel Harper: Apparently not General. But those people are keenly interested to know if your group's action in stealing the Stone of Scone bore any relationship whatever to what you know about Lord Beaconsfield's desires in the Holy Land?

9

General Benson: Not in any sense those people would understand.
Samuel Harper: Please explain yourself General. Your response is of the utmost importance.
General Benson: I happen to know there are those in power who would draw on the influence with the British middle class that the Scriptures hold. They know they can convince the masses of voters that the creation of a Jewish homeland is the fulfillment of prophecy and can cause the party in power and the nation to appear to be conforming itself to the will of Almighty God with powerful impact on the sense of rectitude of ordinary people. But their knowledge of the Scriptures is superficial and their desire to employ the attitude of religious Britons in furtherance of their own policies is cynical and calculated, and will work a great evil. They will indeed fulfill prophecy but not in the sense they believe, and they will throw thousands possibly millions of innocent Jews and a few not-so-innocent ones into a flaming cauldron.
Samuel Harper: Your concerns do you great honor sir, but can you be more explicit?
General Benson: Nothing mankind can do will frustrate the unfolding of prophecy. But only Israel, the true progeny of Jacob, that is, the Anglo-Saxons themselves, can have a legal and historical claim to the Holy Land. The displaced Jews of Eastern Europe are the children of the Khazar Empire who are merely converts to Judaism. They may one day lay claim to and even take up residence there and that event would have to fulfill some aspect of prophecy. We British-Israel people as you call us, believe, that since the Jew rejects Christ's messianic mission, that such event should it occur will perfectly fulfill Luke 19:27 which commands:
"But those mine enemies, which would not that I should reign over them, bring hither and slay them before me."
Nor could anything as pertaining some of those who pull the strings behind the facade of British power be clearer than Revelation 2:9 and 3:9:
"I know the blasphemy of them which say they are Jews, and are not, but are the synagogue of satan."
Samuel Harper: Why could not a convert to Judaism claim title to Palestine?
General Benson: Under what legal system of which you are aware can conversion to a particular religious system give rise to the blood inheritance of another?
Samuel Harper: I see your point though I'm sure my principals don't, for many powerful men are urging this policy upon Her Majesty's government and she herself is persuaded by their reasoning believing, as she does, that the Jews, the Khazar-Jews that is, are of the blood of Israel.
General Benson: No one can be more aware of this than I. You are quite right, I was also at Vienna on the day Russia declared war on Turkey. It was April of 1877. The Queen had only recently followed Disraeli's misguided urgings and permitted herself to be declared Empress of India. My good father, I am sure, rolled over in his grave in far off Bengal. He won a posthumous VC for his valor in the Mutiny, but he had always regretted the supercilious way in which second raters from back home destroyed a sound

10

working relationship of mutual respect he had known — we all had known — with the Indians in the old days. I remember it all too well because I was forced to cancel my leave. I was to be the chief referee at the first All-England Lawn Tennis Championship at Wimbledon that year. My good friend Spence Gore went on to win it, but I was much too busy with affairs of Empire back in Vienna.

Samuel Harper: How different really was it that Disraeli should urge the claim of Jews for a return to Zion, with Russia justifying her moves against the Ottoman Empire on behalf of Rumanians, Serbs, Bulgars and Montenegrans? The Czar's 'Slavic Brothers' were energized to Russia's ends by such rhetoric. Beaconsfield was neither taken too seriously, nor too lightly when he asserted in one of his many forgettable novels that "Race is everything, there is no other truth." He stated in our race-conscious era only what every man knew to be true. If Russia was to carve up Turkey on behalf of Slavs, Disraeli would use similar reasoning to further British moves to feast at the carcass of the sick man of Europe. Even the Prince of Wales, who lost no love for Beaconsfield, conceded it was devilishly clever diplomacy.

General Benson: Agreed, but let's stick to the facts for now, interpret them as we might. Lord Beaconsfield, I gather, prepared a document which he proposed to have published under some other author's name entitled THE JEWISH PROBLEM AS AN ORIENTAL PROBLEM, I recollect. This document in addition to discussing briefly the tensions relating to the declining power of the Turks and the forthcoming demise of the Ottoman Empire also launched the idea of creating a homeland for the Jews in Palestine. It was necessary to have some member of the British Embassy in Vienna assume the responsibility of selecting the person whose name would appear as author, a printer, etc. I can't over-emphasize what an extraordinarily difficult assignment Lord Beaconsfield handed us, in fact, I'm not sure he fully understood the complexities.

Samuel Harper: I think I perceive some of the pitfalls but please assume I don't and enlighten me.

General Benson: My pleasure, of course. First, the concept of creating many small nations out of ethnic groups was itself a matter of hot debate in government circles. Constant talk of creating once again a separate nation of Poland was cause to give rise to the most vehement arguments pro and con. Those opposed feeling that the principle of creating many small nations, each theoretically sovereign but in actuality required to be a satellite economically and politically to a major power and thus allied to such by treaty, simply increased geometrically the chances that each clash of nationalities gave rise to the danger of war between the major powers. Traditional rivalries of the most inconsequential nature could cause a major conflagration. This, of course, was enhanced by the newly found freedom of the press and modern means of transit and rapid communication of information to anywhere in the world. Weapons of mass destruction were increasing at an alarming rate in a world where men still thought essentially in chivalric codes where men battled one on one. The incongruity threatened Europe with total war over and over.

11

Samuel Harper: I follow, and the Jewish issue exacerbated an already explosive matter.

General Benson: Quite. Even stranger, it is difficult for a non-Jew to comprehend the complexity of the issue of a Jewish homeland in the minds of Jews themselves. And it was ultimately this conflict which defeated Disraeli's secret moves as much as anything.

Samuel Harper: How so?

General Benson: It was necessary to select someone with good connections in high circles, someone who knew both Gentiles and Jews and was accepted by both. There were a number of these, to be sure, in Vienna which had a most liberal attitude with respect to the assimilation process. The one selected not only had to pick a phantom writer who would accept responsibility for the writing, meet the press, etc. but also a printer and a member of the press to leak the story to, etc. It was all botched, and I accept full responsibility, though I don't think the Prime Minister himself could have brought it off.

Samuel Harper: Do go on. Also, why Vienna?

General Benson: For reasons, I'm sure, that related to Austria's having no opposition to and no basic interest that was jeopardized by creation of such a state. Austria's only interest was Bosnia-Herzogovina. Germany had great interest in anything that smacked of entrenchment of British power and Disraeli's proposal involved the creation of a Jewish homeland under British rule. It was, of course, intended to protect Suez. Virulent anti-semitism as reflected in the German press and which had been fostered in the German universities for years would not permit serious consideration of such a project by Bismarck if he had wished to. But what finally blew the whole thing up was the conflict among Jews themselves on the issue of a Jewish homeland. Almost without exception, wealthy Jews were vehemently opposed. With but the most tenuous grasp on their social standings, whatever those might be in even the most liberal countries, the wealthy Jews did not wish to sacrifice their hard-earned social posture however slight. The displaced Eastern Jew, the largely Khazar Jew with no status, in many cases not even enough to eat, was therefore pitted against the so-called 'assimilated Jew.' Needless to say an assimilated Jew was, and had to be, chosen for the task. The printer he chose, also a Jew, leaked the document to a Jewish journalist who I am sure he thought would favor the project. But instead of favoring Disraeli's idea, he castigated it. A furor arose in Berlin and all of Europe, as you probably recall, inflaming latent and overt anti-Jewish feeling everywhere. Lord Beaconsfield beat a hasty retreat and ordered the project quashed. We, of course, officially denied all knowledge of the document, but there is no doubt the first major statesman to propose a Jewish homeland in Palestine was British and a Jew, Lord Beaconsfield himself.

Samuel Harper: Most enlightening and the project is still alive, is it not?

General Benson: Clearly so, or you wouldn't be here would you?

Samuel Harper: Very perceptive, General. So we come to the real question — was the theft by you and your band of British-Israel zealots aimed at the frustration of the British Policy in support of a Jewish homeland?

General Benson: You can tell Arthur Balfour for me we had as our objective but one thing — awakening the British to the covenant relationship they formed with Jehovah at Sinai. Any other project impinged by such an effort is but incidental to this main purpose.

Samuel Harper: You know full well that Balfour is but a front for men more powerful than he.

General Benson: Of course, and well they know that if the British ever learned that the Khazar-Jew has no valid claim to the Holy Land their policy would collapse.

Samuel Harper: What I take it you imply is that if the Englishman recognizes himself to be Israel, then the question 'who is the Jew'?

General Benson: Exactly. And when the Khazar is recognized as merely a convert to Judaism, with no blood relationship to Israel or valid inheritance in the Holy Land, then the British policy must fail.

Samuel Harper: I see then that your objectives do indeed jeopardize the interest of men in high seats of power whether that is your specific objective or not. You can be sure there will be no prosecution for your rather innocent 'crimes,' for publicity is the last thing these men desire your project to receive. The entire effort will be characterized as an effort by Scotsmen to gain recognition for their obscure movement for Scottish autonomy by returning the Stone to its original home.

General Benson: I understand Mr. Harper and I can only regret that for all the propaganda to the contrary, we do not have a free press.

Samuel Harper: I understand your desire for publicity, but that great blessing, which can fan the most puny and pusillanimous matter into a national issue, is accorded, when desires of our rulers can be enforced, only to those whose objectives accord with the policies of government. No characterization of your effort is intended, please let me add.

General Benson: Your comments are true enough and no offense is taken, but it is no less a tragedy for the Jews and the rest of mankind.

Samuel Harper: I dare say for mankind, but why the Jews?

General Benson: Hatred for the Jews is primarily, at least in the minds of the masses, because of their crucifixion of Jesus. It is the clearest thing of all that the Khazar Jews, who did not convert to Judaism, as near as the historians can estimate, until some seven or eight hundred years after Christ's death, surely had no responsibility for the crucifixion.

Samuel Harper: That may be true, but the Khazar, like anyone else, is free to receive the Savior. We all, in our various ways, reject Jesus. And we shall all, I suspect, pay the price.

General Benson: There may be hope for you Mr. Harper.

Samuel Harper: Kind of you to think so General. It is all a mystery to me, but mysteries are my bread and butter and your quest is not unlike mine. But I must reach my destination in my own way.

General Benson: Godspeed Mr. Harper, to you and our great nation.

Samuel Harper: Godspeed to you General Benson.

General Benson: Try to remember one thing Mr. Harper. There can be no civilization without Christianity and no Christianity without Christ's chosen priesthood — we are Israel, that chosen priesthood and denying it won't change the fact.

Samuel Harper: General, I hear again, as Britons will forever, I suppose, the siren song of England's divine mission, the dream that will never die.

General Benson: Long live the dream Mr. Harper.

END OF CONVERSATION AS RECORDED AND SWORN TO BY DAVID SKAGGS, PUBLIC COURT REPORTER.

Letter to Samuel Harper
from Arthur Conan Doyle
August 14, 1908 (London)

Dear Sam,

I am sorry to hear that Tony still does poorly. We had hoped the change of your new circumstances might improve her health. Give her our love.

I hope your period of exile will be brief, but while you are away I shall try to keep you informed about vital matters, at least as they might come to my knowledge. I'm sure the significance of Edward's visit to Roman Catholic Italy and the Pope after so many centuries of British working classes' animosity to Rome was not lost upon you. We may have discussed this briefly before your departure, though things were so hectic those last days you were here. He met with Nicholas II in Reval in early June to get a pledge from the Czar that conditions would ameliorate in Macedonia to improve relations with Turkey. Most ominous of all, the German Navy Bill was passed by the Reichstag which provides the financing for four more capital ships. There can be no doubt William II intends to challenge us on the sea, a policy he will soon announce publicly no doubt.

It may not mitigate the pain of your exile to know that others of your ken have experienced the same. I can recall the longing for home I felt during the time I spent at sea, like Melville a-whaling, in my medical school undergraduate years. Since I have achieved a degree of fame (or is it notoriety?) as a 'friend' of Sherlock Holmes, this monstrous creation having taken on a life of his own, my sea trips have been romanticized by others who would portray these undertakings as great frolics.

And while I concede we quaffed a few too many at times, and there was a bit of boisterous camaraderie in these drunken bouts, still for the most part it was homely, lonely, hard work and a great deal of homesickness. But enough! Self-pity is a despicable attribute to both of us.

Jean, my better half (by far) sends her very best and says to tell you the Samuel Harper rose flourishes in her greenhouse and she hopes you're doing at least half as well. We both hope Tony can get better, but if that's not possible, that her last days may be free of pain.

Your remarks, Sam, about the depravity of the nobility and the acquiescence of the working classes were nearly a verbatim quote of remarks of mine to the same effect in my last conversation with Kipling. I wish I could say that King Edward is grief-stricken over the entire affair which turned out so badly for you. Needless to say, such a reaction would reflect a degree of sensitivity to the rights of others that neither he nor the royal family, nor any significant part of the nobility display. Indeed, if they did, either the decadence of our rulers would not exist, or at least we might hope for their repentance. Such is not the case as you well know.

And surely if he possessed any sense of rectitude he would not have occasioned your departure on the spurious assertion that one so familiar with the truth of the Ripper case could not remain. Pure spite! Were your knowledge dangerous to the crown why wait from 1888 to 1908? It was with quite mixed feelings that I knelt before His Highness in the recent ceremony in which Edward touched his sword to my shoulder.

Those who rule this nation are bored with their voluptuous diversions and take enormous privilege and complete lassitude as an absolute right. As for the King, he is now much exercised with the entire German problem which, in his case, is as much a matter of being miffed at the cavalier treatment he receives from his nephew the Kaiser as it is the threat that nation poses to British hegemony.

Last October Joe Chamberlain's anti-German speech in Edinburgh resulted in a breakdown of negotiations toward an Anglo-German accord. I fear nothing will do but an eventual war. What a long way we've come since the days when Carlyle glorified Frederick the Great with not a cavil from anyone. Now Balfour takes time from his ineffable languor to write an introduction to Constable's forthcoming translation of von Trietschke's POLITICS, to make clear what deep exception he (and we) take to the German professor's demeaning attitude toward everything British. I wonder if Germany and England can deflect from this collision course. All the machinery of propaganda is being oiled to prepare the German common man for a coming war. And what a monstrous collision it must surely be if it ever happens.

If you don't already know, Sir Henry Rawlings, your guardian, has been awarded the Grand Cross of the Bath. I am sure you will be greatly pleased by the news. He was like a father to you and Myles for so long. He never failed in the pledge he gave your father to look after you two after your father's untimely demise. He is a dying breed, I regret to say. He stands for the very best that Britain has been able to offer by way of an exemplary life, insurmountable courage and brilliant leadership. They pooh-poohed his warnings in 1875 that England and Russia must collide repeatedly on the Indian subcontinent, but his prescience was established by events beyond doubt. Now, of course, Germany has replaced Russia as the major threat to British interests and Russia a potential ally. Were all the aristocracy like him we would be a greater nation in a better world.

My good Harper, you mention that you have made the acquaintance of Nellie Bly. That must surely have been interesting. She has been creating something of a sensational stir over there has she not?

I confess to you that I don't believe the British press is anywhere near the force for change in British life that the American press is there. I suspect you will agree that had our barons of Fleet Street not had a vested interest in preserving the status quo, the British common man would long since have been incensed at the utter depravity of much of the aristocracy. He might, almost surely would have, swept away the nobility, perhaps the crown itself.

You and I surely know that had the British press not suppressed the Cleveland Street scandal, it's possible the Ripper murders might never have occurred. As the German poet Heinrich Heine has said:

16

"In these times we fight for ideas, and newspapers are our fortresses."

Your remarks regarding the sacred background of the British nobility are noted with considerable interest. You also remark the fact, which I knew would not escape you, that the Masons, that most influential of all secret orders, is a self-declared priesthood and traces its genealogy (I'm told) back to the royal priesthood of Egypt. We could ask Kipling about this as he is big on Masonic. Remember Ruddy's reference to how Masonic membership saved the principal character from death at the hands of the natives who awaited the fulfillment of Alexander's promise that a Mason would come to lead them in his THE MAN WHO WOULD BE KING? How strangely similar to your feelings about the British-Israel groups and as you mention, the British love of tradition, for aren't our hoary rituals really a religious liturgy, more often than not embodying the direct involvement of the clergy?

Ever since you took me to task for what you characterized as 'gross inaccuracies' in STUDY IN SCARLET regarding the Mormons, I have been thinking of proposing a pact to you. Since we both seem to have a deep interest in the spiritual and the metaphysical, and are both interested in deciphering the deepest available mysteries, why don't we apply our talents to this end? Let us explore together that mystery of all mysteries — what lies beyond the grave? Is this just a silly notion of a no longer young man who not too slowly approaches the inevitable sepulchre we all face and therefore feels a certain urgency in the pursuit of the answer to this question?

I look forward to your response.

Your friend,

Arthur

Letter to Arthur Conan Doyle
from Samuel Harper

October 2, 1908 (New York City)

Dear Arthur,

Tony continues to do poorly and I am slowly preparing Leslie for the bad news. We are doing all we can but as you well know, one can quite quickly reach the limits of medical science. And once one has exhausted the meager remedies available, one can but pray.

Were the weather here better, were it sunny with blue skys and fleecy clouds I might not view your proposition with quite so favorable an impression. But we are not enjoying the beautiful autumn weather for which New York City is noted and I view the gray cloudy day lugubriously. Swedenbourg, the gloomy Swedish philosopher and mystic has nothing on me at the moment.

I am fervently in agreement that we should enter a compact such as you describe in yours of August. The 'pursuit of the metaphysical' as you like to term it, has, I am sure, a considerably different meaning for you and me. But whether we concern ourselves only with proving the existence and nature of life after death (which I am sure is your objective as manifested by your interest in spiritualism), or as in my case, whether any source is available to mankind to lead him to the light as the Western world once thought the Bible to do, I suppose is irrelevant. We both seek some deeper meaning to our lives than we presently feel and in that we have a lot in common, not only with each other, but with most of the human race.

You may, perhaps, gain keener understanding of where I stand, metaphysically speaking, at what I regard as the frontier between Knowledge and Faith. What I've learned in this life has given me no strong religious conviction, much as I envy those with a staunch belief like that of my father and Sir Henry. I have gained certain strong convictions about what is wrong with organized religion. Equally strong convictions regarding the fallacies of those who feel they (we) need no form of organized worship. But I confess I have found nothing I could liken in any way to what I've been led to think of as 'faith.'

Still, as a metaphysical matter, I am convinced that faith, whatever it is, must exist. Let me narrate an incident to you which shows how I arrived at this conclusion.

On a cold winter evening in December four or five years ago, Myles and I were sitting in front of a most welcome fire in the Drawing Room at the Diogenes Club sipping our after dinner brandies and engaged in a drifting conversation that bordered on the edge of our lapsing into utter silence. Indeed, there were long periods in which we said nothing at all, gazing into the fascinating flames enveloping a triumvirate of husky oak logs in the massive fireplace. The atmosphere was conducive to the flow of philosophical ideas although, as you are well aware, it is by no means easy to break the surface jocularity that Myles hides behind to get him to discuss anything more serious than the cricket scores.

Then Arthur, somehow the conversation turned to the question of religion. No doubt because Toby Rawlings had just died and both Myles and I were most fond of him whom we had lived with and whom we loved like a brother. I had attended the services for Toby that morning although Myles, due to pressing commitments, was unable to be present.

Suddenly and with no preamble, Myles looked from the fire into my eyes and remarked, "What manner of creator would place the secrets of life under the enormous, unknowable mass of fact, rumor and myth that conceals all our efforts to discover eternal truth? Surely none but an infinitesmally small number are equipped to sort fact from fancy were they so disposed. And Lord knows, not one in a thousand even seems to care. Perhaps I judge too much by our own contemporaries, but surely nothing will more quickly brand one as 'peculiar' in our society than an attempt to turn conversation toward a topic as serious as man's condition beyond the grave."

I recognized at once that Myles was affirming what I've known for some time, that he does not believe that any such being exists. He seems never to have shared the reverence our father, and after his death, our guardian Sir Henry evidenced. And for whatever reason, in spite of my inability to align myself with a religious viewpoint, I, unlike Myles, would prefer to share my father's attitude were it possible. At any rate, the human mind being the contrary thing it is, I immediately interpreted Myle's remark in opposite fashion to the one he intended. I asked myself: If there is a supremely just God, could he make the route to discovery of his nature and that of life after death so difficult and obscure that none but the most learned of men could hope to discover it? As I pondered this, I realized that infinite justice requires that a method must exist which even the simplest of God's creatures can discover. Such being the case, there must be a corollary to this fact: No amount of erudition and intelligence would suffice in one's search, indeed, it might be that the more knowledge one acquires the more one loses the simplicity required to come to an undertanding of the truth. These were most disturbing thoughts and yet they flow quite logically from the concept of a supremely just God. Disturbing, but perhaps unavoidable and irresistable.

Myles, I am sure Doyle, had no such intention, but he had inadvertently set in motion a train of thought that was to have an important effect on my life. I had no idea how it functions, but I was convinced that there must be a means by which all men, however simple their thought processes, must be able to arrive at a conviction of the truth. I was not prepared to term this 'faith,' indeed, I do not yet know what that term involves. But logic dictates that some means must exist by which we can all achieve an absolute conviction of God's existence and of his required code of behavior if such there be. If others call this faith, so be it. I cannot say I have yet discovered how the principle of faith works, but that there must be such a thing is as certain as the existence of a Supreme Being. There cannot be one without the other. And since I believe, for reasons I can't explain, that there is a God, then there must be faith. Perhaps our joint endeavor will produce for me what I have as yet not discovered. Having tried the route of knowledge and gotten no closer to the truth, perhaps I am ready for something less (or is it more?) demanding — utter simplicity.

Nothing speaks more eloquently of the arrogance of modern man nor of his essential, intellectual dishonesty than his attitude toward the learning of the past. If the assertions and opinions of the learned men of bygone eras in any way conflicts with the conception of modern man as the be all and end all of human progress, from the foggiest antiquity to the present, it is summarily rejected. Modern man sees himself as the pinnacle of human evolution and all creatures prior to his time as less noble and worthy of attention.

This is, of course, consistent with evolutionary doctrine which sees progress as beginning in the primeval slime with the development of a single cell which over eons of time evolved into the organism called man. Progress is therefore more or less a straight line ascending from the lowest depths to man's present 'lofty' pinnacle. The pernicious aspect of such doctrine, is lost on even the most objective of scientists. It permits all evidence in conflict with such a presumption to be rejected out of hand.

Modern man, in effect, defines himself to be superior and disqualifies all evidence to the contrary because it is not in accord with this definition. The logical absurdity of such an attitude need not even be discussed.

For whatever it's worth, Arthur, my feelings are that there is a most pernicious aspect to the 'theory' of evolution. Rest assured I do believe that organisms evolve but surely on a much shorter time frame than Darwin imagined, perhaps under the influence of the radiation of cosmic rays, and I don't agree that man evolved from a lower form. Nature does not proceed from disorder to order but rather the reverse. Grains of sand don't evolve into a rock; quite the opposite. Rocks break down into grains of sand. But my cavil with evolution as propounded by those who think man an ape is the damage it does to man's self-image. Well and patiently have you borne with me as I have unendingly expounded to you my conviction that a weak or negative self-image lies at the heart of every crime.

If all creatures began as protozoa in the primeval slime, then, only by sheerest accident is man superior to the other creatures. It therefore becomes unmitigated and unforgivable aggression for man to sustain himself at the expense of any other living thing be it even a succulent scallion.

Whereas Genesis expressly bequeaths the whole world as a gift to mankind, Darwinism views man as claiming all things by brutal aggression. What offense this gives to the sensitive soul. And there is no escape from the vicious ring. Man must live, but in so doing he proves only his superior cunning. Implicit in such doctrine is a bestial definition of the nature of man which cannot be avoided. In contemplation of such philosophy is it really any great extension of thought to equate the crimes of 'Ripper' with the cloddish abattoir worker who butchers the beef of which we Britons are so fond?

Probably few things could speak more eloquently about the spiritual condition of modern man than to describe some of the major events of the year 1859 when we were born.

20

In the year of our birth, Charles Darwin published THE ORIGIN OF THE SPECIES. John Brown raided Harper's Ferry. Tischendorf, with the aid of the Czar, gained access to the remainder of the CODEX SINAITICUS one of many mementoes of the past enlightening mankind's understanding of the origins of his religious beliefs coming to light in our era. Wagner's TRISTAN AND ISOLDE was premiered and the glorification of the ancient racial myths in the modern era was accelerating to its pernicious end. Tennyson published IDYLLS OF THE KING. Fitzgerald published his translation of THE RUBAIYAT exalting further the Eastern philosophies versus Christianity. Karl Marx published his CRITICISM OF POLITICAL ECONOMY and John Stuart Mill published ON LIBERTY. Disraeli's reform bill led to the defeat of Derby's ministry. DeTocqueville died and Teddy Roosevelt was born. Gounod's FAUST premiered. Dickens published A TALE OF TWO CITIES. Baron Rothschild served his first year as the first Jewish M.P. having been seated after waiver of the requirement that he swear the Christian oath. Spain declared war on the Moors. Work began to unify Germany under Prussian rule, and France declared war on the Austrian Empire. The first oil well was drilled in Titusville, Pa.

Without elaborating, it can be seen that all was race, politics, economics and religion and I have long since concluded that all are hopelessly intertwined, indeed, they seem but different terms for the same phenomenon.

Religion, more explicitly, the demise of religion as we know it was complete. Darwin, unwittingly and quite despairingly, saw to that, though such was not his intention. And as the Churches lost the battle with science, there rushed into the vacuum politics and new pseudoscientific theories of race that had not yet, but would later, take on the spurious justification of social Darwinism, the exact opposite of Christianity, the anti-Christian thesis of every man for himself under which the world functions today. Eventually, politics, the politics of social Darwinism, would effectively replace religion.

You and I grew to manhood in an age in which the old was dying and the new was not yet born. And few had yet come to realize, as did Melville, that Christianity is (was) the sole energizing force of Western Civilization. We were so enamored with science and Progress we scarcely noticed the death of Christianity. But all our years have been spent watching mankind's attempts to synthesize this abysmal replacement for defunct Christianity called Humanism.

Let us see, old friend, what we are able to synthesize between us to replace this replacement, for surely no one, including ourselves, can be the worse for our having tried.

I appreciate your kind words and encouragement — much needed at this time. Also I appreciate your information about Sir Henry's GCB. He had written me the news himself. It was most pleasing to see him receive this so richly deserved honor. I hope it will not be too long before I am able to congratulate him in person. He plans a trip to America next summer. It shall be good to see him. Yours,

Sam

21

P.S. I most sincerely appreciate your bits of news of developments there at home and abroad as you hear of them. The Baltic and North Sea Conference during August seems just one more futile attempt toward a peaceful resolution of difficulties only war can resolve.

Letter to Samuel Harper
from Arthur Conan Doyle
Dated November 15, 1908 (London)

Dear Sam,

Give our best to Tony. I am sure you're doing all you can. Once the few palliatives science can offer fail, it becomes largely a religious or (if you prefer) a philosophical problem. Our most sincere feelings are with you.

Public passions are high in Germany right now over the interview Kaiser William II gave to the Daily Telegraph in which he stated that the German public is anti-British but that he is our friend. Truthful no doubt, but he is finding there is no market for truth when a people are inflamed.

Taft defeated Bryan to settle the question of the (your) Presidency for four more years. We British wish a man favorable to Britain to be in such a seat of power at times like these. The public here are fearful of the German challenge, at least enough so that the Naval Bill passed in March, as I am sure you saw. The Reichstag debate over the Kaiser's interview with the Daily Telegraph has embittered people both here and in Germany. It is not good.

As I read your letter and the dossier on Benson I could not help but recall my Vermont visit to Kipling's place at Naulahka in '94. It was, of course, wonderful to be with Ruddy again because just being in his presence makes my creative juices flow. And we devoted most of a week to our favorite pastime in discussing matters relating to the Empire — our Empire which was absent-mindedly, and, I might say half-heartedly taken up and, by many Britons, will be more than semi-gladly laid down.

In his own way Kipling is much like Benson although Kipling is not a believer in British-Israel, at least to my knowledge. But he is what Melville's Captain Ahab is frequently called — a monomaniac of the idea. The idea, of course, in Benson's case and Kipling's is basically Anglo-Saxon superiority, perhaps uniqueness is a better word, however one may explain it.

On that score, I've often pondered just how difficult it is for the rest of the world to have even the tiniest glimpse of an idea of what a wonderful thing it is just to be British.

It is a truly remarkable thing to a person who has seen much of this world that even the lowliest Briton is proud, burstingly proud, just to be an Englishman. This is a condition little seen anywhere outside the Western world and very little in the West. In Germany, I fear the basic problem is the way the press and the politicians play to a general feeling of inferiority to the British. The French are only slightly less guilty never having recovered from Trafalgar. Americans are but a trice from the time they will feel superior to everyone under heaven, including us, but that is only proof of their essential Anglo-Saxonness.

Regrettably, my dear Sam, if I read you rightly, the idea of British superiority can (and has been) deflected to evil purposes by those who would employ it to their own advantage under the screen of 'Empire.' And if I had to sum up Ruddy's primary theme during our week of discussions, it would be essentially that. That we have not been true to a religious and very sacred trust. I know there are those who regard Rud as being agnostic and those who think he is religiously neuter, but I think this ignores the prophetic role in which he cast himself in some of his best and best remembered poetry. Which of his works is quoted as often as the words to the hymn so frequently intoned in churches throughout Anglo-Saxondom as GOD OF OUR FATHERS KNOWN OF OLD which Rud was commissioned by the Times to write for the Queen's sixtieth anniversary?

Permit me to quote what I know you've heard more than once before:
The tumult and the shouting die,
The captains and the kings depart;
Still stands thine ancient sacrifice,
An humble and a contrite heart;
Lord of hosts, be with us yet,
Lest we forget, lest we forget.

Far-called our navies melt away,
On dune and head-land sinks the fire;
Lo, all our pomp of yesterday,
Is one with Nineveh and Tyre;
Judge of nations, spare us yet,
Lest we forget, lest we forget.

Can there be any strong distinction made beween the counsel being offered to Englishmen by Ruddy's lyrics from that delivered by Benson? There may be some difference as to how they arrived at their attitudes, but none whatever as to the problem they perceive and to which they seek solutions. Ruddy writes a poem, Benson steals the Stone of Scone. Their objectives precisely the same. To rouse the British out of the evil ways into which we've fallen, which they feel will inevitably lead to our downfall.

Harper, dear friend, you're probably aware that at Balfour's instigation, Edward bestowed upon me, in addition to knighthood, the title of Deputy Lieutenant of Surrey. The uniform that ceremonial post requires me to wear on occasional public events has about four stone of gold braid festooning it. Each time I see myself in that rig I am reminded of the prophet Samuel's counsel: "Beware of kings." For it is by the dispensation of these honors that appeal to the individual's vanity that monarchs maintain themselves and their power. How many firebrand reformers in the Commons have had their fire quenched by election to the Lords?

Make no mistake, I am not ungrateful to the great nation we call home. Ruddy and I, as well as anyone, are living proof that for all the social stratification that curses our nation, there is upward mobility in our society. Any worthy individual can make his mark if he wills it strongly enough. But we put too much store by half in worldly honors. In those of lower class origins (of which I am one) we see the tendency to genteelize their origins. My mother could bore you for hours reciting her Plantagenet forebears.

I remember one of our conversations with Sir Henry and his brother

Gregory regarding Sir Henry's work in Assyriology. I can't recall the event which occasioned the question, but clergyman that he is, Gregory made a remark manifesting a degree of ire over a British-Israel prelate from somewhere, Rangoon — the Anglican Bishop of Rangoon, I believe, to the effect that the British are Israel and he could prove it. Gregory insisting it cannot be proven looked to Sir Henry for supporting confirmation of his viewpoint.

With hesitancy and much deliberation, Sir Henry ratified that utter, irresistably perfect proof isn't possible. But the very manner of his delivery seemed to indicate he had no difficulty accepting the proposition. Indeed, I believe he did agree with the British-Israel idea.

On the other hand Reverend Rawlings seemed more effronted that the British-Israel prelate would cater to a worldly demand for proof of what could so easily be taken on faith. And I think I read the attitude correctly of those most in a position to comment with professional competence on the entire British-Israel postulation: It is a postulate not in the least inconsistent with the state of our understanding of archaeology and history — but a postulate nonetheless. And in an era producing new archaeological discoveries annually, almost monthly, it seemed to me they perhaps look for that postulation one day to be subject to verification.

It seems to me Sam, that British-Israelism was embarassing to them not because what they propose is thought to be outlandishly improbable but because they claim a spurious proof to demonstrate their case.

Sir Henry made reference, I recall, to the work of Professor Chwolson, a scholar of the National Museum, St. Petersburg regarding the many tombstones in the Crimea indicating that the descendants of the Ten Tribes lived and died for centuries right in the area to which the Scriptures and the Assyrian artifacts tell us the Assyrians deported the Israelites.

But still we're lacking proof for while we know the Goths were resident in the same area, we can't establish that the Hebrews and Goths are one and the same people. And surely many peoples have held sway over the centuries in that part of the world.

The Reverend Gregory pointed out that those of faith can accept upon Scriptural proof the proposition that the Goth is of the house of Judah and therefore one of the twelve tribes of Israel for the Book of Genesis states that there will ever be a son of Judah on the throne of Israel. And we know the Royal family to be of the house of Saxe-Coburg-Gotha! Which reasoning, of course doesn't prove anything more than how completely Gregory accepts the British-Israel postulation.

I fear Benson remains a perfect example of the honorable Briton who, seeing our Empire about to slip from us, would reach for a proof that doesn't exist to flagellate his countrymen over the fact they've abandoned their Israelite beginnings and their covenant with Jehovah. Except the fact is but a postulation subject to the whim of opinion. And in the realm of opinion every man is king.

Sharon Turner's HISTORY OF THE ANGLO-SAXONS began the whole idea of tracing our roots back to the ancient Celts, Goths, Scyths, etc. thereby inspiring, in a race-conscious era, the basically race-oriented works of a century starting with those of Sir Walter Scott, one of my forebears, and surely not ending with Wagner's purely racist operas glorifying Teutonic superiority.

Admittedly, it cannot be without special significance that the ancient Gaelic quatrain, translated into English by Scott refers both to the Sacred Stone and to the tribe of Ephraim, characterized by Hosea (9:17) as 'wanderers':

> Unless the Fates are faithless grown
> And the Prophets' voice be vain,
> Where'er is found this Sacred Stone,
> The wanderer's race shall reign.

Having been 'chosen' for a few august positions in my time, generally when I was absent from the fatal meeting in which my appointment was foisted upon me, I know that chosen generally is indistinguishable from servant. The fatal error for which we seem doomed to pay a horrendous price is that we have corrupted the term of chosen = servant into chosen = elite and privileged. T'will be a sad day when the bill comes due.

To leave you on a more amusing note, Ruddy told me an amusing tale while we were there. With reference to the Methodist background of his maternal grandfather who you may recall was a minister, Lord Stanley Baldwin, Kipling's cousin, reports, according to Rud, that Ruddy's mother once threw a cherished family memento, a lock of John Wesley's hair into the fire with the brazen declaration: "See, a hair of the dog that bit us."

Kindest regards from Jean and me to you and yours. I hope Tony is not in too much pain. Please let us know how she fares and you. Our prayers and blessings to her and you and Leslie.

Your friend,

Arthur

Letter to Arthur Conan Doyle
from Samuel Harper

Dated June 10, 1909 (New York City)

Dear Arthur,

There is no good place to lose a loved one. But I have to believe I could handle Tony's passing better in the familiar surroundings of London than I can here. Much as our lovely apartment here in Brooklyn Heights delighted Tony and me when we first let it, and surely it is as attractive now as it ever was, but in my eyes all things look gray and dismal at the moment.

What I have feared and dreaded for so long has finally happened. Early this morning Tony lapsed into a coma and not long afterward all her vital functions ceased. It is a blessing that she is released from her pain, which was tearing me apart emotionally as much as it was her physically. But the void that stretches ahead without her is vaster and more desolating than lonely vistas of the Sahara I have viewed at their most desolate.

And yet, somehow, I don't feel entirely alone, and that is not entirely because I have my sweet, five year old daughter Leslie to comfort and be comforted by. If ever anything has occurred to me which might cause me to believe in a life after this one, it was at my wife's bedside this morning.

You know better than anyone else how cerebral all my reactions to life tend to be. But this morning just after good Doctor James signified to me that the end had come, I felt a sweet presence emanating from what can only have been Tony's spirit. And how she did comfort me in my hour of grief. I have never felt her love more palpably than at that moment.

I think for the very first time I understand what a strong urge has moved you in your desire to contact your deceased mother. No, I am not about to participate in one of the seances that you, Arthur Balfour and W. T. Stead, the baron of Fleet Street so avidly seek. But for the first time I begin to wonder if the concept of an infinitely just God doesn't require one to believe in a life after death possessing very different characteristics than the clergymen have ever conceived, admitting they are notably weak in telling us how we will spend our hereafter. How else can all the grief felt by those who yearn so deeply at the passing of a loved one (multiply what I feel by the millions who have endured something similar in all the history of mankind) — how can that grief be justified? I suppose the traditional Christian belief in a hereafter will suffice for most, but it will not be heaven for me if Tony is not there and my little Leslie, the only part of Tony that remains.

This past year of Tony's terminal illness has not been without its compensations. I have had to prepare Leslie for what we all knew to be inevitable and at the same time, many of the tiny comforting acts which she usually would have sought from her mother she has now come to seek from me. And what a pleasure it is to have drawn close to this sweet little creature. Something that might not have happened had Tony not been ill.

You, Arthur, surely know what a delightful thing a five year old can be. The other day she and I were out for a hansom ride in the park and we passed a woman on the street. I scarcely glanced at her but after we had passed Leslie looked at me with a smile and said: "Isn't she beautiful?" (Almost anyone you can imagine, however ordinary, is "beautiful.") To which I replied in the spirit of general positiveness and just a measure of preoccupation with other matters:

"Yes Leslie, she is beautiful." A little farther on as the horse clip-clopped along she asked: "Wouldn't you like to keep her?" Slightly shocked and amused, but knowing not to show it I replied: "I think I would have to know a little bit more about her before I would care to keep her."

Leslie thought for a while before making any further remark, then she looked up at me with a glow upon her countenance which seemed to register the turning on of a light, one of Mr. Edison's finest, as deduction closed some mental circuit: "You would have to know her name first wouldn't you daddy?" I couldn't help chuckling as I concurred: "Yes, Leslie, we would have to know her name before we could keep her." Of such wonderful little delights has this last year of being both a mother and father to this small girl been filled.

To the woman who for some strange reason feels the calling of being a wife and mother is somehow inadequate and demeaning I can only say that such an attitude is a total mystery to me for even with Tony's illness I have never enjoyed anything so much as the opportunity to draw close to this wonderful little spirit that some sweet circumstance has placed in my care.

Fortunately, being permanently in control of my own destiny, economically speaking, and having only to work when I choose to, I have been able to allocate a great deal more time that I would ordinarily devote to my consulting clients to the care of Leslie. But I have also succeeded in finding a wonderful old Celt, Mrs. Tumulty whose years I couldn't guess, but which must approximate the three score and ten man is traditionally allotted. She has come to live with us, adores Leslie who reciprocates the feeling, and I shall accordingly soon be more free Mr. Doyle, or should I say, "Mr. Watson," to resume the hunt. I do hope that you and Jean are well. I shall try to come to England in the spring to show my daughter the land of her forebears. In the meantime, please keep your letters coming as, for the first time, I feel nearly unable to proceed without the comfort of old friends.

Yours,

Sam

P.S. Am impressed with Elgar's Symphony #1 in A flat which was performed here recently to my great enjoyment. I note your friend Northcliffe has purchased The Times. I appreciate all your bits of news. Americans can be quite parochial on matters of great import abroad. I share your dismay over the prospects for peace. The abortive London Naval Conference last December, failing as it did to produce any mediation between Britain and Germany, is an indication of how great the perils are. The formation of the

Anglo-Persian Oil Company in January speaks well for our efforts to insure sources of energy for the future. But when will the Admiralty's efforts bear fruit to get the Commons to vote the funds to convert from coal to oil?

Letter to Samuel Harper
from Arthur Conan Doyle
Dated October 13, 1909 (Cairo)

Dear Sam,

I am indebted to Balfour for his frankness in telling me, as he did just before our last seance in August, that certain people take such a dim view of our interest in spiritualism that our names likely will be rejected for peerages. This is a bitter price to pay, but I shall survive, and at any rate, I could not alter my beliefs were it death itself as an alternative. I'm sure he refers to the heir apparent (for the King has never complained), possibly also the Prime Minister Herbert Asquith, perhaps Churchill.

There seems to be no end of marvelous feats mankind with the aid of science is achieving. Louis Bleriot flew the Channel in July and while the common man is thrilled with such exploits, men in power are looking to the possible military applications of aircraft. I think they shall find them.

Henry Ford's Model T bids fair to revolutionize the way mankind not only travels and transports goods but even farms his food.

I hear a man named Hoffman has been able to fabricate a synthetic rubber. Will the wonders never cease? But where is the progress in spiritual and moral matters to parallel our feats in the material world?

I trust all goes well with you. It was suggested to me by Stead that I go to the Peace Conference at the Hague to do a series of pieces on the proceedings. But since Jean and I had long since set our plans to travel for September 16th, neither of us desired to alter our intentions to honeymoon in the Med. (Greek Islands, Egypt and Turkey). The Consul, Sir Eldon Gorst has received us kindly here and has advised us that the Sultan Abdul-Hamid desires to honor Jean and me, I with the Order (2nd Class) of the Medjideh and Jean with the Order (2nd Class) of Niehan-i-Chafahat. The Sultan's chamberlain revealed to us when we reached Constantinople that his majesty likes the Holmes stories.

(Continued October 25th)

In Sophia we narrowly missed being killed by a mob of Musselmen. We had been (most graciously) granted permission to attend the sacred festival of the Night of Power. It was the most marvelous spectacle as from the upper circle of pillared arches we looked down upon 60,000 lighted lamps and 12,000 worshippers, who made, as they rose and fell in their devotions, a sound like the wash of the sea. Sam, you should have been there.

A young woman in our party, ignorant without doubt that we are all infidels to the Musselman and that killing an infidel is a 'ticket to heaven' for the faithful, perched on the parapet and waved at the 12,000 men below. In their tradition no woman could appear at, let alone so defile the proceedings, and a sea of faces, livid with anger, looked up at us. I heard a low deep growl . . . it only needed one fiery spirit to head the rush and we should all have been massacred — with the poor consolation that some of us had really asked for it. However, she was pulled down, and we made our way as quickly and as quietly as possible out of the side door. It was time, I think.

I must admit, I would have loved to have gone to The Hague. Matters of the utmost moment are being considered there. As you will recall the Russo-Japanese conflict interfered with the originally proposed conference. Now Teddy Roosevelt gets to act like a world statesman in attempting to stop the insane arms race in which the major powers are involved. I doubt he will win any major concessions from Germany. They are johnny-come-latelys on the world power scene and will not accept the status quo. These things have an irresistible dynamic all their own.

One need only remember how the German newspapers took the Kaiser to task for attending the Queen's (his own grandmother's) funeral to know that William II rides a dangerous steed. He must cater to the Germans' yearning for power, or he will fall. It is a bad situation that no one controls and for which everyone is responsible.

Russia is close to revolution and the Duma is clearly not a body with much power to satisfy the rebels. Still England and Russia have apparently been able to overcome their ancient rivalries in Asia and Persia which Sir Henry warned of many years ago, albeit only to unite against their potential enemy Germany.

The Kaiser and the Czar met to discuss Germany's plan for a railway to Baghdad. How such an investment can be protected in time of war or justified at a time Germany's resources are so stretched purchasing armaments is anyone's guess.

They might as well plan a trip to the moon. But such is their need to expand in an era when all the coveted plums on the colonial scene are in someone else's hands. I hear the Kaiser even toys with the idea of planting German settlers along the route of the railway to protect it, though I doubt the Sultan will buy that.

The French and ourselves draw ever closer and our resolution with Japan of spheres of influence in the Far East, while it sounds peaceful and benign, has as its primary aim the creation of a secure situation in Asia should Europe go to war. It all sounds good but its portents are ominous.

I would have enjoyed covering the Conference but I have no illusions that Europe will take a radically new direction away from war.

Hope you are all well. Best from all of us.

Yours,

Arthur

31

Letter to Arthur Conan Doyle
from Samuel Harper

Dated July 11, 1911 (New York City)

Dear Arthur,

The summer heat is upon us and I have just returned from a trip with Leslie to Coney Island. We each ate a hot dog a foot long, redolent with kosher spicing which above all involves copious amounts of garlic. Leslie had a hilarious time as we rode on the 'thrillers' as she insists on terming the amusements. We have done quite a number of excursions lately to many places near New York and some even as remote as Montreal so that neither she nor I must think about Tony.

Somehow or other I seem unable to avoid one type of encounter or another with the Mormons since I elected to do an analysis of STUDY IN SCARLET. I am beginning to wonder too, why you ever wrote that piece! And please don't think I raise the subject merely to thrash your buttocks (or 'dewskitch yer nancy' as your literary guttersnipes The Baker Street Irregulars might say.)

I have delayed telling you about the case even though it was clear from the start that nothing of a confidential nature would come out of the assignment. But I feared if I raised the matter sooner you would conclude immediately I was amusing myself at your expense once again.

But since I construe our agreement as requiring me to share with you whatever important conclusions I come to on the subject of religion and/or metaphysics, I feel I am finally at the point I should relate to you some interesting finds.

Not long ago, at high noon, I was sitting at my favorite table at Gage & Tollners, the finest place for food and beverage in Brooklyn Heights, when I was approached by a woman of nondescript aspect, strictly of the working class and distinctly ill at ease to be in a fine restaurant. I asked her to sit down as I rose to greet her, but glancing self-consciously from left to right, clutching an out-of-style handbag popular a decade previously, looking distinctly like some bird might suddenly pop out of the nest on her head that passed for a hat and clutching about her a worn coat, she asked in a slight German-Brooklyn accent if we mightn't have a talk as soon as I had finished my lunch. She volunteered to wait outside and did precisely that, to my considerable annoyance as I felt obliged to rush what might otherwise have been a leisurely and rather sumptuous repast.

Well Arthur, when finally I exited the establishment, there she stood in the bright sunlight looking even frowsier than before. She announced with little delay her purpose. "The Chief of Police, Francis X. Reilly knows me and my family these many years," said she, "and I asked his help with a problem I have. He recommended you Mr. Harper and here I am." She smiled showing a toothless expanse of upper gums. Toothless tho' it was (or because it was) her smile was irresistible and I found myself smiling as broadly as she which put her quickly at ease.

"I can see you're an allright type Mr. Harper. Will you help me?" She looked earnestly at me, her eyes telling me that she needed money and that she somehow believed I could help her in some manner to obtain it.

"That's possible I suppose," I said, "but first would you be good enough to tell me your name?"

"Heusser, Ilona Heusser Mr. Harper; my husband Carl works as a motorman on the BMT and we need some special help sir," she concluded somewhat breathlessly.

She was a woman I judged to be about fifty and her shortness of breath told me her health was poor. "What is the problem Mrs. Heusser?"

"We have something that was given to my mother by her employer. He was fond of mother as well he might be — she worked in his service for over thirty years. He, Mr. Coombs that is, told Mom, my mother, that is, that some day it would be worth a lot of money. He told her it is thousands of years old and Egyptian, from Egypt that is, and we should hold on to it until some day we really need money."

"What precisely is it that you have, if I may ask?" I really had little interest in her situation but desired to be polite.

"It's strange Mr. Harper, with queer marks on it and drawings." She sensed my disinterest and was expressing herself somewhat more dramatically as though my attention might increase with the greater level of animation.

"There's a letter with it that says it's a genuine Egyptian record used by the Mormon prophet Joseph Smith," she looked at me triumphantly as though I couldn't possibly fail to be totally involved after such a disclosure. Strangely enough, she was right! We arranged to meet in the offices of the Curator of Egyptian antiquities at the Metropolitan Museum in Manhattan as I desired to have competent witnesses to all that transpired. But little did I dream at the time of the degree of my ultimate involvement. Doyle, old man, you wouldn't have been able to resist either.

I've heard Sir Henry tell too often of the many times he and my father were asked to inspect antiquities when Sir Henry was President of the Royal Asiatic Society not to know how controlled the circumstances must be to avoid lending one's good name to the most blatant frauds. True enough, some highly unprofessional things occurred in the old days when archaeology was a new science, but the cognoscenti follow strict procedures today. And as science develops new techniques for identification, the methods require even stricter application of professional procedures.

Mrs. Heusser appeared accompanied by Carl, her husband, more ill-at-ease in the august surroundings in which he found himself at the Met than Ilona had been some days previously at the restaurant.

They bore with them a package of some considerable size which observably was burlap bound with stout cords around what I conjectured would prove to be a wooden case probably designed specifically to shelter the artifact. Such it proved to be when all the ceremonies of photographing the package before and after entry and every step of the way were completed. A stenographer standing by took notes in shorthand as we proceeded, accepting the comments of Mr. Howes, the Chief Curator much as a surgeon might, who was recording an elaborate surgical procedure. These notes, of course, would become the basis of any affidavit that might later be sworn.

Well, I surely don't need to tell you above all others these boring details with which you're already too familiar from your med school days and after. Suffice it to say a most curious document was finally withdrawn from the specially built container I had deduced to be inside.

One side is clearly very ancient, the other of much more recent origin and is glued to the back of what Howes and I concur is Egyptian papyrus with hieroglyphs and drawings in the style of a thousand other such documents I have seen over the years. Most the markings are black but some are a faded red.

The material is in no way extraordinary, but the uses to which the hieroglyphs and drawings have been put are quite a different matter. Likewise, I find evidence that leads me to believe that it's possible Joseph Smith possessed a great deal more ability in the ancient languages of the Nile than one could ordinarily attribute to an uneducated, rough-hewn frontiersman.

Arthur, you may not agree, of course, with all my conclusions, but I know you'll find the array of verifiable facts interesting. As you well know, Napoleon's expedition into Egypt turned the attention of the world toward the land of the pharaohs and an interest in Egyptian artifacts was kindled which has tended to increase rather than diminish with the passage of time. Soon Egypt was overrun with both the truly scientific and the outright plunderers in search of any and every example to be found of the cultures of those ancient dynasties.

Apparently, one of those early adventurers was a Piedmontese named Antonio Lebolo who was an agent for one of the powerful dealers in antiquities of the period, Bernardino Drovetti. We don't know the precise year but it may have been as early as 1817 that Lebolo obtained a license to enter the catacombs at Thebes. He found many mummies there, surely more than eleven, the ultimate number of which we have record he possessed. He turned the majority of those he found over to Drovetti keeping an unknown number for himself as his commission. He was returning to France with his precious cargo, stopping en route at Trieste, where he was stricken with an unknown disease, and in a few days died. He is believed to have died in 1823, though we don't know precisely.

It was originally believed that Lebolo willed the find to a Michael H. Chandler who some assert was Lebolo's nephew. More recent evidence seems to indicate that Chandler negotiated with Henry Salt, Representative of the Crown in Egypt. Salt died in 1827 and it is speculated he had set matters in motion sometime prior to ship the mummies to Chandler in Ireland. It is not clear why the mummies went there after clearing customs in London for Chandler was living in Philadelphia.

But by no minor miracle, after all this transshipping in an age given routinely to the purloining of such artifacts, the mummies arrived in New York City and were claimed by Chandler. The customs records indicate that

Chandler paid the duties in 1833 and must have accounted himself a very lucky man that this cargo had escaped the clutches of the antiquity barons, the dishonest agents, the plunderers, etc.

He immediately breached the ancient bindings of the mummies in search of gold and jewels and found none of these, I assume, to his great disappointment. The world had not yet arrived at the level of cultural maturity prerequisite to the creation of high market values for materials of only cultural and historical significance.

To Joseph Smith and his followers, this proved a great blessing for it seems clear that by the time, some two years later, when Chandler met Smith in Kirtland, Ohio, he was still eking out a meager way, charging the public small fees to view these 'curiosities.' And more important, the scrolls he found within the wrappings of one of the mummies were quite willingly sold by him to Smith along with the mummies themselves for several thousand dollars.

I think, Doyle, you will feel it to be as interesting as I do that Smith so impressed Chandler with his ability to translate the hieroglyphics that the latter gave a certificate which asserts that Smith's translation accords in minute detail with those translations by the learned men of the day to whom Chandler gave access to the scrolls. I had to go all the way to Salt Lake City, Utah to see Chandler's letter and I can confirm it was in his hand. So you see I have expended no few hours and dollars on this exotic case.

Smith pronounced the one scroll to be the product of the hand of Abraham, the other to be that of Abraham's great grandson Joseph who ruled Egypt as described in Genesis.

You are probably aware that Mormons cherish scriptures beyond those of the Bible alone. And surely any well-informed person who follows such things knows of numerous incidents in recent years of other archaeological finds that give every evidence of being lost books of the Bible, reference to 16 of which we find in the Scriptures themselves.

To the Mormons Smith's translation of the one scroll became what they call the Book of Abraham. It describes a world quite unlike that in which our divines assert that venerable ancient dwelt. Not a pastoral, bucolic scene, but a world of turmoil, much wickedness and danger, not unlike our own. This has the ring of truth to it to me which the accepted interpretation does not have.

The Joseph scroll the prophet intended to translate, but this did not occur due to Smith's murder. And so its contents are not in the Mormon canon and quite frankly, we don't know what became of that scroll for when Smith was killed by a mob in Carthage, Ill. in 1844, the possibility of his translating same ended and the mummies and scrolls were placed in the safekeeping of his mother Lucy Mack Smith who was, I take it, too old (and possibly unwilling) to journey west with the saints and who died in 1856. With her death the precious cargo began a journey during which the Joseph scroll got separated from the present one.

Mrs. Smith, after Joseph's death, lived with her daughter-in-law Emma, the Prophet's widow who remarried L.C. Bidamon. It was L.C. and Emma Bidamon who signed the letter of sale to one A. Combs (sic) who surely is the Mr. Coombs for whom Mrs. Heusser's mother worked.

One can, of course, conclude that the Book of Abraham is purely a work of fiction. But my independent verification establishes that his translation of the hieroglyphics is impeccable. Whether the events portrayed therein are true or some ancient author's fiction cannot be directly ascertained. The Mormons believe them to be true. Clearly a case in which we scientists wish there were a direct way to verify truth.

For our purposes, Arthur, that fact is perhaps irrelevant. It is clear Joseph Smith was no ordinary man and the movement he founded no ordinary movement. This I regard as one of those circumstances which must be factored in and to which some value must be attached when evaluating Smith's life and works and the organization he left behind. In itself it would not presently appear to prove anything metaphysical, but it does prove he was not ordinary and that those who so portray him are clearly wrong. Therefore, what he has wrought surely, by my lights, should be accorded earnest attention free of the ridicule so many with much to lose if he is right in even a small percentage of his assertions endlessly heap upon him and the group he founded. Ridicule is, after all, the first and last argument of fools.

But there is much more. There is the reverse side of the papyrus which apparently was glued on to hold the pieces of papyrus together when the papyrus through usage started to break in pieces. There are drawings and maps on this side. I was obliged to travel to Kirtland to satisfy myself that certain of the drawings were of the Temple built by the Mormons in the rudimentary stage of that building's design. Apparently the Mormons believe that the dead can accept the gospel and its ordinances beyond the grave because the learning process of eternal truths goes on after death just as before. A more appealing prospect than most I have heard propounded by other religions.

However, moral progress also requires the temple ordinances of baptism for the dead, the sealing of families to each other, etc. so they may dwell together throughout eternity if certain qualifications of righteous living have been accomplished, etc.

I don't mind telling you the thought I might be joined for all time to Tony and Leslie is a most appealing concept to me and one I would dearly yearn for, if true. It also accords with what one would expect of a perfectly merciful Creator.

I became so absorbed in the Heusser's problem I traveled to Kirtland and Salt Lake at my own expense to satisfy myself that there was no doubt the drawings are of the temple there and other referenced matter. I satisfied myself the document is the one used by the prophet in writing the Book of Abraham. I also satisfied myself that the papyrus is genuine and negotiated a reasonable price for the Heussers who sold the document to the Met for the money she needed for a serious operation. She is doing well and embarasses me with her unfeigned gratitude.

However, the residuum of this entire assignment is a lingering question in my mind about this mystery man Joseph Smith and whether his mission was divine or was he but another religious crackpot of whom upstate New

York (where Smith began his ministry) produced so many during the religious revival in what was called the 'burned over area,' so much fire and brimstone having been called down from heaven there by the revivalist preachers.

I enclose a memorandum on Jacques Futrelle who I have known for some time. He desires to chronicle my exploits much as your Mr. Watson did those of your good friend Holmes. Why you complain so much of him I can't fathom, after all he pays all your bills!

Best to you all,

Sam

P.S. Word comes to me that the unconstitutional action of the Lords in defeating Lloyd-George's finance measure in Nov. '09 will effectively prevent, at least for the present, the application of Henry George's tax ideas in Blighty. It would have represented the death knell to the large estates upon which so much English power and wealth is predicated to have untaxed improvements and to have shifted all real property taxes to the land, whether that land was in use or not. I also hear that the Lords perceive that Britain is drifting into a major war and they threatened to withhold their support if the bill was not killed. What a tragedy! Only untaxing improvements can reward the doers and punish those who refuse to utilize their land properly. It would represent a revolution to be sure, but rather a bloodless than a bloody one which one day might come about without the justice this bill would work. Now the General Election Asquith called after the Lords' illegal procedures has broken much of their power for all time.

George V is now on the throne. I am sure I will find him a monarch more to my liking than his father.

Recently enjoyed Elgar's violin concerto which was performed here, but am most sad over the death of my father's good friend Count Tolstoy. Also viewed with regret our loss of Mark Twain who has both amused us and enlightened us for so long.

Memorandum to Arthur Conan Doyle
from Samuel Harper

Dated July 11, 1911

Subject: Jacques Futrelle
Born: April 9, 1865 in Pike County, Georgia
Newspaperman turned author of detective stories. Formerly employed by Boston American.
Married L. May Peel in 1897, also a writer.

His most famous character THE THINKING MACHINE is a rival to Sherlock Holmes in ability but does not seem (to me at least) to draw from the rich background of English society as Sherlock Holmes does and, therefore, is less colorful a figure in a less colorful background. Met Jacques Futrelle quite accidentally in a routine business call to the Manhattan Chief of Police. They (the N.Y. Police) are, as you well know, second to none in volume of business they direct my way for consulting services as to the most advanced detection methods evolving world-wide. As you are aware, I have, in my consulting capacity to Scotland Yard, the Prefecture, the Okrana the Czar's Secret Police, etc. become something of an international clearing house for new detection methods. But also they are second only to Scotland Yard in volume of chemicals and other supplies they purchase for detection kits we have sold them. Manhattan's account alone keeps my company in the black. All our other clients simply make the profit more handsome.

But Chief O'Brien apparently is one source of ideas for Futrelle who clearly has the man's trust, as he has that of many other highly placed individuals.

After I completed my visit with O'Brien, Futrelle suggested we stop for a cup of coffee at a cafe near Police Headquarters. We touched on many topics, some amusing, some serious. All but the one he had foremost in mind — can he chronicle my cases for me? He ultimately got to that but only after a number of additional meetings.

Arthur, he is a man incredibly like Sir Henry in many ways not including appearance, of course, Jacques Futrelle being short and dark, the exact opposite of the Aryan-Anglo-Saxon appearance of Sir Henry. He has a strange interest in many things one would not expect in an American. Admires Carlyle and quotes him frequently as well as Melville, Diderot, Bagehot, Edmund Burke, Ruskin, Descartes and a host of others one rarely hears of today. Extremely well read. Adores animals as does Sir Henry. Great admiration for the French (what man with a name like Futrelle wouldn't?).

But it is in certain other characteristics he seems most like my surrogate father. Like some other Anglo-Catholics which Sir Henry decidedly is, he believes Progress is a modern superstition, that the advance of the idea of Progress (with a capital P) paralleled the decline in belief in eternal life. Heaven on earth, so to speak, to replace the debunked 'heaven in the hereafter.'

Still Jacques Futrelle, like you and I, is not religious and is not certain he wants to be. In that he is decidely unlike Sir Henry. But it is in personal style he is most like him. He likes suggestions and demands of himself and others commitment and enthusiasm. Wants devotion — gets it and gives it. He has no interest in time — however long it takes to complete a task is unimportant, if it's worth doing. He burrows on like a mole until the job is done. It was when Sir Henry was Her Majesty's representative to the Paris Exhibition in 1875 and he took me along as his aide that I saw this characteristic at close range in Sir Henry.

He is also very understanding of my idiosyncracies and comprehends the unorthodoxies of the creative personality. He is most generous and a favor is returned with astonishing generosity. He is impervious to flattery or manipulation. Becomes depressed, cranky, even petty when feels unappreciated or that his methods are not approved.

But he can pull the worst situation out of the fire with amazing ease. Very determined and has unconquerable will power. Naturally lucky. Is always making something astonishing happen. Likes practical jokes (you will recall a few of Sir Henry's more spectacular ones). Conceals his hurts completely. Occasional outbursts of temper. Would delay his own wedding in a crisis. Not always a good judge of character. But rectifies his mistakes quickly, almost ruthlessly. Self-confident and stiff upper lip at all times.

Desperately needs approval and recognition of his merit. Not much interested in past records — formulates his own judgments. Takes people at face value, but can be an utter snob to cut off someone who fails to measure up.

Has a temper, but cools off quickly. Hides his deepest feelings and won't acknowledge dependence on anyone. Can go it alone if he must. Occasionally impulsive and slap-dash. Ever optimistic and enthusiastic. Occasionally gets in over his head. Repays loyalty to the uttermost farthing.

Hates routine. Gets bored easily. Sometimes careless about details (fatal error were he a detective instead of a writer). All of which sounds like Doyle in many ways also. Perhaps that's why I've agreed to give him access to my files (names deleted, of course), for in truth, old friend, I have missed our association since I came to America.

Hope you and Jean are well. If Futrelle has occasion to visit Britain, I will give him a letter of introduction and I hope you two get on well.

Yours,

Sam

P.S. I suspect Britons were dismayed that the Czar would be negotiating with the Kaiser over the Berlin-Baghdad Railway, which might, of course, have great strategic importance in a war confronting Germany and their allies the Ottoman Empire. The Czar got his pound of flesh, needless to say, having now a free hand in North Persia.

P.P.S. The unprovoked aggression of the Germans in the gunboat Panther incident at Agadir, French Morocco, will, I think, convince many Englishmen there is no alternative to war with Germany.

Letter to Samuel Harper
from Arthur Conan Doyle
Dated August 30, 1911 (London)

Dear Sam:

Please forgive my not having responded sooner to your last letter, but Jean and I were on a short holiday and only returned a few days ago. We both needed a rest from the strenuous exertions of having moved into our new digs at Windlesham. We shall be looking forward to your next visit so we can show you around what (thanks to the bills received for repairs and alterations) we are now calling 'Swindlesham.'

Jean and I are ecstatically happy. Now Jean and the children are getting used to living under one roof with each other. All goes well excepting a minor crisis every hour or so.

What a splendid time we had celebrating the Coronation of His Royal Highness King George V. I wish you could have been there. I thought of you as one of the fetes we attended began with a performance by the Covent Garden orchestra of Elgar's new symphony #2 in E Flat — one of your favorite composers.

Russia's recent (July 10) warning to Germany of her commitments to come to the aid of France did not deter the Kaiser from a bellicose speech a few days ago demanding Germany's "place in the sun" to be achieved by her new naval might.

I hear Churchill will soon be called as First Lord of the Admiralty. Things will start happening then I have no doubt.

Your information regarding the Heusser documents are noted with great interest as well as your comments about the Mormons and their founder Joseph Smith. I thought it might be of interest to you to have the opportunity to peruse the notes I have developed regarding them and which I expect some time in the future to incorporate in a book or booklet on the subject. Rest assured I have not really felt that you were 'dewskitching my nancy' at any time.

While the depiction of the Mormons in STUDY IN SCARLET may have been a rather sensational and overcoloured picture of the Danite episodes which formed a passing stain in the early history of Utah, still I think you will see I have 'done my homework' on the Mormons since and as you will note, am impressed in a number of respects with the whole subject, just as you appear to be after your experience.

And I am struck by certain similarities between Mormonism and Spiritualism. First, they feel as we do, that the other creeds which so abound in this world have wandered from the basic simplicity of Christianity as it came fresh from the hands of its founder. Also, both these relatively new systems have attained world-wide influence in a brief time, the one having been founded in 1820 and the other in 1848. And, quite surprisingly, both originated in upstate New York not greatly distant from each other. That the rustics of a single agricultural district should produce two important belief systems strikes me as extraordinary. And, while they seem superficially independent of each other, I believe this superficial difference practically disappears if one concedes that Smith was a medium and simply was unaware of the way things are done when spirits beyond the veil contact the living. I think that if the Mormons understood such things, and if they made allowance for the possibility that Smith was a medium, they might then have an explanation of what occurred which would not diminish in any way their beliefs or the dignity and otherworldly nature of their origins.

I think it is impossible to read a long account such as that we have of Smith's experience without being able to sense whether it is honestly or fraudulently intended. So much of it strikes me as sincerely and honestly stated that I cannot question his honesty though, it seems to me, he was substantially misled in certain respects. He tells of his first experience with mystical forces when he sought guidance directly from the Lord. It is not unlike many such events we have seen in Spiritualism.

He reported that "thick darkness gathered around me" and "when I came to myself again, I found myself lying on my back, looking up to heaven." Is it not apparent this was a mediumistic trance? Not unlike those of Andrew Jackson Davis (1826-1910) the founder of Spiritualism.

After his first contact which he mistakenly believed to be with the Father and the Son simply because he did not know how things are done from beyond, he was then contacted by an angel, one Moroni who quoted extensively from the Bible. It is impossible to credit Smith with the ability to recollect faultlessly as he would have us believe such long passages. We must conclude that much of this was inserted after reference to the Scriptures for pious ends.

Smith seems to have had no further experiences from beyond for three years when contacted by Moroni who lived upon the earth 1400 years previously, a perfectly plausible occurrence. He was visited by this apparition every year for four years, a detail which there would seem to be no reason to fabricate. Ordinarily a person bent upon fabricating a story omits all needless details. It is just this sort of seemingly pointless detail which gives Smith's story the ring of truth.

Now we come to the heart of the matter which forces us to the conclusion that Smith was either an impostor or a most privileged person. Moroni announced that gold plates together with the Urim and Thummim, the seer stones of the Hebrews, were to be found in a hillside not distant from the Smith home in Palmyra, New York. He went there as directed and found them as promised. Then he describes another of those seemingly irrelevant details that so surprise me. A novelist, does not give details having no bearing on the plot. Smith describes that in the stone box with the plates and the Urim and Thummim laid crosswise in the bottom were two stones on which the plates and the Urim and Thummim were laid. It matches the imaginative genius of a de Foe to conjure up those superfluous stones, in my opinion.

He reburied the box and revisited it every year for four years when he was instructed to take these things into his possession. Once again, why such a needless detail? But another evidence that smacks of truth.

He began the prodigious job of translation. The Book of Mormon contains 522 pages of densely printed material. How so much information could be contained on a set of plates that one man could lift is not explained. Also unexplained is how the use of the Urim and Thummim facilitated the translation. Smith left us no enlightenment on these points.

We ask quite naturally if anyone else witnessed the plates in Smith's possession. The Mormons have an answer. Two different groups, one of three people and the other of eight have left written testimony of having seen the plates. And the group of three also attest to having seen the angel Moroni. The moderation with which these statements are made increases our respect for the truthfulness of these assertions.

An interesting event is described. One Martin Harris obtained leave to take a copy of the hieroglyphics to Professor Anthon, a learned man of New York. He said the original was Egyptian and the translation very precise. Some of the untranslated portion he characterized as Egyptian, Chaldean, Assyrian and Arabic. A certificate to this effect was drafted and given to Harris. Upon learning that the source of the plates was an angel, he tore his statement up and abandoned the matter. A Dr. Mitchell gave similar evidence to that of Anthon. It is not possible to ignore this statement of Harris or to doubt he had a document with him in Egyptian characters which had been translated by a rough hewn frontiersman.

Smith began to use Oliver Cowdery as a scribe and from that point on, if working a fraud, Smith was in Cowdery's power. However, Cowdery seems never to have broken faith with the Mormon prophet. But it is at this time it seems to me the system began to decay. Instead of bringing a message to all mankind as does Spiritualism, Smith and Cowdery initiate a priesthood thus creating a caste, formal sacraments and a separate sect such as to divide men and to be antagonistic to other creeds. It is curious that this decay should begin shortly after Cowdery's entry.

Now came the period of conversions, growth and pronouncements under priestly authority such as polygamy which was no part of Smith's original revelation and which is now honestly repudiated. The flow of narrative from here on is pretty much a part of the general history of the century: numerous persecutions, the growth and courage of the Mormon people, their migrations under persecution from their enemies and their growth and prosperity in the valley of the Great Salt Lake. Their extraordinary achievements under the leadership of Brigham Young, one of the many-sided characters of history.

He initiated the methods of modern irrigation as well as many other innovations improvised under the pressures of colonizing a harsh land. It is all a wonderful story and it is with some amazement one meets one of the saints in Utah and learns that a mother or father came across the plains with a handcart company.

There remains, of course, the question of what the Book of Mormon tells us. What story does it tell and is it credible? No question it strains us. But we have seen too much strange in our time to say it could not have happened.

The story is a remarkable one and it is narrated in a number of books which are cross referenced so extensively that an enormous amount of effort, quite needless effort, would be expended to achieve the necessary agreements were it all a fabrication.

It tells of the migration of two families to America from Jerusalem about 600 years before Christ. Over a thousand years of history they evolved into two nations, the Nephites and the Lamanites, finally decimating each other in internecine wars. The Nephites were destroyed by the Lamanites in New York State where Moroni, the last chief of the Nephites buried the plates.

There is some evidence to support such a scenario. The discoveries in Yucatan and Central America with their pyramids and other forms of Oriental construction would accord with an interpretation that supports a Middle Eastern origin. I'm told Egyptian demotic characters have been found there. If true, a remarkable corroboration.

There is the semitic appearance of the Indians. And I should like to hear from some learned linguist as to whether or not Hebrew might be a source of the word roots of the Indian languages. This would bear directly on the question.

At any rate, there are corroborating circumstances in support of the Book of Mormon. It is not manifestly absurd as is the theory that would suggest that the brown-haired, blue-eyed Anglo-Celtic race descends from the ten long-nosed, swarthy tribes of Israel.*

On the theological side, much of what Smith revealed is supported by Spiritualist truths. For example, he states that death confers no new knowledge upon the deceased. This was both new and true. He states that Spirit is superfine matter, once again, new and true. True marriage lasts beyond death, the imperfect one does not. There are many other points I could cite in which the beliefs of Spiritualism and Mormonism are in agreement. But there are others such as polygamy which could have come from no high source.

But, in summary, let it be said I believe Smith was a true medium, but that his controls, the spirits bringing him his revelations, were not adequately held in check, misleading him in the process. I believe that if there was a record on plates it certainly was much smaller than the record left in the Book of Mormon. But all of these reservations having been expressed I am still ready to say that all of the Mormon experience has left us as fine a body of decent, law-abiding citizens as can be found anywhere.

It should be said before leaving the subject that the Mormons have the same high regard for the Bible and that the Book of Mormon is intended to corroborate not supplant it. It is in this process of corroboration I suspect a pious fraud may have crept in.

*It's clear that at the time these notes were prepared, Doyle did not understand the difference between the Anglo-Saxon who under the British-Israel postulation represents the Lost Ten Tribes of Israel and the prototypical Jew, that is the Khazar-Jew, a convert to Judaism of Turkish origin referred to in the Benson Dossier. There is no question that Doyle's reference is to the British-Israel hypothesis.

At any rate, this short analysis of the Mormon faith should give you some idea of the extent to which I have commited myself to learn more about this group whom you suspect me of having so seriously maligned. I exaggerate, of course, but I think you understand the seriousness of my interest in their beliefs.

We all send our best regards to you and Leslie. I will look forward to meeting Futrelle. I have read his THE THINKING MACHINE and I agree his is a genuine talent.

By the way, your remarks about the heraldic indicia of our Israel background mentioned in the Benson Dossier interest but mystify me due to my ignorance. Didn't you write a monograph on the subject and, if so, do you still have a copy you can send me? Hope we'll see you one day soon.

Yours,

Arthur

Entry from Journal of Jacques Futrelle
Dated September 1, 1911 (New York City)

(Entry made available to the editor by the trustee of the estate of Futrelle.)

May and I dined at Delmonico's to celebrate her birthday. She is as beautiful to me now as she ever was. My feelings for her are even deeper than when we married. She has been the greatest comfort imaginable to me. I only hope I've been the same to her. She says so — which is pleasing.

In the middle of dinner I received a telephone call and a most pleasant bit of news — Harper has agreed to let me chronicle his exploits starting in the fall. With but one condition — that under no circumstances can our collaboration include the circumstances of his leaving Britain.

That relates to what May's cousin has disclosed regarding the Royal involvement in the Ripper slayings. Between what Roycroft has told us and what I have gleaned from my own sources in New York and London, it seems clear that Sam must have been regarded as a source of the utmost embarassment to the Crown.

In the summer of 1890 when May and I were in London for the Peel family celebration in honor of the 140th anniversary of the birth of their famous ancestor Bobbie Peel (after whom London bobbies are named since he founded the force while Home Secretary) we were staying with Roycroft Peel and his family. While there I quite accidently became privy to certain facts which established conclusively that Sir William Gull, consulting physician to the Prince of Wales and to the Royal family was guilty with others of the Ripper murders. When I disclosed to Roycroft what I had discovered, I learned he was deeply involved in the entire Ripper matter as a special investigator reporting directly to the Queen.

Roycroft was commissioned by the Queen to complete a secret investigation of the Ripper slayings. The Queen knew of the blackmail plot instigated by the whores or perhaps by their pimps, but she only expected them to be silenced, perhaps committed, but not killed. He had retained Sam Harper to bear the full responsibility as well he might have done, Sam being without question the most competent person in the Empire to complete such a task.

In his usual thorough fashion Sam proceeded to document a sordid trail of facts which demonstrated to Her Highness what she already knew, of course, that the Prince of Wales, the heir apparent and the Duke of Clarence, the heir presumptive, were involved in sexual misconduct of such a flagrant nature as to challenge the existence of the crown itself should the public learn of the facts.

Sam learned that Gull had performed more than one abortion on women of high birth who had consorted with the Prince of Wales behind their husband's backs. Had treated the Prince's gonorreah with which he infected his wife Princess Alexandra because, after several years of the loathsome disease he still was "too busy to cure it." And the Prince had already been named as correspondent and had appeared to testify in one of the most sordid and sensational divorce trials of the century.

Bad as that might be, it seemed a minor pecadillo compared to what was revealed about Eddy, the heir presumptive. Besides consorting openly with homosexuals at a male brothel on Cleveland Street which became the center of a public scandal only with difficulty suppressed by the Prime Minister Marquess of Salisbury, he contracted an illegal marriage with an illiterate young Catholic girl, one Annie Elizabeth Crook, who worked at a tobacconist shop near the Cleveland Street site.

Sam found all the supporting documentation of this liaison together with proof that she bore a child by the Prince, a daughter whom she named Alice Margaret.

Roycroft told me that Sam learned some of the details of the Ripper slayings from Walter Sickert, at that time a little known artist, in whose care Princess Alexandra (wife of the Prince of Wales) had placed Eddy to escape the oppresive treatment the Duke of Clarence received from the Prince of Wales who sensed Eddy was unfit to hold the throne even were he not compromised by events.

Sickert had a studio flat close by both the Cleveland Street location and the tobacco shop in which Annie Crook worked. The liaison between Eddy and the quite lovely young girl was consummated at Sickert's flat and with his full knowledge.

Sickert knew many of the prostitutes in London's East End and used many of them as models. Apparently he disclosed, wittingly or otherwise, to them the nature of the Duke's indiscretions, of Annie Crook's having been placed in a mental hospital to silence her and of the daughter born of that union who ended up as Sickert's charge (and later his mistress).

When several of the prostitutes who learned of the facts decided to blackmail the Crown, it was decided by several of the Prince of Wales' Masonic brethren that they would ingratiate themselves to the Marquess of Salisbury, the Prime Minister, and at the same time obtain leverage over the Prince of Wales and therefore, the Crown itself (when he acceded to the throne) by eliminating the bothersome whores.

Sam did not believe the Prime Minister, the Marquess of Salisbury to have been complicit in the killings, but was of the opinion he simply communicated his desire to be 'rid of the problem' thinking Gull would certify the whores to be insane as he had done Annie Crook. His suggestion however was regarded as tantamount to a license to kill by Gull who elected himself executioner, whose utterly ghastly crimes had then to be covered up by his fellow Masons, Salisbury, The Home Secretary, the Commissioner and Assistant Commissioner of Police. Gull wielded the scalpel and John Netley drove the hansom, a rolling abbatoir in which the crimes were committed, all the participants except Sickert and Netley being Masonic brethren of the Prince of Wales. Netley apparently was chosen because it was in his hansom the Duke of Clarence would arrive at Sickert's flat on Cleveland Street.

But they needed someone to identify the whores and for this they enlisted the help of Sickert who agreed to or was coerced into going along to identify the victims.

46

Apparently Sam prevailed upon the Queen to get Annie Crook's baby Alice released to Sickert's care after Annie's confinement in a mental hospital where she was sequestered to keep her from talking.

How Sam got Sickert to tell him the details I cannot say but Sickert's bad conscience over his complicity in the entire affair may have moved him to speak to ease his feelings of guilt. Also it appears he felt he had betrayed the trust of Princess Alexandra to whom he may have been lover and who placed Eddy in his care. Also he was apparently quite genuinely fond of the Duke of Clarence who came to such a tragic end almost surely kept deliberately under deep narcosis until his 'death from influenza' in 1892 at Sandringham barely a week after his 28th birthday.

The Marquess of Salisbury had apparently decided in 1885 shortly after the birth of Annie Crook's child by Eddy that the Duke of Clarence could never hold the throne. That decision became cast in concrete with the Cleveland Street scandal and the Ripper slayings.

Sir William Gull who wielded the knife in the slayings died but two years later in a mental hospital, apparently sequestered as Annie Crook had been to silence him.

Since the crimes Sickert has talked to whomever would listen about the Ripper slayings and his paintings are replete with arcane clues and references to the affair and its principals.

Sam's expulsion by Edward after the King came to power was apparently demanded by the Masonic brethren close to the throne who feared Sam might scotch the game of blackmail they were working over the Royal family. Sam, they feared I gather, didn't care enough whether the Crown was besmirched or not. They judged he wouldn't hesitate to do what was necessary to bring to power a member of the Royal family less randy than Edward and in that I suspect they were right.

Perhaps the most intriguing of the revelations given to me by Roycroft were included in a curious document he later let me read without any comment on his part whatever as to what he conjectured regarding its nature. It possessed neither an address nor a signature, but it is my supposition that it was written by Walter Sickert to Princess Alexandra after the death of the Duke of Clarence under decidedly mysterious circumstances. I transcribed the text verbatim:

"Eddy is dead and the world has been told he died of influenza at Sandringham Castle on January 14, 1892, barely a week after his 28th birthday. Rumor has it he actually died in a rest home at Ascot, drugged into unconsciousness for months. Whatever the truth may be, my utmost sympathy is with you over the death of your loved one, a fine young man I had come to love like a younger brother.

"I somehow knew, that last day, the day they raided my Cleveland Street flat taking Eddy and Annie away to their separate fates that I would never see him again. I hope it is not too painful for you to have me discuss these things, but my heart is filled with pain to overflowing and there is no one else with whom I can confide nor unburden my feelings.

" 'Pas auf die schlecte mechte die umkreisen auf!' "* I cried out so often in my nightmares about Eddy and where I feared he was heading. He and I often spoke in German both so I could keep my mother tongue fluent and so that he and I might discuss private matters when others such as Annie were about, for she knew no German. But I never gave him a warning in German nor any other language. For the die was cast long before you placed him in my charge. Do not think I hope to excuse myself for whatever responsibility I might have in your eyes for what has occurred. But Eddy did not need someone to lecture him. Had I done so, no possible relationship could have existed between us. He had had all the lecturing he or a dozen others needed from his father. And while you cautioned me that none of his actions were to be permitted to come to either the Queen's or Bertie's attention, you also charged me to honor his humanity and to be a true friend to him.

"I admit that these two commandments soon came into conflict with one another. But I had to make a choice. Besides what could he possibly do that would exceed in its licentiousness the examples of his own father? Forgive me, I mean no unkindness to you in so saying.

"How unfortunate it was that Eddy never wished to shoot or ride or do any of the things so admired by his father. Their relationship could have been so different had the H.A.** felt him more of a man. And Eddy could have come to know the fellowship of Bertie's Masonic brethren and they would have felt less threatened by the prospect of his holding the sceptre of power. I will venture a prediction that those responsible for the Ripper slayings will attempt to brand Eddy now and for future generations as the culprit. And neither he, nor you, nor anyone else will be able to defend him against such a charge without disclosing so many other things that cannot be allowed to surface.

"My family has been too close too long to the Royal Courts of Denmark and England for me not to have learned a thing or two about the lives of Royalty. What sacrifices are demanded of those poor unfortunates born to the Royal colours. Many so born would willingly forego all the trappings imagined by the commoners to be benefits and privileges if the very structure of society would not be threatened were they to do so.

"But it has occurred to me that the enormous pain suffered by Eddy at the hands of his father, the derision so openly heaped upon him by the H.A. finally had to be recompensed. And Eddy struck the ultimate blow of defiance in the direction of his father and the Crown. It could almost have been predicted.

"But the blow was not the murder of some really rather innocent whores. It was to have married without the consent of the Queen, without consultation with the Masonic brethren who so jealously guard the privileges they derive in manning the seats of power in the Court, to have married a commoner and a Roman Catholic when Englishmen despise the Pope and all the claims of Rome to superiority and priority over the Church of England, and to have

*German for "Beware of the evil forces that surround you."

**The Heir Apparent (Prince of Wales)

sired a child by her, this lovely and entirely lovable girl who was the first person to take him for exactly what he was. For she had no knowledge of his background before she gave herself to him and fell truly in love with him. She was certainly the first person, other than yourself, to do so. For Eddy that was a unique and irresistible circumstance. It is really no wonder he could do the things for which the Prime Minister now calls him to have been 'quite mad.'

"Salisbury has one eye on the Kaiser, wondering if he will dismiss Chancellor Bismarck and let Germany's agreements with Britain, France and Russia lapse threatening peace in Western Europe. The quick succession of crowned heads in Germany threatens the balance of power and the P.M. wonders if the ancient Anglo-German alliance will go by the boards.

"To what extent I do not know, but I have often wondered if this entire outreaching for power by Bertie's Masonic associates is not merely an extension into modern times of the Norman Conquest. Are we really seeing jealousy at work over the fact England's Crown sits upon the heads of a German family? I can only guess, but it's a sad day when the very ones guilty of the Ripper murders are able to aggrandize themselves by their own crimes and hold the Royal Family at blackmail in the process.

"The comfort I feel in the presence of common people, even the East End denizens, the pleasure I enjoy in their company brands me a true Saxon, I suppose. But these men close to Bertie do not honestly believe in democracy. All their actions are grounded in the desire to preserve their own privileges and those of the ruling classes. It is understandable enough, but the hypocrisy apparent in their pandering to the public disgusts me.

"It is bad enough that the Liberals occasionally unseat the Tories and take power. But unthinkable that the Socialists or Communists should gain admission to the Establishment merry-go-round.

"My frankness puts me at your mercy, but I say these things in defense both of Eddy and my role in the tragic events so recently brought to a close by his death. I loved him as you commanded me to do. And I love you as you long have known. When you dandled me on your knee at the Yellow Palace,* I but a child of five and you a young woman, you knew of my love and saw through the flimsy excuses I found to kiss you or be kissed by you. Those were not the innocent kisses of a child you thought them to be for I was sexually drawn to you even then. But who knows whose eyes might see this. Burn it after you've read it or we both may suffer.

"For now I am left with my last sight of Eddy as they hauled him away to his terrible fate and no guess when I may once again be blessed to have the opportunity to see you."

*The summer home of the Danish Royal Family.

Letter to Arthur Conan Doyle
from Samuel Harper
Dated September 15, 1911 (New York City)

Dear Arthur,

Autumn approaches and our weather is heavenly. The unbearable heat of the summer is past and the days are now warm enough to be pleasant and the nights are cool enough to permit a sound night's sleep. Was aroused from a deep slumber at 2 a.m. by a courier from the Russian consulate. He brought an emergency request from the Czar that I accept a special assignment, depart at once for Moscow and take charge of the investigation of the assassination of Prime Minister Peter Stolypin. Most regretfully had to decline due to my other commitments. The Czar simply cannot accept the fact that only the removal of the throne will satisfy the radicals. The very name Russia, perpetuating as it does the name of the Viking ruling class (the Rus, meaning blonde), must go, in their view. Russia is a land of many races most of whom despise the Aryan minority who rule. They will not stop their agitation until the Czar is deposed.

I read with great interest your notes on the Mormons and while I noted a few inaccuracies (some major) they were on the whole accurate as to Mormon theology. Your observations relative to the similarities with spiritualism are of interest. No Mormon would, of course, attach any credence to them, but such I am sure you already know.

I would point out that your reference to the Ten Lost Tribes and their swarthy skins and long noses betrays still your confusion about the Khazar-Jew who fits that description but is not of the blood of Israel. The role of the Khazars who are converts to Judaism is one of the most important points covered in J.B. Bury's new book which I believed you to have read. Please get it out again and review the discussion of the Khazars as it is most important to understand the distinction between true Israel (the Anglo-Saxon-Celtic peoples) and the Khazar-Jew who is not of the blood of Israel but who practices the Judaic faith.

Your letter states: "I should like to have the opinion of some learned linguist as to whether any Indian words could be traced to the ancient Hebrew root." In that vein you are as one with both Ben Franklin and Thomas Jefferson who speculated on the same subject. Much work will yet be done on this very topic, but as early as 1816 Elias Boudinot in his book A STAR IN THE WEST brought together some interesting facts which he, in all modesty, credits others for discovering. Bear in mind that speculation as to the whereabouts of the Ten Lost Tribes was a major topic of scholarly theological interest in a predominantly religious era.

The Creek Indian word for deity he reports is Y.HE.HO.WAH corresponding to the Hebrew Jehovah; their word for the great first cause is YOHEWAH. Their word for "Praise the first cause" is HALLELUWAH, correspondingly to the Hebrew Hallelujah. Their word for man ISHTE is not unlike the Hebrew Ish with the same meaning. Their word for father ABBA is identical to the Hebrew Abba for the same. The Creek word for now, NA is identical to the Hebrew NA — same meaning. To pray = PHALE in Creek = Phalae in Hebrew. ALE the Creek word (another name for deity) = El in Hebrew. The Creek word KORA for winter = Cora in Hebrew.

The Mohegan word for I (1st person singular) is NIAH versus the Hebrew Ani; this tribe says KEAH for thou or thee; the Hebrew word is Ka. "This man" in Mohegan is UWOH corresponding to Huah in Hebrew. And their word for we or NECAUNUH is not unlike the Hebrew word Nachnu of the same meaning.

Boudinot also remarks that the Mohawks, who were the law-givers to all the other tribes in the northeastern area of the American colonies may derive their name from the Hebrew word MHHOKEK which in that language means law-giver.

To your credit, you seem more willing than most to attribute a divine origin to the Book of Mormon, or, let us say, to concede that the material it contains might be of an otherworldly origin. Unlike most people, who, if antagonistic to Mormonism which many are, simply characterize it as a fraud and fabrication, if not the product of Joseph Smith, then of someone else, Solomon Spaulding or whoever.

I submit that there is no possibility that the document is a fraud. It is simply not possible statistically for anyone to have falsified its contents, surely not an uneducated frontiersman. Indeed, not even the most learned specialist in the antiquities, at the time it came forth could have originated such a document. In fact, the more learned its author in the ways of the ancient world as they were then thought to be, the more surely his fraud would be exposed in the present day because so much believed by the learned then has been found in our day to be false.

If I cannot prove that an angel delivered the book, I can surely demonstrate that its origination must have just as unlikely an explanation. It is as easily explained as being from an angel as anywhere else. The facts cannot be explained in any ordinary way.

But leaving generalities behind, let's examine certain aspects of the book that defy conventional explanation. We moderns have ridiculed much of the wisdom of the past because until probably 1100 A.D. there was next to nothing written down, at least, for the ordinary man. Prior to such time we are required to rely upon what has been recorded by the clerics of what we characterize as the 'oral tradition,' and this only for kings. And the monks, in reducing to writing the genealogies of the kings tended to embroider. It therefore must be regarded not so much as a criticism of the oral tradition as a commentary upon the sycophancy of the monks, that genealogies which include a generous sprinkling of Biblical progenitors for kings are not today regarded as reliable.

Nonetheless that the oral tradition existed and was regarded as reliable prior to the embellishment of the monks is unquestioned. In our day we have no idea whatever of the extraordinary extents to which the ancients went to facilitate the reduction of history to memory, nor the seriousness of the crime of attempting to corrupt these traditions.

51

There is little doubt that the exalted position of the bard in the Irish tradition is primarily because his ability to render the tribal history to meter and rhyme facilitated the memorization of these vital records. More than in our time was it anciently recognized that a people without a tradition to uphold will soon be relegated to the dustheap of history.

It was the primary duty of all members of the tribe to protect the tribal record. The Book of Mormon itself describes how Nephi killed his uncle Laban for attempting to withhold the plates containing the family record. Such an occurrence would be fully credible in that era. As the Spirit counselled Nephi when he hesitated to kill Laban to obtain the plates: "It is better that one man should perish than that a nation should dwindle and perish in unbelief." Such a philosophy was predominant amongst the Hebrews. The tribal record also embodied the tribe's relation with Jahweh or Jehovah, and the code by which the Israelites were enjoined to live by their God. It was thus a doubly sacred tradition, to be preserved at all costs.

It was recognized by the Hebrews that the use of parallel structures in literature facilitated memorization. This device we call chiasmus, though surely I needn't tell a writer like yourself about such things. When I was a boy my teacher illustrated chiasmus in the phrase: "She went to Paris; to New York went he." This use of chiasmus in the Scriptures was something with which all students of Holy Writ were unconsciously familiar. Matthew 13:13-18 says: "Therefore I speak to them in parables: Because they seeing see not: and hearing they hear not. In them is fulfilled the prophecy of Esaias, which sayeth; By hearing ye shall hear not; and seeing ye shall see not."

But as early as 1820 an Englishman, John Jebb published his book SA-CRED LITERATURE focusing attention on the chiastic principle in the Bible. Interest in chiasmus in Scripture can be dated as of that time. In 1854 a Scottish scholar John Forbes published his work THE SYMMETRICAL STRUCTURE OF SCRIPTURE which dwelt in greater length on chiasmus and fully awakened the academic world to a general knowledge of chiasmus and its use in Scripture.

There can be little doubt that the origination of the use of chiasmus was to facilitate memorization in an era when paper and ink were generally unavailable and when the vast majority of the people were required to memorize their tribal histories including the greatest of all tribal stories THE HOLY BIBLE. As a side point I believe the weight of the evidence to support the proposition that the Hebrew tribes carried much of the Holy Scriptures with them wherever they went, transmitted orally from generation to generation. This would explain why once the Bible in printed form was made available after the Dark Ages, the use of the Scriptures spread like wild fire throughout the western world. It was simply a matter of their oral tradition becoming available in a handy compendium.

Be all that as it may, the fact that chiasmus is used so extensively throughout the Book of Mormon is unassailable proof first, that it is of ancient origin, and second, that no unschooled person could have constructed the elaborate chiasmi contained in the book.

As for the proposition that a highly trained scholar originated the Book of Mormon which somehow came into Joseph Smith's hands, that scholar would have to have known much that we have only recently discovered. He would have had to invented two hundred original nouns for the most part names of individuals, cities, mountains, rivers, valleys, monetary units, animals, foods, religions, architectural features, political offices, a metal, a sea, an insect and more. And none of these could be found to conflict with the present state of our knowledge of the idioms of those ancient peoples.

To an Egyptologist two names are bound to stand out. Paanchi and Pahoran, both first encountered by the western world in the Book of Mormon have the PA beginning. We now know that the most common type of names in the late Egyptian Empire began with PA. I could go on almost endlessly in the same vein.

But to summarize, the appearance of esoteric linguistic materials only now known to be validly of Hebrew and Egyptian origin and not so known at the time the Book of Mormon came forth establishes conclusively that not even a highly learned scholar could have forged the document. And there is at present, after untold thousands of attempts, no case in which it has not been found to accord perfectly with the latest understanding of the scholarly as to the circumstances of the cultures it purports to describe.

Strictly as an evidentiary matter, one must conclude it to be truly an ancient and valid document. Draw your own conclusions as to whether Joseph Smith's story of how it came forth is true.

I regret I can no longer locate any copies of the monograph I wrote on heraldry. I am sure all that sort of thing is either still in the boxes I left with you upon my sudden departure, or has been hopelessly lost.

However, if I might encapsulate what in my more verbose days took 25 pages, I will try to give you a quick course on the subject.

We are often told that the use of heraldic emblems came into use with the invention of armour which rendered it impossible to otherwise indentify warriors encased in their defensive gear. Undoubtedly it served such purpose well, but to imply that this is the earliest use of heraldry is to commit an error of perhaps three thousand years. As a booklet published by the U.S. government indicates quite correctly: "Heraldry is as old as the human race, and the carrying of banners has been the habit of nations since the beginning of time." As for such usage by the tribes of Israel, it is stated in Numbers 2:2: "Every man of the children of Israel shall pitch by his own standard, with the ensign of their father's house." The second chapter of Numbers goes on to state that, when not on the march, the Twelve Tribes encamped in a definite order around an open space at the center of which was the tent-like enclosure for national worship called the Tabernacle. It is frequently assumed the tribes encamped in the form of a square but the Bible does not actually say this and there are some indications it may have been round or oval. At any rate, Numbers tells us that Judah encamped on the east side of the enclosure with Issachar and Zebulun at Judah's flanks. On the south side was encamped Reuben flanked by Simeon and Gad.

On the west side was Ephraim flanked by Benjamin and Manasseh with Ephraim and Manasseh representing their father Joseph the son through whose intercession with Pharaoh, Jacob and his eleven sons and their families were saved from starvation. On the north side the tribe of Dan staked out, flanked by Asher and Naphtali. The Levites or the professional priesthood encamped next to the Tabernacle.

Having established that the tribes employed ensigns during the exodus while Israel was wandering in the desert let us explore the origin of the symbols employed by each of the tribes. We see that the book of Genesis (Chapter 49) gives us the counsel of Jacob (or Israel) to his twelve sons on his deathbed. Each son was characterized by the old man, these characterizations related to events described in the scriptures regarding each of the sons, and became the origin of the emblems employed in each tribe's standard or ensign.

To state concisely what the experts have agreed upon after much discussion and contemplation, the symbols, primary and secondary of each of the sons are as follows:

	Primary	Secondary
1. Reuben (the oldest son)	A man	A body of water
2. Simeon	A sword	A fortified gate of a castle
3. Judah	A lion recumbent	Three Lions A sceptre A vine flowing over a wall
4. Dan	A serpent	A horse (usually white) and a lion
5. Naphtali	A hind or stag	none
6. Gad	A knight on horseback	A lion
7. Asher	A cup or vessel	none
8. Issachar	A laden ass	none
9. Zebulun	A ship	none
10. Ephraim	An ox	A unicorn
11. Manasseh	A bough (or olive branch)	A cluster of arrows
12. Benjamin	A wolf	none

The Levites, as the priesthood tribe encamped with the Tabernacle and had no emblem.

It will be of interest to you that in the parish church of St. Lawrence in Eyam there are traces of paintings of the emblems of the Twelve Tribes that are several hundred years old, and that underneath these ancient paintings there are visible traces of others even older.

I am told too that in certain Masonic degrees known from the most ancient times the symbols set forth in Genesis 49 representing the tribes have been employed.

That all of these symbols would survive the early emigration from Egypt, the later downfall and deportation of Israel and nearly three thousand years of war, separation and migrations would be impossible to predict or expect. But strangely, of these twenty-two symbols or emblems at least nineteen are, or until very recently have been, employed as emblems of one or another group of the Anglo-Saxon-Celtic peoples.

History records few, if any, instances of the use by one people of the emblems of another tribe. Sound military practice would dictate otherwise. This being the case, it is safe to assume that where found these symbols signify beyond doubt that those using the emblems were of the origin indicated by the emblem.

To give but a few examples before exploring the symbolism of the crest of the British Crown, the Castle Gate symbol of the tribe of Simeon is widely used among the Celto-Saxons including the Arms of the following: Winchester, Exeter, Swansea, Carmarthen, Dunbar (civic emblem), Plymouth, Bedford, Doncaster, Northampton, Newcastle, Wigan, Edinburgh, Stirling, Aberdeen, Limerick, Carlow, Athey, Tralee, Dublin, Londonderry, Ballymena, Drogheda, Dungannon and Carrickfergus.

It likewise appears in the heraldry of the clans and ancient families of Lord Elphinstone, Mackinnon of Mackinnon, Machlachlan, Maclean of Duart, Macleod of Macleod, Macnaughten of Dundarawe, Macneill of Earra, Macquarrie of Ulva, the Captain of Clanranald, Malcolm of Poltalloch and Spalding of Ashintully.

The Lion of Judah, besides appearing in the Arms of Britain also appears in the Arms of Scotland, Northern Ireland, Canada, Norway, Sweden, Finland, Denmark, the Netherlands, Belgium and Luxembourg, as well as in the emblems of many of their provinces and cities.

The serpent of Dan appears in the Arms of Buxton and Barrow-in-Furness in England, in the Crest of Livingston, Earl of Linlithgow and in those of the Chiefs of the Robertson and Morrison Clans in Scotland. In the Netherlands it appears in the municipal Arms of at least twenty communities. It was nearly chosen as the national emblem of the United States in lieu of the eagle and was the official emblem of several of the military and naval units of the U.S. Revolutionary forces.

The white horse of Dan appears in the Municipal Arms in Denmark of Horsens, Holstebro and Augustenborg. In the Netherlands a horse appears in the Arms of Assendelft, Hoogkarspel, Westerbork, Zuidlaren, Baarn, Renkum, Workhoven and others. It is also the emblem of several of the former

German municipalities and of Lithuania. In England it is the emblem of the County of Kent and it also appears in the Arms of Ramsgate and Margate. In Scotland the white horse appears in the Crests of Cochrane, Earl of Dundonald, Dunbar of Mochrum, Hepburn, Earl of Bothwell, Trotter of Catchilraw and the Arms of the Chief of Clan Cumming.

The cup or goblet of Asher appears in the Arms of Barnsley and Warrington; in Scotland it is a prominent feature in the Arms of Greenock and Paisley and in the Arms of Carnegie, Earl of Southesk and of Schaw of Sauchie.

The ship of Zebulun appears in the emblems of nineteen places in Scotland and in the Arms of Clan Chiefs Argyle, Burntisland, Bute, Caithness, Campbelltown, Greenock, Inverness, Kirkwall, Largs, North Berwick, Oban, Orkney, Queen's Ferry, Renfrew, Rothesay, Rutherglen, Stranraer, Wick, Zetland, Campbell, Clan Chattan, Clanranald, Gunn of Kilernan, Hamilton, MacAllister, McBain, MacBean, MacDonald, MacDonell, MacDougall, Macfie, MacGillivray, MacIain, MacKinnon, MacLaren, MacLauchlan, MacLean, MacNeil, MacPherson, Menteith and Shaw of Rothiemurchus.

The ox or bull of Ephraim appears in the national emblems of Iceland and Denmark. It appears in the emblem of the District of Alborg and the municipal emblems of Rodovre, Tyrstrup, Bov and Dalby.

It appears in the Crest of the Macleod of Macleod and in England we still give our native land the nickname of 'John Bull.' Hundreds of other examples could also be shown not only of the use of the Bull but also of the secondary emblem of Ephraim which is the Unicorn and of the other symbols of all the sons of Israel. Which leads us quite well to a discussion of the Royal Crest of England.

To the left we see the Crowned Lion representing Royal Judah and to the right we see the Unicorn of Ephraim, the family from whom the Royal family of the Ten Northern Tribes who separated from Judah after the death of Solomon. It might be well to recall at this point that after the revolt of the Ten Northern Tribes and the establishment of Ephraim as the Royal House of the Ten Northern Tribes whose capital became Samaria the distinction between Judah and Israel (The Ten Northern Tribes) is quite consistently maintained in the Scriptures. Prior to such time, of course, the term Israel meant all twelve tribes but not so after the revolt. Nonetheless, we see that the Book of Genesis (49:10) promises that there will ever be a son of Judah on the throne of Israel; likewise it is stated that the sceptre will never depart from Judah. It thus takes on special significance when we see that the Royal Arms of Britain incorporate the symbols of both Judah and Israel. We also see in the Royal colors the Harp of David. David, of course, was of the house of Judah and the six-pointed star of David appears in manifold applications in British heraldry.

The obvious conclusion is that those of the Royal Family proclaim themselves through their heraldry to be descendants of David of the House of Judah, the Royal line ruling over both Judah and Israel. No other conclusion is possible.

Some may assert that this only proves that those claiming these heraldic emblems believed themselves to be of the Twelve Tribes but that the issue

56

remains unanswered whether they were in fact, of such descent. I suppose at one point in my life I fell into such a category myself. I think at present I find the evidence irresistable that our ancestors both thought themselves to be Israel and were in fact the descendants of the Twelve Tribes.

The question with which I wrestle now is not whether they were Israel but what religious significance should be attached to that fact. Precisely, is Israel a Chosen People as the Scriptures state in a special relationship with God and how does the idea of a God who would choose a single people as a Holy Priesthood equate with our concept of an infinitely just Creator? I have enormous difficulty believing these two ideas are not entirely inconsistent.

At any rate, suffice it to say that the heraldry of the European nations lends enormous support to the proposition that these nations are descended from ancient Israel. Each man must decide for himself what significance to attach to that fact. I hope this highly condensed approach will suffice for your purposes.

Leslie and I send our best to you, Jean and the brood. I hope it shan't be long before we can get together in London, New York or Timbuctoo.

Fondly,

Sam

Excerpt from Letter to Arthur Conan Doyle from Samuel Harper

Dated November 1, 1911 (New York City)

The flicker of gaslights on mahogany in Gage & Tollners was comfortingly like that so fondly remembered at the Diogenes Club; Futrelle was finishing an enormous section of nesselrode pie that fittingly capped off a dinner of enormous lobsters we had enjoyed with a carafe of cold chablis for me and sparkling water from the gasogene for Futrelle who is allergic to alcohol.

I had drawn him over from Manhattan to my favorite restaurant close to my flat in Brooklyn Heights.

Gone was the despondency with which I quit England, greatly deepened by the death of my lovely wife. How I had missed all my favorite haunts, the Cafe Royal and all the rest, when King Edward advised me he could no longer 'insure my safety' in the affair of the Duke of Clarence.

Not that any man need insure my safety, but it surely would not do to have another breath of scandal however small associated with any member of the Royal Family. And no minor scandal could result if I should take a life in defending myself from some paid killer in the hire of the well-born Ripper killers, and should Scotland Yard's investigation then lead backward to some key Mason in the Home Office or other high position and thence, by the King's membership in that powerful fraternity, to the throne.

Futrelle was most direct in addressing himself to the matter of my departing England. "I must tell you Harper," he said crunching the great shreds of chocolate on the surface of his pie, "that there is a great deal I already know about the case which has caused you this extraordinary inconvenience, and a great deal more that I've conjectured without proof, but probably, by intuition, not too far from the truth."

I began to interrupt. "But before you interrupt," he said smiling, "let me state I shall never pursue the matter with you or press you for any details as I know the ethics of your calling make such matters privileged information even were the case not fraught with the immense political overtones only a fool could miss."

I returned his smile. "You are well informed at least on the point of what ethics require of me in such matters."

He shrugged his shoulders modestly as he plucked a succulent morsel of dessert from his plate with his fork. "However painful to you," he said, a look of utmost understanding and compassion upon his visage, "England's ill fortune at losing your talents is America's blessing and mine."

"You are kind to say so," I replied, determined never again to advert to the Ripper case or any aspect of it with Futrelle. But the Ripper case was not and has never been, since it played out its bloody obscenities in 1888, far from my mind that autumn evening in 1911 when I enlisted in the person of Jacques Futrelle my second Boswell, a chronicler of events second only to you my dear Doyle, a chap who bids fair to become one of the world's great writers of scientific detective 'fiction.' And he, like you, is always seeking grist for his mill which, he trusts, I can supply be letting him fictionalize some of my exploits.

We surely never dreamed, as the revolving door of the restaurant whirled us into the street, that he would ever become directly involved in a case, but no sooner had we turned toward the river and drawn close to the entrance to the alleyway running alongside the restaurant in which we had just dined than a moan of profound and terminal pain reached our ears and told us that some fell creature lay mortally wounded not five yards away on the filthy cobblestones behind a dozen or so large trash cans.

We approached with haste and Futrelle struck a match to lighten the poor devil's features as I strained to observe his condition, bending over him. Pale and flickering though it was, the matchlight revealed enough to sicken the heart of me. A man of forty-five or fifty lay dying and at a glance I recognized all the characteristics of England's greatest 'unsolved' crime. The throat slashed, I knew it would prove under the coroner's scrutiny to have been cut from left to right, as was his breast and his belly. The stench of punctured intestines and blood was overwhelming, but to his credit Futrelle didn't betray anything but complete control. I was aware briefly of a feeling of admiration for his levelness. Something more than I bargained for.

But I was absorbed at once in trying to determine if the poor creature could still be alive or had the moan we heard been his last? I felt for his pulse but could find none. Still as Futrelle moved the match close to his distorted and bloody features, his lips moved in an enormous effort, his last to be sure, to speak.

I strained to hear his words, but when they came they were surprisingly strong. "Balfour . . ." he paused to summon his remaining strength. "Balfour will die . . . if . . . you don't warn him . . ." And with that he was gone.

I left him precisely as he was, concealing my surprise to hear him verbalize the name of one of my oldest friends, a former Prime Minister and a man deeply involved in matters of the utmost consequence to His Majesty's government.

I took a pencil and notebook out of my coat pocket and recorded his last words as well as perhaps twenty-five or so salient features of the scene while Futrelle summoned the police. They arrived remarkably swiftly, or so it seemed, and when they determined his identity from his wallet which, incidently contained five thousand dollars in large denomination bills, they were good enough to give me his name and address.

"We've not seen you lately at the station house Mester Horper," said a constable with a heavy Irish accent, "odd it should be you to find this royal mess." "Quite so Officer Moran," I said scrutinizing him closely to see if any special meaning lay behind his words, "odd it surely is."

Having given them our responses to their remarkably few questions, Futrelle and I took our leave of the scene and proceeded slowly to walk down the street toward the subway Futrelle would take home. "An auspicious beginning to our new association," said Futrelle, his eyes searching my face. "What do you make of the precise, almost ritual slashing?"

"Not unlike another case with which I am familiar," I said between puffs on my pipe. "That would be the Ripper case no doubt?" he queried. "Ripper indeed — could be a coincidence of course."

"Not likely, I think," Futrelle said with an irritating certainty. If Futrelle is correct, I conjectured silently, then Isaac Fenster as we now knew him to be named surely made the mistake of crossing some powerful figures, knowingly or unknowingly. But I reserved comment on his statement by a non-committal "Hmmmm." Where, I thought, had I heard the dead man's name before?

We agreed to meet the following day at the home in Manhattan of the victim, a wealthy Jew, Isaac Fenster, a Wall Street banker. What was he doing so far away from his fashionable home neighborhood, all alone in the hands of the most evil of men, right here on Samuel Harpers' home grounds?

I shook Jacques' hand and he was gone into the bowels of the BMT, a look of mixed amazement, anticipation and foreboding on his countenance.

Then I moved swiftly in the darkened streets toward my home. Several times I stopped to glance behind but the dimly lit streets glistening from the moist air blown from the East River condensing on the cobblestones revealed not a sound or a sign of life except an occasional cat. Out on the river I could see the solitary lights of a slowly moving tugboat and heard its mournful whistle penetrate the blackness of the night.

Best ever,

Sam

P.S. I read of Churchill's appointment as First Lord of the Admiralty. He will have his chance now. He should be able to accelerate the process of modernizing the fleet, especially the switch from coal to oil. Ever since the Russian fleet had to sail for the Orient, during the war with Japan, with her guns incapacitated because of the coal piled on the decks (extra fuel for the long journey which was beyond the ships' designed range) Navy men everywhere have been preoccupied with the need to switch to oil. It shall begin now.

I hear Balfour may soon resign the leadership of the Conservatives. Do you hear the same?

Letter to Samuel Harper
from Arthur Conan Doyle

Dated November 16, 1911 (London)

Dear Sam,

I note with great interest your description of the death of Isaac Fenster and its similarity to the Ripper slayings. I await additional news of the case with great anticipation. I can think of no reason why anyone would mimic the Masons in the manner of his execution, but then I know nothing of the man or his circumstances. Please keep me informed.

Balfour has indeed resigned as of November 8th. He will be playing more tennis now, I suspect.

It is too bad you were unable to honor the Czar's request to investigate the assassination of the P.M. Stolypin. I would have appreciated some recent word on the condition of things inside Russia.

While they call it a "Jewish Revolution" in the councils of the Czar and, indeed, the Khazar-Jews as you and Bury have brought me to calling them, are the chief fomenters of the Czar's problems, still, there is massive discontent to be exploited amongst all of Russia's minorities. It is a pernicious thing to lead every ethnic group to yearn for and demand their own national status. And how, once ignited, do all these minorities surrender their grievances for the common good in a pluralistic state like Britain's Empire or in America? Mankind seems to possess unlimited ability to embrace contradictory objectives without even recognizing the mischief such contradictions create.

Since my last letter to you I have thought a good deal about some of the things Rud and I discussed during our last visit together. We were reminiscing about our childhood experiences and sharing personal reactions to our circumstances.

Raised as he was in India, one would have expected there would be very little we would have in common. And yet, perhaps childhood is childhood wherever it is experienced. We discovered we had much in common in spite of the exotic setting of his and the squalid circumstances of my early years.

I suppose it is not really so surprising that we should each have come to our present stations in life devoted to the crown, the Empire and the status quo. After all, in spite of our meager beginnings, we've managed to prosper. And any country which allows that can't be all bad. Rud has received the Nobel Prize for literature and I've been knighted as you surely would have been but for your exile.

Sam, I know you dwell now in a country that has abandoned all such distinctions, but it serves a good purpose that a nation can so express its appreciation for the accomplishments of its citizens. That may sound pompous and self-centered but I know you will not so regard it.

I am greatly humbled that my simple scratchings have brought pleasure to so many, and that in expressing their appreciation they have created my present prosperity. Perhaps it is these very blessings that made me contemplate so seriously at this fairly late stage in my life the deprivation and squalor in which I began.

But perhaps of greater relevance to our present endeavor, devoted as it is to the question of where this whole mystery we call life takes us, is the impact of childhood on our religious development. People who haven't been raised under the constant fear of hell-fire can have little in common with those of us raised in Roman Catholicism. Even though Melville was not raised a Catholic, I sense in his writings that he experienced the same horror as I in enduring the fire and brimstone Calvinism of his childhood, and that his breaking away from that code was as difficult as mine.

Rud, although he came from an only mildly religious family of Methodists, had a surprisingly strong appreciation for my fears of hell-fire. He described to me the terror he experienced when, as a small boy, he first learned of the Hindu custom of suttee, the burning of the surviving widow on the dead spouse's funeral pyre. Nightmares in which he saw in vivid detail this immolating fire apparently troubled him for weeks. Rud predicted that if England ever left India to govern herself that suttee as well as slavery and a host of other evils outlawed by the British would return in a week. The Christianity our colonial government took our far-flung Empire may have been a lukewarm version of the original, but it rendered a great service nonetheless to the benighted nations in those lands.

But Rud lived like a maharajah compared to my family. Lockwood K. may have only been a curator but the Kipling family enjoyed the services of a staff of servants on his meager (by the standards of home) salary.

The most vivid memory of my childhood, Sam, is the stench of human sewage that permeated Edinburgh, "auld reekie" as we called it. There was no escaping, at least in the poorer sections where we lived. Crime abounded, and between the confinement of our threadbare surroundings, ever closed up against the stench and the ruffians, and the restrictive code of Catholicism is it any wonder I yearn for the freedom of the out-of-doors be it skiing, motoring, cricket or what-have-you?

Even my choice of a philosophy if you can't call spiritualism a religion, may have been dictated by the circumstances of my childhood. We may suffer the derision of our fellows for our beliefs, but we enjoy the knowledge that the spirit is free to return, even across the valley of death.

I yearned for travel and adventure and freedom when I was a youth. Especially to be free of the fears and terrors of hell-fire. Unlike some, I was not seeking to live licentiously. But I did yearn to be free of my fears of the hereafter.

And my choice of the profession of medicine had a part also. I recall how compelled I felt to question if there could be a God who would leave mankind in the cesspool of the London slums even if the conditions were man's own doing.

I recall once being called out late at night to a home in Seaside where my impoverished practice of medicine began. An old woman led me into a darkened bedroom, that I doubt had ever seen sunlight. The stench of human excrement permeated all. In the bed a mound indicated the presence of some creature though of the most diminutive proportions.

"What is it?" I asked. "My daughter," said she. "Why doesn't she die? She's nineteen and has spent her entire life in that bed." I doubt man or mankind is perfectible, and if the fatalism of the Orient goes too far and insures that the squalor of the backward races will never be undone, still I can understand how hard it is to believe in a God who permits such suffering to occur.

But if Catholicism would not do, still I could not live without religion. It is too much a requirement of the Celtic nature, I guess. And after years of searching and having lost so much with the deaths of so many I dearly love, I had to find a belief which would meet my needs.

That the spirits of the dead live on and can communicate with us may not be everything. But it is a beginning and I'm perfectly willing to devote my life and all my wealth to discovering the rest.

Yours,

Arthur

Letter to Arthur Conan Doyle
from Samuel Harper

Dated November 18, 1911 (New York City)

Dear Arthur,

We are at last seeing the delightful autumn weather I remembered so fondly in my recollections of New York prior to our departure from Blighty. The trees in Central Park still are in leaf and we enjoy a symphony of colors, red and orange, yellows of every shade and magenta. I come to life in the fall just as I once was given my life being born in October. Hope you all are well, as are we.

The coroner's report on Fenster is unusually detailed. A clue to the great importance of the man in the affairs of New York City. There was no alcohol in his blood or other type of drug. Death was from bleeding although there was severe damage done to vital organs in slashing the belly, as in the Ripper cases, that would have occasioned death had he not bled to death first. For a man his age he was remarkably healthy and likely had many more years to live but for his murder.

We now know definitely what I surmised, that he was taken to the death scene and dumped there, as there was not enough blood at the scene for the deed to have been done there.

We've traced his movements the evening of the murder and have a report that he dined at the Harvard Club with a guest who could not be identified by the staff of the Club. Fenster was well known at the Club to which he had belonged for years. Many of his usual dinner companions are known to the staff, but not the man with whom he dined on the night of the murder. He is described as having had a heavy accent, possibly German, and Fenster and this man are reported to have conversed entirely in German during dinner. The waiter who served them is from a German immigrant family from the Bay Ridge section of Brooklyn where many German immigrant families live.

The waiter, one Harry Albert, reports that each time he drew near the table to serve them they ceased talking quite abruptly and did not resume until he departed. He says it was clear they did not wish to be overheard.

Albert says he could readily identify Fenster's companion if he saw him. He smoked black middle eastern cigarettes and drank heavily in contrast to Fenster who, by custom, did neither. He was a swarthy man of perhaps forty years, possibly an Arab or Turk.

The doorman at the Club says he flagged down separate cabs for them and they departed separately, each alone.

I don't know, Doyle, whether to attach great importance to the man talking German. The Fensters are German Jews and have many relatives in Germany where the deceased spent several years in school.

The confusing aspect of the autopsy results is that elements found in Fenster's stomach that clearly entered the alimentary tract subsequent to the meal at the Harvard Club are not included in the ingredients we have established were employed by the chef at the Club in preparing what Fenster ate. A number of these are employed in preparing cuisine of the ethnic groups in the Levant. If I had to guess at an explanation, I would speculate that upon leaving the Club Fenster either visited a home or restaurant in which he dined upon cuisine prepared by a middle Easterner, possibly a Turk. It all leads me to speculate that Fenster may have been approached by interests representing the Austro-Hungarian Empire and/or the Ottoman Empire. Were this correct, we might conclude that he ran afoul of persons intending to frustrate Balfour's goal of a Jewish homeland in Palestine. Turkey will surely fight at Germany's side in any war breaking out between the major powers. If Fenster uncovered a plot to kill Balfour as a means of derailing Arthur's plan to carve a Jewish homeland out of Turkish territory, a homeland under British protection employed to protect the route to India, they could have killed him in spite of his opposition to Zionism. For the time being, this is my theory of the reason for Fenster's death. It is subject to revision if evidence adduced later should invalidate the theory.

True to our commitment made the night of the killing, Futrelle and I met at the Fifth Avenue mansion (should I say 'palazzo'?) of Isaac Fenster. It was 10 a.m. and a police officer was stationed at the door, a member of the small force assigned to the Fenster home as a protection to the dead man's family. I wondered to myself whether my good friend the Police Commissioner was not as concerned with the possibility of further Ripper-style vengeance upon the family of the deceased as with keeping the curious away. The constable waved us in when he saw my identification. "We were told to expect you Mr. Harper."

Futrelle and I entered the impressive foyer of the Fenster mansion. Futrelle's expressive eyebrows raised to express the impression these lavish surroundings made upon him. I smiled, expressing my agreement. We awaited the appearance of some emissary from the Fenster household.

"My inquiries with some contacts that know Wall Street in general and the Fenster firm in particular advise me that the victim recently published a revealing book about the inner workings of the financial world," I said.

"Revealing in what sense?" Futrelle asked.

"For now I must confess to be ignorant as to the answer," I responded, "my contact could not take the time to tell me, in fact he seemed most reticent about the whole subject, as though acutely embarassed to be calling the matter to my attention, but he has arranged to deliver a copy of the book to me which should be in my hands by tomorrow. I shall make it available to you as soon as I have perused it." We fell silent once again and directed our attentions to a more minute examination of our resplendent surroundings. I was struck by a sudden realization.

I realized that I had been here before on several occasions though it was not then owned by Fenster and had been completely redecorated. The former owner (whose name you surely recall) was Emerson Morgan the first to report the loss of a Sickert painting. Out of an art collection worth millions a single canvas stolen! Not long afterward Morgan sold the house and moved to the south of France. He must have had a sense of great concern, Arthur, over the ease with which so many people he regarded as faithful could be suborned for one not terribly valuable painting. By now, of course, Sickert's insatiable need to discuss the Ripper case was causing whispers in many high places.

Also, I had had occasion to interrogate the deceased when I was on special assignment to Theodore Roosevelt in connection with Emma Goldman's possible role in the McKinley assassination. Roosevelt is a friend of Fenster's father who contributed large amounts of money to Theodore Roosevelt's campaigns. Theodore Roosevelt told me that Fenster pere quite innocently, he believed, sponsored the entry of "Red Emma" Goldman into this country as well as scores of other East European radicals, under his program to help his coreligionists escape the pograms of the Czar.

Out of regard for Mrs. Fenster's bereavement for she was prostrated by the circumstances of her husband's demise, we interrogated her private secretary, Mrs. Cornelia St. James, a lovely blonde woman with cool blue eyes who did what to Jacques must have seemed a most curious thing. She looked at Futrelle then back to me and said, "Do you trust Mr. Futrelle, Mr. Harper?" I saw a look of bemusement on Jacques' face. I realized at once that she had worked for the former owner of the house, had seen me on these premises and was familiar with my efforts on the Goldman case as well as with the fact I possessed the confidence of former President Roosevelt.

I looked directly in her eyes as it was clear no evasion would suffice with such a person. "Mrs. St. James, I have personally known Mr. Futrelle for years," (an exaggeration of course), "and beyond the familiarity with his good character that implies, I have checked his background as thoroughly as that of a common criminal." I was greatly amused at Futrelle's look of surprise. But was there a suspicion in her mind that I believed her to have been one of those suborned in the theft of the Sickert painting?

"You are too keen not to know now when we've met before Mr. Harper. I must tell you that I was decoyed from this house when the theft occurred you came here to investigate."

"Your protestations are unnecessary as I had already determined the truth of what you assert," I responded. "Now, if we might confine ourselves to the distasteful matter at hand."

She reflected her relief and gratitude in her wonderful eyes, "How can I help, for I shall surely do all I can." Doyle old man, you would be as impressed with her beauty as I am.

Futrelle and I gently interrogated Mrs. St. James for over two hours in considerable detail about Fenster's movements the fatal evening as well as his overall behavior recently. I was about to terminate our conversation and had just cautioned her to be especially careful of her own movements and safety. Futrelle had not said a word for perhaps thirty minutes. He fixed Mrs. St. James most directly, "Did Mr. Fenster keep any kind of a personal diary which might help us?"

She responded directly, "Yes he did but, perhaps three months ago, he complained it was missing. I told Mr. Fenster that the disappearance of the journal coincided with the resignation from his service of Rebecca Kopoloff, a young Jewish girl whose entry into this country from Russia he had sponsored. Mr. Fenster dismissed the idea of any connection, or seemed to."

Futrelle and I exchanged a quick glance. "Mrs. St. James, you are more than kind. May I beg you to regard this as only the beginning of our association, for I think it entirely possible we may have further need for your services." The look in those keen eyes assured me of her willingness to help. "Of course, Mr. Harper."

Futrelle and I made a detailed examination of the premises with special attention to the private office of Fenster from which his journal was purloined, then we departed.

As we walked along in the brisk late autumn afternoon, the nurses in Central Park pushed their prams with their precious cargoes, the children of the elite, the most influential American families, scions of the wealthy Wall Street merchant bankers. "I wonder," Futrelle turned toward me as I spoke.

"I wonder by what means we might locate Fenster's journal, for it's imperative we review its contents with all possible haste."

"Perhaps there is a way I can be helpful," said the dark-haired scribe as we took leave of each other in the evening chill, both deep in thought about the case of the death of Isaac Fenster.

Hope you and Jean are both well. Any comments about the Fenster case?

Yours,

Sam

P.S. I now discover that the copy of the dossier on Cornelia St. James which I sent to you when we were interested in the disappearance of Sickert's paintings from collections around the world, is likely the only one still in existance (if it still is). Regrettably, the original file is either lost, stolen of strayed (or more likely, misfiled). Would you be your usual wonderful chap and send me a copy of yours? It now is clear that she figures importantly in the Fenster murder case. Fenster purchased the mansion vacated by Emerson Morgan. You will recall his name. He was one of those whose Sickert was stolen about three years ago. We interviewed him and her at the time. She was Morgan's personal secretary and Fenster kept her on in the same capacity when he purchased the house. I badly need the file to review what we learned about her at that time and we will, of course, update ourselves as to the intervening period.

P.P.S. The enclosed copy of a letter from Isaac Fenster to our friend J.B. Bury was found when I reviewed matters in his office. I thought you might find it interesting.

Excerpt from Letter to J.B. Bury
from Isaac Fenster

Dated October 1st, 1911 (New York City)

Dear John:

I am pleased to receive an advance copy of THE HISTORY OF THE EASTERN ROMAN EMPIRE with your kind inscription. I read with great interest the portion devoted to the Khazars, and while I realize you regarded it as beyond the scope of your book to discuss what became of these converts to Judaism after Ghengis Khan vanquished their empire, I still could have hoped some discussion on the topic would have been included.

It is beyond question that enormous numbers of these Khazar-Jews migrated to the centers of Eastern Europe where they are found today — the Karaites in the Crimea, the Polish and Lithuanian Jews who have received so much financial aid from my father and me to migrate here. That they are numerically the dominant group, 75% or more, in Judaism today is also beyond question and while I can understand that your conservative nature precludes your asserting more than the historical evidence will justify, I believe that privately you might accord greater recognition to the evidence accruing every year in the records we keep in connection with the waves of Jewish immigration to this country under our sponsorship.

It is precisely because I know you to be free of any interest in matters religious that I value your conclusions on these topics of such great interest to me.

To those of us who follow the Zionist Movement closely, but who have little sympathy for it, the recent assassination of Stolypin is a matter of utmost dismay. Probably the most liberal Prime Minister ever to serve under a Czar, the most willing to express his attitude in concrete legislation to ameliorate the admittedly bad situation in Russia, the man holding forth the most hope for a peaceful resolution of the problems of the minorities in that vast, polyglot empire, and I have no doubt when the facts are known there will be found to be a significant representation of Khazar-Jews amongst those who plotted the assassination as in all past political murders of Czars and ministers.

It is, perhaps, an oversimplification to call it a 'Jewish' revolutionary movement as the Czar does, but there is a generous element of truth in the assertion, nonetheless. And surely my father's financing Japan in her defeat of Russia in 1905, a defeat which finally convinced even the petit bourgeoisie of the corruption of Czarist rule and swung the scales against the Romanoff dynasty, indeed, the monarchy itself, has not lessened anti-semitism anywhere.

But whatever the complaints against the Jews or those of the Jews against the regime when the pograms of 1881-82 were unleashed and the Russian people were, in effect, given a hunting license to kill Jews, the movement to establish a homeland abroad, long in germination, finally took flower. And though the Khazars were not Israelites, they were converts to Judaism, and the ancient Israelite dream of a return to the Holy Land lived in their daily observances and captured their imagination. It is understandable enough why they fixed upon that long promised return as a solution to what had become an intolerable situation in Russia. I suppose the most interesting aspect of all this to me, historically speaking, is why the Khazars did not assume the same stance as other national minorities seeking a restoration of a national homeland in the scenes of their former greatness, the Crimea and environs??? The Poles, the Croates, the Serbs, the Montenegrans and a dozen or more other minorities at least spoke in terms understandable to the Czar and other heads of state in pleading their nationalistic schemes. Nationalism and ethnic autonomy are the great common language of the era, the common currency of international understanding. How strange they alone chose another language in which to convert their dreams to reality.

Until I discovered Mormonism and understood that a solution can exist for the Jews in becoming converted to the restored Gospel, I too could not resist the idea of a Khazar-Jewish homeland in the Holy Land. Now I see it will only lead to a more horrible fate than that they flee in Eastern Europe.

This, I know, means nothing to you since you are not a Mormon, but as a trusted and true friend of mine, I wish you to know how I justify my own attitudes toward Zionism. I may not affect the outcome of these matters in my lifetime, but there is a solution and to know that and to believe that solution will ultimately come to pass is all that saves me from utter despair.

Sincerely,

Isaac Fenster

Letter to Samuel Harper
from Arthur Conan Doyle

Dated November 30, 1911 (London)

Dear Sam,

I follow your progress on the Fenster case with great interest, although I regret I can't see any way I can be of much help from a distance of three thousand miles. I appreciate the way you are keeping me informed and let's hope that at some point I can be helpful. I found the letter to J.B. Bury to be especially interesting. Fenster was well informed about matters in Russia.

You probably have heard or read of the series of seances in which Balfour, Stead whom you call "The Baron of Fleet Street," and I partook at which photographs were taken that were originally thought to reveal a likeness of the control or spirit with whom we were in touch. It caused a bit of stir and I came in for my share of ridicule.

I am aware that much has been made of my interest in faeries, leprechauns, etc. just as I am aware this is all attributed to my Irish background, the world assuming that the Irishman expects to find a faery under every bush. But no one seems disposed to tell me why it is the English are not reputed to be interested in the metaphysical in spite of the fact there are more haunted houses in Britain than in all of Ireland and Scotland put together. And no one in a position to know has the slightest doubt these places that are visited by spirits of the dead are 'peculiar.' I have too much first hand knowledge of such places not to be forever convinced. It is something one never forgets.

Yet, if the churchmen have staked out the spirit world as one of their areas of special expertise, why do we receive no explanation of such metaphysical realities?

The stately homes of England as they are so admiringly called, as often as not have a room, perhaps a wing or maybe merely a passageway which is religiously avoided by the family, having conceded it to be the special province of a family ghost. I know that many Americans consider such matters to be a subject for ridicule.

To his good credit the Mormon prophet Joseph Smith did not think so. I am indebted to an American fan (probably a Mormon) for sending me an article by one O.B. Huntington entitled THE PROPHET ON OLD HOUSES from a Mormon church publication called the YOUNG WOMAN'S JOURNAL for July 1891. Huntington narrates as follows: "I will relate one circumstance that took place in Far West, in a house that Joseph had purchased, which had formerly occupied as a public house by some wicked people. A short time after he got into it, one of his children was taken very sick; he laid his hands upon the child, when it got better; as soon as he went out of doors, the child was taken sick again; he again laid his hands upon it, so that it again recovered. This occurred several times, when Joseph inquired of the Lord what it all meant; then he had an open vision, and saw the devil in person, who contended with Joseph face to face, for some time. He said it was his house, it belonged to him, and Joseph had no right there. Then Joseph rebuked Satan in the name of the Lord, and he departed and touched the child no more."

Now whether you agree, Sam, or not, as I surely don't since I don't believe in satan, you have to admit Smith didn't regard psychic phenomena as something to ridicule as most of the clergy do. To his credit I must say. Hope you're all well as we here are.

Yours,

Arthur

P.S. It took a bit of doing to find the enclosed file on Cornelia St. James. Three years is a long time. It was not in my actives but was stored in my dead files. Happy to help. I have reread the file and if she is still as beautiful as you described her then, I envy you your duties. Besides, it's time you considered remarriage if you will forgive a word of advice from an old friend.

Dossier on Cornelia St. James

(quoted in part)

White, female, hair blonde, eyes blue, wt. 110#, Ht. 5'4"
Born November 26, 1874, Ogdensburg, New York
Citizenship U.S.A.

Parents: Unknown, orphaned age 3. Raised in part (13 to 18) by aunt and uncle. Foster homes prior to that.

First encountered Cornelia St. James in 1908 on one of my first assignments in New York City when went to home of E. Morgan who had reported theft of a single painting, work of Walter Sickert, from his mansion on Fifth Avenue. The place is all it has been reported to be by the press. Managing it, which Cornelia St. James does in addition to her secretarial duties is a genuine undertaking. She is situated to know a great deal about the menage that Morgan himself could scarcely know. Cornelia St. James is outspoken to the point of bluntness at times, although, I don't believe she ever intentionally gives offense. Possesses a keenly logical mind unlike many of her gender. I would guess that she not only never lies, but likely is incapable of doing so. I'm sure many a one exposed to her occasional rapier thrusts has wished she could. Can be sarcastic but is truly amazed when she discovers she may have given offense by her remarks, confirming that she is not intentionally inflicting pain but does so quite unintentionally though this is of no comfort to the victim. In my judgment she is fearful of nothing whatsoever and must surely have lowered whatever estimation she held Morgan in over the craven way he sold the mansion and moved after the theft of his Sickert demonstrated he had a traitor in his employ.

Comes from a small town upstate New York. Parents died in her infancy. A difficult childhood in and out of foster homes. Appears to have traveled extensively in her capacity as secretary to some outstanding individuals in American industry and politics. Those I have checked confirmed they retained her for her efficiency and honesty, not to mention her beauty, and in spite of her occasional bluntness. Speaks beautiful Parisian French although she can lapse into the French Canadian argot at will since many of her relatives come from Quebec Province.

She has a temper which is not always, though usually, well controlled.

I saw her vent her spleen on a domestic in Morgan's employ whom she caught in some petty theft.

She is optimistic and high spirited and tends to test those around her as to their firmness in commitments. Hates weakness in others but will respond to requests (never to orders).

Is married to Thomas Myers who I have determined works as an assistant manager in the commissary at the Plaza Hotel. Cannot determine if the marriage is happy or not. He apparently has a drinking problem insofar as my inquiries seem to indicate. They have no children after several years of marriage. She appears only to admire men who are highly directional and moved by some great dream. She is usually charming and at times almost pollyana.

Is coldly analytical of the world exactly as it is, but still is highly idealistic and seeking something (or somebody?) to cling to.

Extremely eager to demonstrate her integrity and cannot bear to have same doubted, still I've found she can easily leave out the main point of matters I press her on.

At times quite breezy in her manner, she is usually reserved and almost shy. Seems contemptuous of society (with a capital S) and indeed of all hypocrisy.

A figure of great beauty, still she is occasionally clumsy physically. Romantic to the core; loves beauty and truth and feels deception or hypocrisy to be the ugliest of all things.

In spite of the efficient way she manages Morgan's affairs including sizeable sums, she does not seem much motivated to acquire great wealth herself. Can be quite extravagant in spite of her impecunious state.

I judge her to be utterly trustworthy to those to whom she has given her allegiance. A woman I judge a man could count on in all events if he doesn't much care about bad cooking which she outspokenly confesses to with great candor.

Dresses well, hates sloppiness in all its forms. She is so much an optimist that gloom and pessimism seem to make her physically ill. A real friend to, and almost conspirator with Morgan's children. Quite a child herself really.

The range of her interests has made her quite helpful in this case. I judge her to be a complete non-conformist which may be why we get on so well. Very helpful in the Sickert matter thought she did not betray Morgan's confidence in any sense.

Letter to Arthur Conan Doyle from Samuel Harper

Dated December 28, 1911 (New York City)

Dear Arthur,

We are in the heart of the Christmas season which every year seems to lose more of its sacredness and takes on more aspects of crass commercialism. I admit that when you have a little tyke about it all takes on a special meaning; the scent of the Christmas tree in our living room, the glow of the fire on the hearth reflected in the glistening ornaments on the tree. There is a staggering display of goodies for Leslie under the tree for which I confess I am solely responsible. With New Years it will all be over for another year and good riddance. I am sorry we cannot, it seems, return to the simplicity of the first Christmas.

Your remarks about the Prophet Joseph Smith and 'haunted' houses are noted with interest. But I am impressed once again with what seems to me to be an unwillingness on your part and that of others interested in spiritualism to recognize how clearly psychic phenomena of the kind you cite have been described in considerable detail in the scriptures. In Matthew 12, verses 43 through 45 we are taught: "When the unclean spirit is gone out of a man, he walketh through dry places, seeking rest, and findeth none. Then he saith, I will return into my house from whence I came out; and when he is come, he findeth it empty, swept, and garnished. Then goeth he, and taketh with himself seven other spirits more wicked than himself, and they enter in and dwell there; and the last state of that man is worse than the first. Even so shall it be also unto this wicked generation." I know it shan't be lost upon you that such places are haunted by <u>unclean</u> spirits. Just as in the case you refer to involving Joseph Smith and the illness of his children. Perhaps you can now understand why I view the practice of spiritualism as being fraught with such dangers. It is the spirits of those who yielded themselves up to the sins of the flesh who haunt the scenes of their past transgressions and how much good can come of any contact you might have with such spirits? The spirits of those who died in righteousness have no need of a medium as they are at peace in their home beyond the veil and hard at work teaching the gospel to others, if the Mormons are right.

J.B. Bury writes that he spent a weekend recently with you and Jean. Did you get to discuss his new book with him? He asked me to review an early draft of the manuscript and I thought it a scholarly effort that did him great credit. It's about the history of the Eastern Roman Empire and contains some fascinating material.

I do wish Arthur Balfour, who it seems to me, is absolutely determined to throw the power of the British government behind the move to create a Jewish homeland in Palestine would read it and digest it. J.B. points out that the Khazar Empire, once a major force in the east, converted to Judaism some time prior to 1000 a.d. The present day descendants of the Khazars are a major component in modern Jewry. These are the 'unassimilated Jews' of Eastern Europe that Arthur would repatriate to Palestine in fulfillment of Scripture. But, if these Khazar-Jews are only converts to Judaism, and not physically of the blood of Israel, what possible claim can they have to the Holy Land? And who in the world today would concede that even true Israel, were some people suddenly to arise, claim and prove themselves to be such, can even have a claim to the Holy Land, the Scriptures, that discredited source in the minds of so many, being the only basis of such claim?

I'm sure Arthur's objectives are largely grounded in what he regards as Realpolitik and in the needs of the Empire to protect our approaches to the Suez Canal. And while I agree we need a base in the Eastern Med., why inject such an inflammatory issue as the creation of a Jewish homeland?

Why not see if you can get Balfour to read J.B.'s book? It would probably do no good, knowing Arthur as I do, indeed he may already be familiar with the points the book raises, but it seems one way to alert the Earl of Balfour what a pandora's box he is threatening to open in case he needs this new intelligence.

If the British-Israel group are correct, only we (Anglo-Saxon Israel) have a valid claim to the Holy Land which, of course, would be no more welcome an assertion than the claim of the Eastern Jews to the Palestinians and the rest of the world. So our 'rights' if any, must be those of the conqueror.

While the B-I people can't prove they're right, more important in a matter like this, we can't prove they're wrong. And since we don't any longer (and probably never did) have a majority in the British nation who believe in the British-Israel identity, British public opinion won't accept such a justification for the move. Surely the Arabs whose genealogy derives from Abraham, would not take kindly to a claim by us that we alone have title to the Holy Land. I doubt they will take more warmly to our attempts to 'repatriate' the Jew there either. It is a great mischief he is engaged in and a totally unnecessary provocation. Be a good man, Doyle, and convince him to stop.

If the Turkish Empire falls, as surely it will some day soon, we should take what we can, but why some high-flown enterprise grounded in Scripture and a false interpretation of Scripture to boot? I see dark clouds on the horizon if the Earl of Balfour persists in this bull-headed endeavor.

Since we formed our compact I have more consciously devoted thought to religion. The matter of life hereafter being of such importance how is it that I have so much difficulty allocating but 15 or 20 minutes a day to the topic? Shows how disproportionately we value our worldly pursuits when viewed in this light. Still we know this life and can value it for good or evil in the light of recollected experience. What do we know about where we go after death?

As I pondered such things the other day it occurred to me we know perhaps even less about where we came from before life. Yes we're told life sprang into existence at the moment of conception, but is this necessarily true?

Poet Laureate William Wordsworth, a great favorite of Sir Henry, obviously didn't think so. Do you recall his lovely lines:
> Our birth is but a sleep and a forgetting;
> The soul that rises with us, our life's Star,
> Hath had elsewhere its setting,
> And cometh from afar:
> Not in entire forgetfulness,
> And not in utter nakedness,
> But trailing clouds of glory do we come
> from God, who is our home . . .

A lovely passage, is it not?

It is not difficult to believe we existed before we came here, but if so, did man's spirit always exist, as Plato believed? And, if so, what a new concept of creation comes into view for in what sense is God our creator if we always existed? If we existed before, how much of our present personalities came with us and if any, then what is the contribution of heredity? These are important questions. Is it not so???

Questions arising from such speculation can lead from one to another endlessly. Why are some born crippled or blind? Is this the work of an infinitely just God? Why is one born poor, another to a noble family? Is the man born to riches truly luckier than he who is born in the peasant's hutch? The poor man surely feels him to be luckier, but is he? If so, where is infinite justice?

From a cosmic viewpoint, Doyle, that of a truly just God, is one being treated as even-handedly as the other? If so, how are things evened out? And what about those who are born never to hear the gospel of Christ? What about the millions born in India only to die of starvation in their first five years of life?

These are the types of things which mystify me. What about the woman who wishes she were born a man or vice versa? How do they come to terms with their lot? It surely will not be easily done, but it is questions like these I must discover answers to.

You ask to know more about Nellie Bly. I can't, I fear, treat this question with my usual professional detachment, not quite completely. I was at one time seeing her socially and I found her attractive and very pleasant company. Whether more might have developed is difficult to say. I didn't feel very ready to rearrange my life over her as would be required were I to remarry.

Nellie's husband died quite suddenly in 1910 and she has been operating his manufacturing plant, but not with total success. She has talked of selling what's left of the business and moving to Vienna. Her husband was fifty years her senior and so now she seems ready for a romance with someone closer her age.

She is a true daughter of Mrs. Pankhurst, the Suffragette, and I must say she forced me to analyze all my viewpoints before giving voice to an opinion that might, only in the most subtle way, be grounded in the male point of view. It is a trifle discomfitting, but since we were not undertaking anything more serious than an occasional dinner together, I found her amusing good company.

I really wonder if women have the slightest inkling of what happens to a man's attitude when he is confronted by a woman who wishes to marry and yet rejects the traditional female role? Why would a man undertake the support of a woman who has no desire to accommodate the only needs for which he desires to marry — a home, children, consortium? It makes little sense, but there it is. They can't have it two ways as they will some day realize, I fear, to their great sorrow.

But let me get to the matters which prompted your question about Nellie in the first place. You may recall Nellie married in 1895 and retired from the newspaper field. Her exploits were, to say the very least, on the sensational side. She broke all the old rules. Shunning the polite and genteel little pieces to which the few women journalists were given at the time, she wrote about slums, political corruption, treatment of the insane, sweatshops, etc. Her technique usually was to disguise herself and learn about her subject as a victim of the system. It's a method that's been repeated often since then, but Nellie was among the first to use it and was almost certainly the first woman to do so.

Her efforts duplicating the Jules Verne story AROUND THE WORLD IN EIGHTY DAYS (Nell did it in 72 and I josh her still about it) may have been the thing most remembered about her career. But she was a serious reporter with more courage than ten men. She smuggled herself into Mexico to expose the regime there and had she simply disappeared, not a thing could have been done to help her, not even by the President.

She brashed her way into the office of Joseph Pulitzer at the New York World and dared him to give her a job. He did! She has been a thorn in the side of many pompous and/or venal (sometimes both) persons ever since. If her muckraking hasn't accomplished all the good it should have, you have only the limited attention span of the public to blame. For Nell did her part.

About 1889 Nell was doing a piece about Johann Most, editor of the inflammatory rag FREIHEIT which was mostly read by the anarchistic and/or Bolshevistic Jewish emigres from Eastern Europe. Nell met a 20 year old Jewess named Emma Goldman, 'Red Emma' you surely know about. In 1901, after President McKinley's assassination, incidentally just eight months after the death of her Highness the Queen and the accession to the throne of my erstwhile friend the Prince of Wales, Kodiak (Teddy Roosevelt) asked me to determine if Red Emma had conspired with the assassin Czolgosz to commit the murder. It was entirely due to the good terms on which Nell stood with Emma that I was able to meet with the lady anarchist and interrogate her. Emma narrowly escaped a trip to the electric chair with the somber Czolgosz. I take no credit for her good fortune. I objectively judged that, on the basis of the facts I could muster, it could not be proven she did so conspire. But Red Emma seems to have appreciated my objectivity if not my 'help.' To her I guess they seemed one and the same.

So now you understand somewhat how Nell has figured in my checkered career.

Hope you're both well; the Happiest of New Years to you both. I enclose a copy of the dossier on Red Emma.

Yours,

Sam

P.S. News reaches us that Amundsen has made it to the South Pole. What a triumph of human determination!

P.P.S. You have not missed I am sure the passage of Britain's Official Secrets Act. I view this with mixed feelings. While I concede that national security often requires that officials have a high degree of discretionary authority regarding the release of information, having been privy to the offenses committed in the name of national security in the Ripper case, I expect there will be many abuses committed in the name of the national interest.

Ravel's Daphnis and Chloe ballet was performed here recently much to my delight. See it Doyle at your first opportunity.

Dossier on Emma Goldman

My correspondence with the Secret Police of the Czar indicate they have but a modest file on 'Red Emma' as the New York City Police call her. Not surprising since she left Russia when she was only 20. But she had already come to their attention as an agitator.

Born Kovno, Russia on June 27, 1869. First child of Abraham and Taube (Bienowitch) Goldman. He has two daughters from previous marriage, one of whom Helen Zodokoff came to America with E.G. Father failed as a shop-keeper in Kovno. Family moved to Popelan where he kept an inn and managed government stage-coach. Failed at this also. Family moved to Konigsberg, Prussia. She attended Realschule there for few years. She appears to have done well in literature and music and prepared herself for Gymnasium exams. Passed these but was not accepted because religious instructor refused her a certificate of good character. Personality seems to have been formed by bitter father whose own failures and disappointment that she was not born the son he desired subjected her to sarcasm and ridicule. Family moved to St. Petersburg in 1881. Was employed by a cousin in his glove factory. Became active in nihilist and populist student groups. Arrested twice by the Okrana, the Czar's secret police for agitation. Read widely in radical literature advocating dethronement of Czar. In 1885 she and her half-sister emigrated to America settling in Rochester, N.Y. Deeply embittered at exploitation of their fellow Jews by factory owners who employed her. Became highly critical in U.S. of German Jewish (assimilated) capitalists who employed and exploited Eastern European Jewish emigres.

In 1887 had unsuccessful marriage to Jacob Kershner, a fellow factory worker. He was apparently impotent. Divorced. Reconciled. Divorced again, permanently. Moved to NYC August 1889. (NYPD source of much of info from 1889 forward). Met Johann Most, editor of FREIHEIT and Alexander Berkman also Russian emigre, revolutionist-anarchist. Emma Goldman and Berkman planned to assassinate Henry Clay Frick, steel magnate. Berkman served 14 years in Pennsylvania's West. Pen. but Emma Goldman escaped prosecution for her part in attempt on Frick's life. In 1893 served year on Blackwell's Is., N.Y. for advising a Union Square audience of unemployed "it was their sacred right" to steal bread if starving and demands not answered. Worked in prison as nurse. Studied midwifery in Vienna 1895-6. Apparently has come to reject violence and theory that "end justifies the means."

In spite of energetic efforts by authorities, could not convict her of com-plicity with Czolgosz in assassination of President McKinley although Czolgosz had followed him through Cleveland and Chicago speaking engagements right before he went to Buffalo to kill the President. (See accompanying transcript of conversation between Samuel Harper and Emma Goldman pursuant to assignment from Kodiak to ascertain if Emma Goldman involved in death of President.)

Dynamic speaker. Frequently lectures on birth control, women's move-ment, anarchism, free speech.

Upon Berkman's release (1906) they published monthly MOTHER EARTH. Lectured extensively arousing concern of radical groups over threat to free speech. Also on new drama, Ibsen, Shaw, Strindberg, etc. Concept of new women (influenced by Ibsen). Advocate of free love. Attacked 'conventional lie' of marriage. Advocated 'uncoerced mutual regard of two persons.'

Dismissed demand of women for vote as a 'mere fetish' probably because she had little faith in democratic process. In 1908 was deprived of citizenship when government denaturalized her missing husband.

Emma Goldman charged with complicity in bombing of Los Angeles Times (Oct. 1910) but was unable to satisfy myself this was true when I was retained by the Otis family to investigate.

Formed strong friendship with Nellie Bly who sought her out for a story as ready to ridicule her as not. Forms strong friendships and inspires great loyalty in others. Boundless courage, extremely loyal. Will stand against the crowd no matter how great the danger. In midst of national hysteria would not refrain from statements sympathetic to Czolgosz and narrowly escaped his fate. Clarence Darrow himself warned her to refrain or incur the wrath of a nation in a paroxysm of frustration over the assassination of the President who led the nation to imperialistic victory over Spain. Just when nationalism was hitting its stride in U.S. and when the Anglo-Saxon majority felt certain that American glory would exceed that of Rome and Britain combined, to see a 'foreigner' cut the President down and then be defended by a radical Russian Jewess was more than public opinion could tolerate. Emma survived only by the skin of her teeth.

The vitriol unleashed was difficult to believe. Immediately after Czolgosz was electrocuted the top of his head was sawed off to analyze the insane brain that conceived the dastardly act and a carboy of sulphuric acid was employed to destroy his body.

INTERVIEW WITH Emma Goldman (in the presence of Nellie Bly, transcribed from notes taken by Nellie Bly in shorthand)

Emma Goldman: Nell tells me you wish to talk to me Mr. Harper.
Samuel Harper: That's right —
Nellie Bly: Sam is fair Emma. He will not prejudge you.
Emma Goldman: It would be nothing new if he did.
Samuel Harper: I'm sure that's true Miss Goldman. You were lucky to be released from prison in Chicago, and now you return to New York City risking arrest and being taken to Buffalo where the President was killed and where, needless to say, feelings run high.
Emma Goldman: Even Nell's paper, The World, insists I inspired the killing.
Nellie Bly: I didn't write that Emma.
Emma Goldman: I know that Nell, but The World is the one newspaper that I hoped might avoid the hysteria.
Samuel Harper: Too much to ask Emma. Having seen the public enthusiasm in Britain when the spirit of Empire was at its peak, I can tell you you're possessed of the utmost good fortune you weren't summarily shot in Chicago.

Emma Goldman: This is America Mr. Harper, not England.
Nellie Bly: Easy Emma. Arguing can't help.
Samuel Harper: It's all right Nell. I understand her state of mind, and even that has a certain value. What they call 'mens rea' in the law; relates to the question of guilty intent. Were Emma guilty and trying to convince me of her innocence, she would presumably be more pliable.
Emma Goldman: What do you wish to know Mr. Harper?
Samuel Harper: I've satisfied myself Emma that Czolgosz was present in the audience that heard your talks in Cleveland and Chicago. You went on to St. Louis I'm satisfied of that, and Czolgosz went on to Buffalo where the murder took place. I need to know if you traveled together, talked together or had any connection of any kind with Czolgosz, during those stops at Cleveland and Chicago.
Emma Goldman: The easy thing would be to say there was none. But Czolgosz was in both instances, among those who came forward after the conclusion of my talks. You couldn't see him once and not recognize him. He was a pathetic figure, totally lost. I've seen his kind by the thousands, alienated, bordering on dementia, silent, somber and a bit frightened as well as a bit frightening. Always alone, strictly a loser. I don't think Cleveland and Chicago were the only times he came to one of my appearances. I'm sure I saw him at other meetings. But not close up as in the last two. I can't be sure.
Samuel Harper: Where do you think he may have heard you before?
Emma Goldman: Possibly at some of the meetings in New York City.
Samuel Harper: Was he still hovering about after your talks?
Emma Goldman: No. Had he done I would be sure. No, he didn't come close until Cleveland and Chicago. But I recollect a man that could have been him attended at least two meetings in New York.
Nellie Bly: Emma have you considered getting a lawyer?
Emma Goldman: Clarence Darrow offered his services free. But I can't think of anything more likely to be interpreted as an admission of guilt.
Samuel Harper: Quite right Emma, that is precisely how the public press would interpret it. But I recommend you think about it. It's by no means certain how this all will turn out and a lawyer could almost surely buy you some time. Time usually brings more dispassionate judgments.
Emma Goldman: Your advice is good Mr. Harper, but I have a feeling my case is being tried inside Mr. Harper's head, and a lawyer can't help me there.
Samuel Harper: I can only express my opinion to my client Emma. But since all the evidence collected fails to support the concept of a conspiracy between you and the assassin, I must recommend that no action be taken against you.
Emma Goldman: You're very kind Mr. Harper.
Samuel Harper: Not kind Emma, merely objective.
Emma Goldman: Kind or objective, it's all the same to me. Usually I'm dealing with the antipathy only a Jew can know. In my world objective is kind. Better than automatic dislike.

END OF TRANSCRIPT

Doyle:

The above assertions were substantially corroborated by the testimony of other witnesses deemed to be reliable.

Sam

Entry in the Journal of Samuel Harper

For December 29, 1911 (New York City)

Futrelle having been called out of town on personal matters, I would have to visit Cornelia St. James without him. As I rode up Fifth Avenue in a hired motorcab, I wondered for a moment why I felt so elated, and realized to my surprise, that I was anticipating with pleasure looking once again into those cool blue eyes and gazing upon her lovely countenance. No woman had seriously interested me since the death of my wife, but this one surely did. But she is married, I recalled and dismissed her from my thoughts. But the feeling of pleasant anticipation remained all the same.

Having obtained an appointment by telephone, Mrs. St. James came to the door herself as I rang, only what seemed a very brief moment elapsing before she came to the door, a lovely smile upon her face. Was she as eager to see me as I her? I dismissed the thought as childish.

"Mr. Harper, how wonderful to see you," she smiled. "The most fortuitous of circumstances," I responded, "require me to request additional help from you." There was no wedding ring upon her finger.

"Mrs. St. James," I began.

"Cornelia will do, if it makes you more comfortable," she offered.

"A lovely name to be sure, but perhaps your husband would object?" I asked.

"Not likely," she responded, "he — Tom died only a few years after our marriage, four years ago."

"I'm sorry that you must have been very unhappy," but I was elated to know she was unattached, or was she? "Perhaps your fiance would object?"

"There is unhappily, no one," she smiled wistfully, "and as a Mormon, it is even more difficult."

"So you too shared the religion to which Mr. Fenster was converted," I responded, mildly surprised.

"He was instrumental in bringing me to the gospel," she smiled.

"He was a wonderful man Mr. Harper, a follower of truth wherever it led him. And as you see, it led him into the hands of satan."

I was not sure I truly understood her remarks, but was uncomfortable at the direction our conversation was taking, involving as it did metaphysical overtones where I. wanted merely facts. "Then should I conclude that you believe Mr. Fenster's religion was a contributing factor in his death?" I asked.

"Only insofar as it may have helped him to understand the devil's plan and thus to be in a position to frustrate that plan," she responded.

There it was again, an uneasiness once more assailed me and led me to fear I could not rely on her opinions at all and perhaps not even her view of the facts.

But I underestimated her. "You will find," she said, "that a devout Mormon, as Isaac Fenster decidedly was, lives in a different world than do most modern people."

"Different? In what sense?" I responded.

"It relates to our understanding of the nature of God and of man," she smiled her loveliest smile, "we believe that God is an exalted man — as man is God once was, as God is man may be — that tells it all. Modern man views God as a mystic and unfathomable force, unknowable in any way. But this has the convenient result of relieving us of any responsibility, for what can we owe to a God who is unknowable?"

"Perhaps I begin to see, but do go on," I urged.

She leaned forward in her chair and touched my hand for just a moment as we sat facing each other in the sumptuous Fenster sitting room. She just as quickly withdrew her hand and I mine as though we had each felt an electric shock.

"It relates too to the plan of salvation and the role of the adversary in that great unfolding drama," her eyes looked into mine. "Mr. Fenster was about to become a great force in the conversion of the Jews to the gospel, that is the real reason he is dead, although you will undoubtedly find that evil men had their own cynical reasons for killing him. How satan attains his ends is not as important as the fact he does attain them. The Jews must be converted before the Savior's return and Mr. Fenster above all was in a position to be instrumental in achieving this."

To a degree I lost my feeling of uneasiness; her reasoning was lucid within the framework of her beliefs. But I could see it was imperative for me to learn more about Mormon doctrine if I was to be able to filter out her perceptual biases.

I decided upon another approach. "You will be interested," I said, "in a case I worked on the first year I resided in this country. I was approached by a woman who wished to have the authenticity verified of an ancient document. Her title to that document led back to a man named Bidamon."

"That will be the man Emma Smith married after she apostatized," she said.

"Apostasy is not, I think, a word to which Mr. and Mrs. Bidamon would have taken kindly," I said. "But you are very acute in your discernment; it was none other. She had in her possession a document the authenticity of which she desired me to establish so that she could sell it."

"How fascinating!" she exclaimed. "What sort of document?"

"It was an Egyptian papyrus," I responded, "which apparently served as the foundation of one of the accepted works of your church, or so it was asserted."

"That would be the Book of Abraham," she observed, "what did you conclude?"

"The document was undoubtedly genuine — I suspect it was a document used by some ancient priest to help him recollect the elaborate temple ceremony connected with one of the Egyptian rituals," I said. "I cannot attest that whatever purpose to which Joseph Smith employed the document is worthy or valid, but the papyrus was undoubtedly genuine."

"How interesting," she exclaimed with quite apparent delight.

"You are not totally unfamiliar with our Mormon background."

"Not totally, but I shall surely welcome any additional insights you feel may contribute to my understanding of how Mr. Fenster's conversion to your beliefs may have been a causal factor in his demise," I urged.

"There is, of course, the possibility I have misread," she conceded, "but I think I am safe in saying that Mr. Fenster perceived himself to be a great threat to the world banking system, and anyone who read his book may have shared that point of view. He believed the references in the scriptures to Babylon relate to the similarity in the way international bankers use gold to the way in which Nebuchadnezzar the king of Babylon did."

She gazed at me with a tentative glance that asked if I were able to follow.

"The most fascinating aspect of what I have read in his book," I offered, "is the part about how the price of gold has, in fact, been severed from the supply of paper obligations upon which the world of credit functions."

"You're right, I am sure," she conceded, "but I must confess that little of what he says in his book has any meaning for me. But I assure you that from the time he first allowed a publisher to read the manuscript I had a premonition that great danger hovered about him."

"There can be little doubt," I offered "that many powerful figures in the world of finance and government might desire to see that manuscript suppressed, but I fail to see how killing him would achieve their purposes when, in fact, he had already determined to publish the book himself. Quite the contrary, killing him would insure the book a tremendous vogue — the exact opposite of what they would want."

"You're a better judge of such matters than I," she conceded, "but whatever the connection, many powerful forces were working against him. To those of us who cherished him for his manifold kindnesses, it was a great anguish to see his peril but be unable to help except with our prayers."

"I suspect you spent more than an hour or two on your knees," I consoled gently.

"You're most understanding Mr. Harper," she smiled, her eyes glistening with tears.

"I'm sure you can give me," I suggested, "some names of persons whom I can contact for a clearer picture of his activities the last year or so before the murder."

"Of course," she responded, "there were many but that's the problem. A man of Mr. Fenster's vast connections has almost more than you could contact in a meaningful way."

"I understand, but surely your intuition must tell you something about where I should begin."

She smiled a wonderful smile. Was I mistaken or was it more than that of a mere acquaintance?

"Were I in your position," she said after a considerable pause during which she gazed out the window at a hansom being drawn slowly by an ancient horse down Fifth Avenue, "I would begin with Lord Balfour."

My increased interest must have shown on my face at her having mentioned the name of Balfour as had the victim.

"Yes, Lord Balfour," she emphasized, "you see Mr. Fenster was aware of Balfour's desire to influence British policy toward a declaration favoring the return of the Jews to Palestine. Isaac Fenster felt that the return of the Eastern Jews to the Holy Land could be nothing less than a death sentence for all who returned."

"Surely you're mistaken?" I urged.

"Not at all," she insisted. "He was all too aware that many, perhaps most Jews have no valid claim to the Holy Land since they are not of the blood of Israel. And if they could not be there as holders of the birthright, then surely they must fulfill some scriptural role. He feared it could only be the fulfillment of the reference in Luke 19:27: But those mine enemies, which would not that I should reign over them, bring hither, and slay them before me."

"Then," I said, "he could have been slain by Zionists?"

"Yes, of course," she replied, "but he may also have stumbled into a plot to kill Balfour."

It had now become clear to me I must take an entirely different approach to the matter of learning what Cornelia St. James knew and yet be able to filter out her perceptual biases based on her religious beliefs.

"I realize this may seem a trifle unorthodox Cornelia." Her eyes reflected her pleasure at my use of her first name. "But I wonder if you would be willing to see me socially, perhaps for dinner a few times so that, as I work my way through this matter, I can have the benefit of your enlightenment on questions as they arise?"

The look in her eyes told me the idea was acceptable, perhaps even one to be viewed with pleasant anticipation. I was pleased that she seemed pleased.

"Of course, Sam. There is really so much to cover it may be the only way," she smiled a smile that told me we were becoming more than friends. "Tell me what your wishes are and I shall do my best to help."

"I desire nothing more for the moment than to take you to dinner on Saturday evening. Is that," I asked, "acceptable? By then with luck I will have read the rest of the book and even Mr. Fenster's journal may be in my possession. And I can be prepared to ask some relevant questions."

She seemed somewhat astonished by this last statement, shaking her head and smiling at my self assurance. "I will be delighted to see you Saturday whether to discuss those documents, or just to learn more about Mr. Harper."

My journey home to my flat in Brooklyn was filled with pleasant contemplation of her lovely face. And I realized for the first time how very lonely my life had been since Tony's death.

Journal Entry of Samuel Harper

December 30, 1911 (New York City)

At Futrelle's urging I had made my way to Manhattan late on that cold December evening and now we sat in a booth nursing hot drinks in the dark, oaken surroundings of O'Shaunnessy's Bar, a landmark all denizens of the Bowery know as a haunt of the fourth estate. We chose a booth which gave us command of the front door through which we expected our informant to enter.

"Your sense of mystery Jacques is a touch on the dramatic side." I smiled and sipped my toddy observing his features.

"Not at all," he smiled, "I am merely testing your fabled powers of deduction."

"Ah so! You expect me to tell you that Nellie Bly will soon enter that door and that after a moment's conversation she will lead us to the Lower East Side where we shall meet Emma Goldman who is sheltering the young Jewish girl who disappeared from Fenster's home with Isaac's journal." I smiled as Futrelle's eyes widened in amazement.

"Quite a feat, my friend, quite a feat." His unfeigned appreciation showed in his voice. "Explanations are in order, sire."

"You labor at the same disadvantage as the yokel from upstate who wanders wide-eyed into a nickelodean on Broadway in the middle of a moving picture show, not knowing any of the origins of the story being portrayed on the screen." I puffed deeply on my pipe, exhaling a great cloud into the air above our heads.

"First, we sit in O'Shaunnessy's, a place known by the cognoscenti to be practically the private preserve of the newspaper world, indicating our informant is of the press. Second, our informant must lead us to someone conversant with affairs inside the household of a Jewish prince — one of the elite of Wall Street. Lastly, as you are possibly aware, not only does Red Emma draw the members of her race who are ducking the law for any reason like iron filings to a magnet, but her entry into this country was sponsored by Fenster's father and word comes to me off the street that Emma has vowed to run Fenster's killers to earth or die." I didn't say that Nellie Bly, once America's best known woman reporter, whose husband having died in 1910 and who was attempting a comeback after several years of retirement had been my liaison with Goldman when I was attempting to determine if Emma was a conspirator in the murder of President McKinley.

"Deftly done, but you only guessed it was Nellie Bly." Futrelle raised his glass in a mock salute. I responded with mine.

"Call it intuition. I believe our bearer of tidings good or ill approacheth." He turned his eyes toward the entry as the lady reporter entered through the frosted glass door to O'Shaunnessy's. A draft of cold air and crystals of frost wafted into the pub causing the babble of voices to subside amidst a raucous chorus of "Nellie shut that door." With a smile and a wave, she slammed the door defiantly and loudly declaimed, "Shut up you drunken hacks."

A reporter seated nearby smiled at her and said, "Sure good to see you back Nell." She returned his smile, "Many thanks, Bob."

Now all smiles and glowing with charm, even at forty-six still a comely figure, she crossed toward Futrelle and me, her gloved hand extended. "Jacques, it's good to see you." Then looking at me, "We meet again Sam — what a pleasure."

"Having gone around the world in 80 days, more or less," I joshed her, "what grandiose newsgetting scheme are you machinating now?"

"72 days, if you please," she responded, then sotto voce, "The Titanic," she whispered very low so that her compatriots of the press could not overhear and preempt her. "In the spring, I will ride the Titanic on her maiden voyage and report the foibles of the wealthy from on board by Marconi. We will sign exclusive rights with the White Star management in the morning."

Futrelle with his ex-newsman's nose for a good story snorted appreciatively, "What a coup!"

"Tell a soul and I'll have your scalp," she playfully but seriously threatened.

"I'm sworn to secrecy," he pledged with a smile.

Then looking directly at me Nellie said, "I haven't seen you Sam since we ran into each other at the Johnson-Jeffries fight last year in Reno. I believe," Nellie said, "you made a killing betting on the black man."

"I'm never one to let my love for the Celts rule over my perception of the odds," I teased.

"Well, no one's perfect," she teased right back, her Irish smile beaming. Then leaping to a new subject, she glanced almost imperceptably at Jacques and said, "I thought the death of King Edward might have induced you to go home at last?"

"With Lloyd George and the Liberals in power," I responded, "how could an unreconstructed Tory like me go home — I've lived amongst you barbaric colonials so long, no well-mannered Briton would have me in his presence."

"Enough of your banter you ruddy, aristocratic, Irish-oppressing — you — you," and she burst out laughing, unable to continue her mock diatribe.

Futrelle interjected, "But that's not what we're here for, is it?" "Quite so," I said smiling ever so conspiratorially at Nell, but nonetheless happy to be getting to the point. "You have some important intelligence Nellie, I presume."

"Not even a meager toddy for a poor wench before you pry my goodies from me?" she said, feigning deep pathos.

"How crude of us Jacques," I waved to a waiter signaling for another round, signalling that Nell wanted the same as mine by pointing first to my glass then to her.

"Jacques, Sam, you know I don't do these little errands for nothing — what's the pay-off for lovable Nell?"

"The usual," Futrelle replied, "an exclusive insofar as anything at all is made public."

"Then my terms are 'the usual' also — I accept your assurance and my exclusive, but I remain free to publish anything I am able to dredge up on my own, including the material I assume you are trying to recover," she said, her direct gaze banishing any air of former playfulness.

"Well done, Nellie," I said, "your terms seem most reasonable. Now where are we to see Red Emma?"

"You are a terror," she smiled complimenting my deduction. "I've rented a motorcab outside to take us downtown."

Outside in the glow of the streetlights sparkled the dry, cold flakes of snow falling softly to earth in the winter's first storm. We boarded Nellie's rented car and instructed the driver to take us to the Jewish district on the Lower East Side. I looked forward with the same old sense of excitement to the pleasures of the hunt.

Nellie Bly had led Futrelle and me to the rundown lower East Side of New York into which each day there poured hundreds of Eastern European Jews. They who had been lucky enough to come through the vague screening procedures of Ellis Island. Some ended up with names other than their own simply because one of the immigration officials couldn't understand their foreign tongues, or couldn't spell, or simply didn't like the name he heard and arbitrarily chose a new one. Used to the slow life of the tiny shtetls of Poland and Russia, the pace of a major metropolis added to the anxiety of leaving home, of enduring a squalid sea voyage, of relentless poverty.

Some stayed a while and moved on when money became available, saved only by the most rigorous thrift from the poor wages of 'sweated labor,' to join kinfolk in Cincinnati or Chicago or Atlanta.

Many remained and the cultural melange in this portion of the city became more like an Asiatic bazaar than anything else. By day the streets were filled with pushcarts dispensing food that all wished were kosher. Only Elohim knew for sure and the orthodox took no chances. People from the shtetls found that in place of village boundaries were now the limits of their neighborhood. And beyond their own block lay another village, another people and a mix of other cultures, Irish, German, Italian and unnumbered others.

By day the streets teamed with life, people jostling each other on crowded sidewalks and in the streets. Horse drawn wagons, motorcars and pushcarts moving slower than a person could walk through the jostling crowds.

Some stood talking animatedly in Yiddish, gesticulating broadly. Irish speaking English with a Gaelic lilt and syntax. Others ported huge bundles of much-worn clothing. Women wearing shawls, sitting at windows above the street shouted to children below in Yiddish or German or Italian.

The roar of street sounds, overwhelming during the day, were never totally silent even at night. And always there were the odors of cooking, of unbathed bodies, of fresh-dropped manure, and a hundred others. Like the underworld haunts of London, there were the dangers of pickpockets, mashers and worse.

Into this cauldron that spawned doctors and drug addicts, musicians and murderers we went, Nellie, Jacques and I in search of Red Emma, and the

Fenster journal. Our motorcab dropped us off at an address only Nellie knew. Up a flight of rickety stairs in a smelly, ancient tenement building where bags of garbage stood outside every door contributing the redolent odors of fish and coffee grounds and greasy foods now cold.

In response to our knock, a sound of shuffling behind the door and slow movements. Finally the familiar face of Emma Goldman was visible in the opening of the door against its chain bolt. The door closed again as she removed the chain and then opened widely. Nellie was the first to speak. "Emma, Sam you know, but please meet Mr. Futrelle. Jacques and Sam are jointly working on the Fenster case."

Emma Goldman: Mr. Harper, a pleasure to see you again and in circumstances less threatening to me.

Samuel Harper: Yes, Emma, a pleasure indeed. I hope you'll feel perfectly at ease with Jacques. He is worthy of your trust in all things.

Emma Goldman: Mr. Futrelle (shaking Jacques' hand) you come well recommended. Please feel at home.

Jacques Futrelle: Please call me Jacques for, if you don't object, I should like to call you Emma.

Emma Goldman: Not at all Jacques. As you can see, Sam, Nell and I are old friends and we stand on little ceremony.

Jacques Futrelle: And I feel likewise Emma. We're off to a fine start.

Emma Goldman: (Looking at Harper) Nell has told me of your search for Rebecca Kopoloff.

Samuel Harper: Yes, we learned of her from Mr. Fenster's associate Mrs. St. James who suspects that the coincidence in time of Rebecca's leaving Fenster's employ, and the disappearance of his journal, were enough of an indication that she might have taken it when she left. Perhaps even was introduced into the household for no other purpose.

Nellie Bly: I told Emma, Sam, of your suspicions.

Emma Goldman: Your hunch or was it Mrs. St. James' is quite on the mark Sam. And that is why I cannot produce Rebecca herself. She is afraid to show herself to me or to you. I was only able to obtain this (crossing the room and taking up a large book from a small table in the corner) by employing extraordinary threats and the services of an intermediary. (Hands book to Harper).

Samuel Harper: Then you don't know who engaged Rebecca to penetrate the Fenster household?

Emma Goldman: I cannot say for certain, because the rabbi who located Kopoloff for me and retrieved the journal could only obtain it upon his promise to protect his sources. And had it not been Issac Fenster whose death was involved, it would have been utterly impossible for me to assist in any way.

Samuel Harper: I think it's also fairly certain that once whoever hired Kopoloff knew the contents of this journal he had no reason to object to its being released to you.

Emma Goldman: A probable surmise.

Jacques Futrelle: What do we know about Rebecca Kopoloff, Emma, really?

Emma Goldman: Not much really, Jacques. She was among the many whose passage was financed by the Fenster Foundation. There are the usual supporting documents, a rabbi's letter, her school master, etc.

Samuel Harper: I have finally received a response to my cable to St. Petersburg. And, about as I expected, she has a record there of student agitation, some Jewish Zionist activities, but it's very sparse, largely, I suppose because she's so young.

Jacques Futrelle: As I suspected, we will likely learn as much as is helpful, from her activities since coming to this country.

Nellie Bly: I take it Jacques you've been sleuthing the girl's movements since her arrival?

Jacques Futrelle: Yes, she spent a short time, perhaps six weeks at Henry Street Settlement doing menial chores. Nothing especially unusual about her noted by the people there. Then to work for the Fenster household.

Samuel Harper: Mrs. St. James indicates that Mr. Fenster himself directed the girl be hired. She is under the impression a Jewish friend of Fenster recommended her, representing to him the girl had worked for an acquaintance, was honest and hard-working and likely to go far with proper training.

Nellie Bly: Emma, does the journal indicate why Fenster hired her?

Emma Goldman: It very well might, but I haven't gotten far into it and so far I am not up to the time when she entered his service.

Jacques Futrelle: I am not yet certain but I hope soon to have located this girl. Indications are she is working for the head of one of the Wall Street firms that is often in the syndicates organized by Fenster's firm to make new offerings of bonds.

Emma Goldman: She can't be still in Manhattan or I surely would have found her.

Jacques Futrelle: You're quite right she —

Emma Goldman: Nor can she be working for a Jewish firm.

Jacques Futrelle: Right again. You've been very thorough Emma.

Emma Goldman: Let's say that I've taken Fenster's death quite personally.

Samuel Harper: I would dearly love to know Emma why you are so involved.

Emma Goldman: You didn't know Mr. Fenster, Sam. Perhaps if you did it would be less of a mystery.

Samuel Harper: Perhaps Emma, but I know enough about you that not all the great Jewish philanthropists of Wall Street are viewed with as much affection.

Emma Goldman: Had you been sweated as we have been by those who professed only the desire to assist their co-religionists, you would know that something less than charity is involved in many cases. To many the immigrant Jews are a commodity — cheap labor — to be exploited like cheap cotton, like the cheap fabrics we run up for fourteen hours a day in the garment district for a few dollars a week. But Mr. Fenster was the exception. He really loved people, even us, the lowest dregs of the social order. There are not many like him and I'll do all I can to repay his killers or die trying.

Nellie Bly: We shall help Emma, but we need to know all that you've found out about Rebecca Kopoloff. Who do you think she was working for?

Jacques Futrelle: Or to phrase it another way, who wanted Fenster dead?

Emma Goldman: That's not going to get us far. The Fensters financed the

Japanese government bond issue that permitted the Japanese to defeat the Russians in the war of 1904. So the Russian government might have desired revenge. But others did also. I think we shall have to seek out every possible clue. Mr. Fenster was not a man about whom people were neutral. He aroused as much hatred in those who opposed him as he did love in those who were beneficiaries of his many kindnesses.

Nellie Bly: You found no clue in the journal?

Emma Goldman: I've only had it in my possession for 24 hours and now you must take it from me. I think Sam is better able than I ever would be to discover any clues that journal might contain.

Samuel Harper: I hope you're right Emma. I assure you I will try.

Emma Goldman: And I'll keep trying to contact Rebecca Kopoloff.

Jacques Futrelle: She might surface but I doubt it. We'll have to dig her out.

Samuel Harper: You say she was a Zionist, Emma?

Emma Goldman: Yes, her dossier indicates she was, and as you may know, Fenster, like most rich Jews, was against Zionism. That opposition alone would not ordinarily lead me to suspect the Zionists of his death. As much as they regret the opposition of men like Fenster they do not kill them over the issue. They need the support of the rich Jews and a murder over that issue could destroy the Zionist cause for all time. But Fenster's opposition was different. Most rich Jews feel threatened by Zionism. They fear their acceptance by Gentiles, however tentative it may be, will be destroyed if the goyim come to think the Jews' allegiance is to a foreign government. Not Isaac Fenster. His opposition challenged the power structure within Judaism. Even his own father opposed him —

Nellie Bly: Do go on Emma, it's fascinating.

Samuel Harper: Yes, do go on.

Emma Goldman: Fenster did not believe the Zionists could justify their claim to the Holy Land. He felt the time was soon to come when all the world would know that the Eastern Jews are not of the true blood of Israel. He felt, as I understand it, that even if they succeeded in taking a stance in Zion, it would cause great suffering and bloodshed when the Christian and Moslem worlds realize the Eastern Jew is but a convert to Judaism. The Christian world might support the Zionist movement in the belief that the return of the Jews fulfills scriptural prophecies of the return of the Jews to the Holy Land prior to the Second Coming. But let that perception change and the Jews will lose the support of the British and be wiped out.

Samuel Harper: How could you know this Emma, if you haven't read the journal?

Emma Goldman: Many Jews in New York know that Isaac Fenster became a Christian and why. He was not bashful in telling the Zionists they had no claim to Palestine. It is one thing to oppose Zionism because of the fear of social repercussions from the Gentiles. It is quite another to challenge the very idea of Jewish Chosenness.

Samuel Harper: You are most persuasive Emma. May I ask your attitude toward Zionism?

Emma Goldman: You're entitled to that. I view it as ludicrous. The Jew demands nationhood so that he can impose all the evils of nationalism, the source of so much Jewish suffering, on his own kind and others. Karl Marx saw the end of the nation-state. It is historically unavoidable. The Marxist dialectic laughs at nationhood. We seek the international brotherhood of all workers.

Samuel Harper: I suspect you are as far ahead of your time as Fenster was. The nation state may disappear but not in our lifetime.

Jacques Futrelle: Be all that as it may, let's stick to the case at hand.

Nellie Bly: I agree with Jacques, you're digressing.

Emma Goldman: Perhaps but maybe Sam is trying to see where my sympathies lie so that he can validate my opinion.

Samuel Harper: Keen — very keen, Emma. But I need to ask a very tough question. In your judgment could Fenster's challenge to the rabbinical power structure have brought about enough opposition to result in his murder?

Emma Goldman: It wouldn't be the first time would it?

Samuel Harper: Precisely, Christ before the Sanhedrin. Let us assume that you're right. We thus have one potential set of motives and one group of suspects. It could be someone or some group from within the Zionist movement. And we know the Russians had good reasons to desire his death. What about the banking community?

Nellie Bly: We won't know the answer to that until we read the book he wrote about banking will we Sam?

Samuel Harper: And maybe not then. I've read it and I am trying to get an opinion from a friend who knows about such things better than I. But it's a possibility we must entertain until disproven.

Jacques Futrelle: It almost seems we could multiply suspects endlessly where Fenster is concerned. But what about his dying words that Balfour must be warned? "Balfour will die if you don't warn him," those were the words he most needed to speak with his dying breath.

Samuel Harper: That leads back to the Zionists for all influential Jews know of Balfour's fixation with the idea of repatriating the Jews.

Jacques Futrelle: Not necessarily Sam. Balfour beats the drum for a Jewish homeland, but who believes the cynical Earl of Balfour gives a damn for anyone but himself and as an extension of his own interests, the British Empire. The Germans I doubt credit him with altruism. I'm sure they see his pro-Zionism as a smokescreen behind which British hegemony in the eastern Mediterranean will be strengthened.

Emma Goldman: Remember Fenster was a German Jew and had as much influence there as he did in America. What if he learned of a German plot to defeat the British plan by killing Balfour?

Samuel Harper: Not impossible by any means, and not an easy matter to investigate. Anti-semitism has been a virulent force in Germany for years and in the most respectable circles. But I shall see what we can discover from my German sources.

We enjoyed Emma Goldman's hospitality over cups of strong coffee for another hour before departing. Jacques took Nellie home and I took the subway to Brooklyn. I was eagerly devouring Fenster's journal as I rode and nearly missed my stop. I was pleased with the evening's accomplishments.

Letter to Arthur Conan Doyle
from Samuel Harper

Dated January 6, 1912 (New York City)

Dear Arthur,

True to his word, Jacques succeeded in locating Rebecca Kopoloff. Thus we found ourselves rattling along the irregular roadbed of the Long Island Railroad, drawn in a dingy coach toward the North Shore. Presently we would see the homes of the barons of Wall Street which emulate in grandeur the dwellings in Belgravia, those of their counterparts from the City of London.

At the Glen Cove station we were met by a Rolls Royce driven by a liveried chauffeur in the employ of Michael Redwood, one of the wealthiest men in the world of finance.

Jacques finally had set aside the book in which he had been absorbed on the train since talking over the din was most uncomfortable. It was Henry George's PROGRESS & POVERTY. I glanced at his book and remarked: "Hard to believe, isn't it that that is the book which broke the power of the House of Lords?"

Futrelle seemed mystified. "I don't follow you."

"You're unaware, I take it that the tax reform measures George set forth in that book were incorporated into Asquith's budget in 1909. When the Lords vetoed that budget their power over fiscal matters was removed for all time. And if Count Tolstoy is right, either the Czar must embrace the principles of Henry George or the destruction of Czarist Russia is assured." I puffed on my pipe and observed the look on Jacques' face.

"I knew George's ideas were well received abroad but I was neither aware he caused such a crisis in Britain nor that you knew much about him," he said.

"An Englishman would have to be obtuse indeed not to know a great deal about Henry George. It is no exaggeration to say that the ideas of George as expressed in that book you hold came as close to breaking up the power structure of Britain as is likely to happen and very close it was. Amongst a more volatile people it would have been enough to destroy the aristocracy for all time. Besides but for Henry George, Teddy Roosevelt would have been Mayor of New York City in 1886 and Kodiak told me quite a bit about that campaign and his redoubtable opponent Henry George."

I watched our progress over gracefully rolling hills along a road bordered by white wooden fences bounding well manicured expanses of lovely meadows. "Everything about the place reeks of money," I muttered.

"As J.P. Morgan once remarked," Jacques smiled, "if you have to ask the cost you don't belong."

"Quite," I agreed, "brief me on how you traced the girl here."

"It is somewhat complicated," he began, "but first I called upon our mutual friend, the one you refer to by my favorite code word 'Kodiak.' You're aware I'm sure that he was, a number of years ago, one of the most powerful members of the Police Commission."

"Yes I well recall. The New York Police were still shaking their heads over him in that role," I said, "when I first came to America."

"Well," said Jacques, "he still is able to ferret out information in this town. He was a great admirer of Isaac Fenster who contributed hugely to several of Kodiak's compaigns."

"So, with a few well placed phone calls," I ventured, "he was able to learn quite a bit, I take it."

"Indeed, he was. It was Fenster's good offices with the Japanese," Jacques continued, "that persuaded them to let Roosevelt intermediate in their war with Russia. They could have attained more decisive hegemony in the Pacific had they pressed their advantage."

Our chauffeur pulled slowly into the drive of one of the largest estates we had yet seen. Enormous aggregates of native stones cemented into great pillars were stationed at intervals along an enormous wrought iron fence whose spear-like points curved outward at the top so as to impale any intruder. A sign next to the electrically activated gate said simply 'REDWOOD.' Then we began a slow drive up a meticulously manicured avenue of immense, overarching oak trees. "What," I asked, "did Kodiak unearth?"

"Enough to make him think the Russians were keeping Fenster under surveillance and that Kopoloff was insinuated into the household for that purpose." Jacques hesitated and I looked at him quizzically.

"What puzzles you?" I asked.

"I don't really know," he said. The Rolls drew slowly over a rise and there appeared before us at a distance of about a mile what could have been Balmoral Castle moved stone for stone to Long Island.

"Just a real place to rough it," Jacques intoned with a smile.

"Barely tolerable," I agreed.

"Back to my problem," Jacques resumed. "It seems too pat to explain Kopoloff's presence in the Fenster employ and surveillance for the Russians as flowing from her Russian nationality. In truth she probably hates Russia, why would she aid them, especially to the detriment of her benefactor. Yet if we assume she was there for some other reason such as to steal the journal we are led to the conclusion that the banking community may be responsible for Fenster's death. But if that's the case why would Redwood agree to our interrogating the girl?"

"Your perplexity is understandable," I commiserated, "so let us consider what other possibilities might operate. Where are we led if we assume Fenster's death relates to Balfour and an attempt on Balfour's life. The most apparent explanation, of course, is that some group is opposed to Balfour's policy of creating a Jewish homeland in Palestine. But who and why?"

Futrelle, with furrowed brow, pondered his response. "You mentioned Balfour's cynicism. I take that as an indication you think he may be interested in a Jewish homeland in Palestine only as an extension of British power in the area."

"If you knew the Earl of Balfour as I do —," I smiled.

Jacques smiled and winked, reflecting his understanding. "I am mystified

96

by one thing in particular," he said. "Why, with the Turkish Empire up for grabs sooner or later, would England seek any justification other than the needs of her own power base in India and free access to it via Suez?"

"We shall have to ask Balfour that." I looked out the window as the Rolls drew to a halt at the front entrance to the palatial digs of Michael Redwood.

As the chauffeur opened the door at his side, Futrelle made one last remark over his shoulder. "Both Fenster and Balfour might be the targets of the Germans. I wonder if Rebecca Kopoloff speaks German?"

We exited the Rolls under the watchful eye of Redwood's chauffeur. "Balfour yes, but not Fenster who was helping rid Europe of the Jews German intellectuals so despised."

Jacques' face reflected a triumphant feeling. "True enough but he may have fallen victim to his own discovery. Having uncovered the plot to kill Balfour, he had to die himself."

"A possibility, of course," I admitted, "but so many people had good reasons to kill him, I would have to conclude the odds are against such an accidental explanation."

We were admitted to the sumptuous home of Michael Redwood by a butler who took a considerable time in responding to our ring. The massive oaken door which finally opened to admit us was not thick enough to keep from us the sounds of much coming and going inside. The expression of misery and distress which downcast the features of a tailcoated domestic bespoke a calamitous happening in this wealthy household.

Futrelle and I exchanged bewildered glances as the butler, attempted with one hand to smooth the few hairs disarrayed on his balding head. "Mr. Harper — Mr. Futrelle —," he stammered. "You arrive at — oh my — how can such a thing." His eyes were rolling, his countenance flushed. Jacques and I entered a massive foyer. From upstairs the distressed wailing of female voices could be heard.

Suddenly Jacques and I realized the nature of the calamity that had befallen the household.

"Where is she?" I asked the butler. He gestured toward the top of the stairs at the left of the foyer with an effete movement that perfectly expressed his inner feeling of helplessness. Futrelle and I bounded up the stairs. At the top of the stairs we looked down a darkling hallway entered upon by many chambers. All the doors were closed but one. Outside this doorway, gazing in horror at some spectre in the room, was a gaggle of chambermaids, moaning and wailing aloud.

Jacques and I rushed to the doorway as all the chambermaids gave way to let us through. There, hanging by knotted bedclothes lashed to one of the oak beams overhead, her body swaying ever so slightly, her face a deep purple, her tongue forced from her mouth and obviously quite dead for at least an hour, was Rebecca Kopoloff.

The simple room was meticulously clean. Her few meager and tattered items of clothing were neatly arrayed in her drawer. The room was entirely unremarkable in any way. Aside from the stool lying on its side on the floor which she had kicked over in effecting her own execution, the impeccable atmosphere of the chamber was complete.

On a small desk lay a copy of the Bible. Beside the book lay a short list of scriptural citations. Through mere habit I took out my notebook and copied them down. Then Jacques and I began the long wait until the police should arrive.

Best ever,

Sam

P.S. My sources tell me you have been helping the Prefecture's people in their efforts to recover the Mona Lisa which was stolen from the Louvre. Let me know if I can help.

Journal Entry Samuel Harper
January 8, 1912 (New York City)

The face of Michael Redwood, even in repose, perhaps especially in repose, was downturned at the corners of his mouth, revealing, I suspected, a negative mindset. I couldn't help but be filled with wonder how one blessed with every possible material advantage as I knew him to have been, could yet feel so negative about the world, a frame of mind which could only be a reflection of his own negative self-image.

As I reflected upon this I was sardonically amused that I should still be filled with wonder at encountering a personality that had enjoyed every apparent advantage and yet could only raise himself up by bringing others down. Amused, for having encountered the same phenomenon in a multitude of cases amongst the British nobility, I should no longer be surprised. And no one knows better than I that the negative personality is its own proof that whatever the material advantages might have been, or appeared to be, still there has to have been lacking the loving treatment that makes a person self-confident and whole.

The lowliest cottager can send forth into the world a sounder, more creative son or daughter than the most exalted peer of the realm, if he but love his child and bring forth the spirit of self-love in his offspring. Indeed, more than once have I reflected upon the possibility that the deeply entrenched sense of class to which the British nobility cling so steadfastly and which prompts so much opposition to social change is rooted entirely in the self-hatred of the upper classes. A more self-loving and self-confident society would be more open.

Having been exposed myself to the brutality of the public* school system, I know how deprived the children of the upper classes have been of parental affection and of the evil perversions born of such neglect.

Futrelle, a native of America, born to the egalitarianism which America embodies, could not, I think, have shared my ruminations as we entered Redwood's sumptuous Wall Street offices. Still I detected the slightest attitude of deference in Jacques — nothing definable — the most minute degree less movement, a trifle less emphasis in the voice.

"Mr. Harper, Mr. Futrelle, please come in." Redwood spoke from his desk, not a trace of a smile gracing his features, weatherbeaten from the sun and salt-spray, the evidence of leisure hours spent at the wheel of his sailboat on Long Island Sound.

He did not rise from his desk, a manifestation we were there only at suffrance. "Please sit down," he gestured authoritatively from his desk. Then looking directly in my eyes, "What can I do for you Mr. Harper?"

I had determined from Redwood's demeanor he was a hostile witness who would not willingly give his cooperation to further our investigation. Still

*In England a 'public school' is, in fact, private.

he didn't dare give the appearance of not cooperating.

"Mr. Redwood," I began, "we wish to know everything you can tell us about Rebecca Kopoloff." I watched his eyes as I said the dead girl's name but not the slightest reaction was to be seen. Clearly, I was dealing with a cool customer, possessed of little sympathy for the needs of any but himself.

"I shall tell you what I can, which is very little. After all Mrs. Redwood is responsible for engaging all domestic help," he responded.

"That's not entirely true, is it?" I had decided I must shake his complacency.

"Are you calling me a liar?" He was quicker to rise to the bait than I had expected.

"If indeed you are lying, then you've saved me the trouble of so characterizing you." He was now starting to show some awareness of the seriousness of his situation.

"What is it you wish to know Mr. Harper. I cannot be responsible for the welfare of every menial staff member. We have fifteen or sixteen such girls coming and going at all times." He was now showing a bit of a flush.

"No doubt true Mr. Redwood, but I happen to know Rebecca Kopoloff was, for some reason we desire to discover, more than just another domestic," I said.

"In what way more?" he impatiently asked.

"That we are here to discover. We know she was hired for your staff to sequester her outside Manhattan while the New York Police were seeking to interrogate her regarding the murder of Isaac Fenster." Once again I watched his eyes closely. There was a slight dilation of the pupils at the mention of Fenster.

"I know nothing whatever about Fenster's death," the volume rising noticeably.

"Of that we must convince ourselves, Mr. Redwood or you are indeed in a situation of considerable embarassment, or worse." I dropped the emphasis of these last two words, making them sound more ominously in the silence of his vast office which was broken only by the majestic ticking of an enormous grandfather clock in the corner of his sumptuous office.

Futrelle looked briefly at me with a non-committal expression. He seemed slightly surprised and, I couldn't determine which, either amused or embarassed at the audaciousness of my approach. "I will tell you what little I know," Redwood remarked, his haughtiness gone.

"That would be most helpful," I responded. "Who," I asked, "suggested you employ Miss Kopoloff?"

"You are aware," Redwood began slowly, "that my firm has been one of the lead houses in underwritings of foreign governmental financings. Some we manage ourselves, some we are principals in offerings by other houses and some of those, of course, are under Fenster's leadership." He paused to assure himself we understood. "We led in the issues on behalf of the German government, Fenster in those we did for the Japanese."

I nodded my understanding and asked for his permission to light my pipe. This he granted with a nod of his head and continued.

"The floating of these issues may seem like a perfunctory business to the public, Mr. Harper," he said, "but I can assure you issues of the highest moment in international diplomacy are at stake in each."

"I have no doubt of what you say Mr. Redwood, do go on." I puffed at my meerschaum.

"The entire question of who will dominate Europe is at issue in these financings and Fenster's motivations in financing the Japanese were no secret." Redwood looked at me for a sign that I understood.

"You refer, of course, to his antipathy to Russia over the pograms against the Jews." I met his inquiring gaze.

"Exactly, Mr. Harper. As the leading U.S. banker for the German issues, we were made aware that the government of the Kaiser favored our assisting Fenster in the Japanese offering as a means of weakening the Russian regime who are," he paused, "regarded as potential adversaries in any major European conflict. Russia covets Turkish territory and Turkey is an ally of the Kaiser."

Futrelle and I exchanged glances. But I did nothing to interrupt the flow of Redwood's narrative. He paused before he continued.

"I was asked by influential persons in the German embassy to give Miss Kopoloff a position. There is nothing more I can tell you. I hadn't the slightest idea she was connected in any way with Fenster's murder."

"It is, surely, most unusual," I said, "for people of such influence to exercise their power to affect the hiring of a domestic." I stared directly into Redwood's eyes, but, unflinching, he returned my intensity.

"Of course," he replied, "but just as surely, if matters relating to this girl were of such import as to prompt the request, they were likely such that I had no desire to know about. Requests of this type are not entirely unusual. She could have become an embarassment to someone for more mundane reasons. The girl was not sexually unattractive, I'm told."

"To be sure and apparently quite bright also," I conceded. "But I take it you knew nothing about the Fenster journal this girl stole from the Fenster home, which theft was apparently the prime purpose of her being insinuated into the household of the slain man?"

I watched Redwood's eyes closely and believe I detected the slightest flicker of a reaction at my question.

"You force me to discuss personalities in a way I find repugnant Mr. Harper." He met my gaze directly.

"To be regretted Mr. Redwood," I said, "but, I fear, unavoidable. Please proceed."

"Isaac Fenster was regarded as the eccentric son of the redoubtable Jacob Fenster," he smiled in a derisive way, the first sign of even black humor he had shown. "He was known to harbor many ideas bordering on the incomprehensible — an embarassment to his father and therefore to me whose primary connection with the Fenster firm is with Jacob, even though the day-to-day details of our joint dealings were run by Isaac Fenster."

"Eccentric in what way?" I asked.

"I'm not sure I can be specific. The world of Wall Street is like any other," he glanced first at Futrelle then at me as though we surely agreed with his statement. "The individual who in any way questions the basic rectitude of the way things are, is automatically an outcast. One rarely knows or bothers to find out why people are placed in such a category. Everyone who counts in Wall Street regarded Isaac Fenster as an odd-ball. I doubt anyone at my level has the vaguest idea why. There was the matter of his book, of course, but I doubt anyone read it. He just wasn't to be taken seriously — that was the consensus and I knew no reason to challenge it."

"That sounds plausible enough," I said, "but conveniently unenlightening."

Redwood showed considerable irritation. "Mr. Harper, if you are quite through, I have my duties to pursue." He indicated his intention to terminate our conversation.

Futrelle and I arose. "I recognize how busy you are Mr. Redwood and we have been helped considerably by your remarks." He drew his shoulders back and looked down his nose at me. I determined to keep him on the defensive. "But be aware it may be necessary for us to trouble you further if our investigative pursuits raise any questions about the testimony you have just given."

"I am always here Mr. Harper," he said, a note of irritation in his voice as he pressed the buzzer summoning his secretary to show us out.

In the street Jacques and I directed our steps to Fraunces' Tavern, the nearest pub. Comfortably ensconced, a warming drink in hand, we shared our impressions of the circumstances surrounding the suicide of Rebecca Kopoloff and our encounter with her employer Michael Redwood, one of the world's most powerful men.

"You like to beard the lion in his den," Jacques said, his eyes twinkling mischievously.

"Not at all," I replied, "it's just that men who wield great power soon lose touch with world of harsh reality as experienced by us lesser mortals. You can only penetrate their insensitivity by reflecting disdain for their accoutrements of power."

"He proved pretty thin-skinned at that," Futrelle observed.

"And well he might, the very least he might be charged with is accessory after the fact," I said, lifting my glass to my lips.

"You think then," my companion asked, "that we can establish facts linking him to Fenster's killers?"

"Not really, but he doesn't know that, or how much we do know. In fact, all he knows is that we believe an employee of his was involved in a man's death. The fact she killed herself in his home involves Redwood in something more distasteful than murder — adverse public notice," I said, "he will cooperate to avoid more bad press."

"Do you think he is really ignorant of Isaac Fenster's death?" Futrelle inquired.

"It seems likely to me he is telling the truth. Fenster lived in the world of ideas. He was a man of great erudition — the antithesis of the type found in Wall Street. Had he not been born the son of Jacob Fenster," I said, "he would not have lasted a week in the firm."

"In my experience," Futrelle remarked, "the investment bankers value money before brains. They profess to need both, but when push comes to shove, they need money absolutely. Brains are a luxury and not always one they can afford, especially," he smiled, "if the possessor of that intelligence does not honor all the holy cows of the Wall Street liturgy."

"What do you make of the German connection?" Jacques asked.

"It would displease my countrymen to know how large a body of pro-German sentiment exists in this country," I intoned into my glass as I took a draught, "it will make it most difficult for America to decide upon whose side she will fight in the event of war in Europe — a possibility I regard as all too likely."

"You think the Germans might have hired Kopoloff?" he asked, "perhaps entirely without Redwood's knowledge."

"If they did hire her, I can think of no reason they would want Redwood to know. The question is," I watched Futrelle's mobile features, "Why would they want Fenster dead? Balfour I can understand. Turkey will fight at Germany's side and Balfour intends to carve up the Ottoman Empire and give the Jews a morsel. But Fenster was actively fighting the creation of a Jewish homeland on Turkish soil or anywhere else. It can only be one of two possibilities, one, either he accidentally discovered a plot to kill Balfour or, two, they approached him to aid in their plan, disclosed the plan to him, he refused to help and had to die. I doubt it's the latter."

"There remains a third possibility," Jacques opined. "The book made it desirable to remove Fenster and they simply decided to kill them both. Somehow Fenster learned of the plot and warned us about Arthur."

"But how did he learn about the plot against the Earl of Balfour?" I mused aloud.

A moment of silence hung between us. Both Futrelle and I were struck at the same moment by an idea.

"Could Kopoloff," I asked, "have somehow informed Fenster?"

"A possibility, of course," Jacques said "but one I can't see how we would learn about with the girl dead."

"What we need," I ventured, "is more information about her post mortem."

"Now there I might be of some assistance," Jacques volunteered.

We soon bid each other farewell with Jacques moving determinedly toward a destination known only to him. I headed for my digs in Brooklyn Heights.

Journal Entry Samuel Harper
January 13, 1912 (New York City)

"Your friend, Isaac Fenster," said my old friend W.T. Stead, his eyes twinkling with mischief, "was a very bad boy." He twirled his glass on the table in the bar of the University Club looking about to assure himself no one was near enough for our conversation to be overheard. He chuckled loudly at his little joke attributing Fenster's objectives in part to me by the reference "your friend."

"I scarcely knew the man existed," I protested, "until some ruddy blokes decided to leave his mutilated body in an alley near my home."

"A bad boy nonetheless," he repeated. "You should be more careful who you associate with." He thought it high humor to ignore my protests.

"Have your fun," I said, "but tell me why a bad boy?" Stead was taking time out of one of his frequent trips to New York City to give me his opinion of Isaac Fenster's book.

"You don't have to be a Hindu to be offended when a holy cow is gored," he playfully and cryptically responded, determined to prolong his badinage as long as possible.

"Tell me about the holy cow, and leave off the ribbing," I smiled briefly, quickly resuming a serious demeanor in the hope I could affect a like change in him.

The best known publisher in London, the proprietor of the Pall Mall Gazette finally adopted a serious visage. "You really don't know why that book could get its author killed, do you?"

I was starting to squirm in discomfort, which was the exact result he desired. "Would I ask your help if I did?"

"I suppose," he mumbled into his glass, taking a draught before resuming. "Fenster was determined to expose the whole ruddy game once and for all."

"What game? Stop being so cryptic," I urged.

"How is it the Americans come up with these dreamy reformers? This Fenster was a man cut of the same cloth as Henry George. They are two of a kind. They nonchalantly advance, sword in hand, prepared to thrust to the very heart of the aristocracy's most valued perquisites and expect their victims not only to accept their losses, but to assist in their own destruction. George would tax away the value of all land including natural resources. But Fenster exposed the fact that there is a way for the Old Lady of Threadneedle Street, The Bank of England to retain control of the world without a colony to her name." He looked at me obviously expecting some dramatic show of surprise. I was all attention, but surprise is not my style.

"You don't seem much impressed," he continued.

"Attribute that to my ignorance," I smiled, "but do go on."

"You desire to know the best kept secret of the Exchequer," he continued, "and all you can say is 'do go on.' Give me one good reason to cast my pearls before swine," he chided.

"To save the life possibly of your good friend, fellow believer in spiritualism and frequent seance co-participant, the Right Honourable Arthur James Balfour."

At this I clearly impressed him enough to cause his demeanor to change, and he was instantly serious. He emitted a low whistle and cocked his eyeglasses, his perplexity and great curiosity overwhelming his recent efforts at self-amusement at my expense.

"You are full of surprises Sam," he said. "First a book as explosive as dynamite and now this. What do you do for excitement?"

I ignored his little joke. "This book surfaced as possibly a key element in a murder I am working on," I said, "a man was killed, ritually slashed precisely like the Ripper slayings, except that no trollop died this time but a prince, one of the wealthiest men on Wall Street."

Stead made a thoughtful delay in responding. "That book could do it. A hundred men in the world of finance both here and in America would have a motive to do in the author of that work. Come to think of it, there are probably not a hundred men in the world, at best a handful who understand what Fenster is saying. But once widely recognized, the information in that little tome would rock the world."

I said nothing, waiting and hoping my reticence would bring him to the point. Like many men who are both intelligent and articulate, he was organizing his thoughts carefully before resuming.

"What do you know about the commodities market, Sam?" Stead asked watching my face closely.

"Very little," I responded as honestly as I could.

"Not surprising," he rejoined, "not one in a million even very well-informed people do." Then he paused, "you are about to learn the secret of how men acquire and keep power through the ages. And, you'll find this amusing, you won't believe it and if you do, you'll never be able to confirm that what I'm telling you is true, or even get anyone to believe you are anything but a fool or worse."

"You fascinate me," I said, "but how you do tease. Can't you come to the point?"

"Too simple, you are, by half," he laughed, "and not enough fun. My teasing you is the price you pay to pick my brains."

I sighed and shrugged my shoulders.

"That's more like it — do relax old man; I will get to the point by and by. But even a most intelligent bloke like yourself will need for me to go slowly."

"Have it your way," I sighed, "I am at your disposal."

"Come to think of it," he said changing pace, "I will give it to you concisely — a veritable nugget, immensely compressed, and why not? Were I to take a year to tell it, it would still mean nothing to you."

"Try me," I said.

"Indeed I shall, my wise friend." He was now still apparently joking, but with a sardonic overtone in his voice reflecting possibly regret he was saying anything at all?

"Both Doyle and Balfour want me to help you," he said, "or rest assured I'd tell you not a word." His gaze was icy.

"My genuine appreciation 'WT'," I said with utmost sincerity. "It really is quite important."

"We are talking about how the money markets of the world are controlled. Nothing less than the key to power, supreme world power, the means of controlling all mankind for good or evil," his serious demeanor adequately emphasized the importance of his words.

"You mean the banking system?" I asked.

"Only in part," he replied, "but a typical error."

"The key to what's possible in the banking system is the price structure of commodities. Money doesn't go very far," he nodded in my direction, "if commodities prices rise. Still most people think controlling bank draughts is the key. Not so, before money in the form of paper can proliferate, thus making fortunes for the powerful, prices must remain stable and this can only happen if there is a means to keep commodities from soaring."

"And how," I asked, "is that to be done?"

"The few men who really run this world," he said as though he proceeded only regretfully, "know that the price of gold controls the price of all commodities."

"Not so startling," I said, feeling more confident.

"You really are an ass," said Stead, "but I'll go on bravely."

He clearly suffers fools ungladly. "Please do," I said penitently.

"Do be still," he said taking a breath and looking out the window of the University Club at the crowd on Fifth Avenue collecting his thoughts. "Even Nebuchadnezzar knew that, but he knew much more we don't find revealed in the Book of Daniel. To control the price of gold and therefore the price of all other commodities, it is absolutely necessary to control the means of refining the precious metal."

"Logical," I said, "but still not earth shaking."

"Why do I bother?" he said, a weary tone in his voice.

"I shall be silent as a tomb," I resignedly stated.

"A great improvement, to be sure," he said, a disgusted look on his face. "It really is such a waste of time, but I shall finish, I promised I would — what a foolish thing to do really."

I said not a word, fearful he would leave off for good.

"Oh my," he sighed and paused, then resuming, "For a gold exchange to work someone must stand ready to buy when there are no buyers and sell when there are no sellers."

"Even I can understand that," I said, not a trace of sarcasm intended.

"Hmmm," he snorted, "perhaps. But you really can't imagine the money to be made by those who stand ready to so serve the marketplace. If you control enough refining capacity, you can sell against future capacity and frustrate almost any amount of buying interest. Then having, unlike King Canute, turned the tide of buying interest, selling claims against your future capacity with a neat profit on every transaction, you then buy back these worthless pieces of paper, once again at a profit on every trade. Without so much as having delivered a single ounce of gold, the market can be permitted to run up and back down again with gold having returned approximately to its original level. The object of the game is to hold the price relatively stable while profiting hugely whether market oscillations are up or down."

I tried to summarize his ideas. "What you are saying then is that price stability in commodities is related to stability in the price of gold, not the availability of paper currency — is that correct?"

"Jolly good," he said embarassing me at the tone of surprise in his voice. "But the tough part comes now. Everyone can see that a stable gold price means relative stability in other commodities. What they don't see," he paused to heighten the drama of his remarks, "is that if one controls the very limited amount of gold refining capacity in the world one can amass untold profits by controlling the clearing of transactions on the gold exchanges. And beyond these enormous profits, one can now expand the supply of paper currencies endlessly without affecting the price structure which is based on commodities all of which follow the price of gold."

"I think I begin to see," I offered, "the colonial possessions of the European nations all wish to be free of imperial control. But each of the economies of these colonies is based on one or more commodities. By controlling the gold market, the Old Lady of Threadneedle Street has at its mercy every emerging nation whose economy is based on commodities. By setting the gold price the merchant bankers of the City of London perpetuate the power of England by forcing commodity exporting nations to sell at depressed prices. Meanwhile to finance their development they must borrow from the Central Banks and pay interest on the paper money these bankers manufacture out of thin air."

Stead looked amused and amazed. "There may be hope for you Harper."

"You're too kind," I rejoined a tinge of sarcasm in my voice to repay his former cavalier treatment.

"But perhaps you are beginning to see how Britain can control all her colonies," he said, "even if they break away as they are threatening to do in search of their precious 'freedom'."

"I do indeed," I responded, "and I see a good deal more also. I see precisely why the men of the ilk of those who committed the Ripper slayings would be happy to do Fenster in for a good deal less than the publication of his revealing book."

"You are not," Stead announced as he concluded our conversation and rose to his feet, "totally without the ability to comprehend quite complex matters, Harper."

"You are too kind by half," I sarcastically rejoined.

Letter to Samuel Harper
from Arthur Conan Doyle
Dated January 23, 1912 (London)

Dear Sam,

I appreciate your sending me a copy of your notes from the meeting with Stead. I can't say that I understand much of it, but I do get a feeling of the importance of what Fenster has to say in the context of world politics. People have urged for years that the Empire be dissolved and we've all thought about what it would mean. But coming, as it does, at a time when we all feel certain we are drifting into a war with Germany and her allies, and when we feel the need for every able-bodied Territorial, I can't say the thought of dissolving the Empire is very comforting.

As you well know, I have stood for years four-square for Anglo-German friendship. The first tremor to this centerpiece in the arch that has so long supported British (and German) policy, to my way of thinking, came in 1902 when they interfered with our efforts to end the Boer War. Then in 1906 when they bullied France into the Algeciras Conference I began to wonder. But I confess I was not utterly convinced at that time that Germany would challenge us, who have, for so long, come to the aid of their interests on the Continent until the trouble Germany stirred up in 1911 when they sent their gunboat Panther to Agadir.

That whole affair spoiled the atmosphere of the Anglo-German auto race in Germany in July while the Agadir crisis unfolded. Having committed myself to participate in the race many months before, I could not and would not withdraw. But for all the elegant courtesy of the German officers who hosted us, I could not enjoy myself, wondering as I did how much longer before our British military men in the race would be killing the German contestants and vice versa.

We have indeed had it all laid out for us sixteen different ways. Professor von Treitschke has discovered British transgressions that Germany must avenge going back to pre-history as though any nation, including ours, could not multiply such examples endlessly. But, by his book GERMANY AND THE NEXT WAR, General von Bernhardi, speaking as he surely does for the topmost echelon of the German High Command, has finally overcome whatever reluctance I felt any longer to draw the bitter conclusion that it must be war between us. Nor was this the only warning. Von Edelsheim also spoke out on the subject of how Germany will dispose of America when the time comes.

I am convinced now there will be a war. The only remaining questions are when it will occur and how long it will last.

The question of when is difficult to answer. Better heads than mine predict that Germany dare not commence hostilities until they have widened the Kiel Canal to allow their larger ships to have access to the North Sea from the Baltic. This is presently scheduled to be completed in mid-year 1914.

Perhaps more important is the question of how long the war can last. I scarcely think it can last long. The Germans must win it quickly or negotiate a peace as a war of attrition they cannot win. I doubt in a costly war of heavy casualties, as modern weapons insure a long war will be, we will find them to be the 'deep patient Germany' Carlyle so admired.

As I have read the literature spewed out by so many Germans for so long I have sought to answer the question of why the world should find itself arrayed against Germany and her allies, Germany the nation conceded by all, including ourselves, to be superior in so many material accomplishments to the rest of the world.

I have concluded the real cause of war is a universal national insanity infecting the whole German race, but derived originally from a Prussian caste who innoculated the other with their megalomania.

This insanity is based upon the universal supposition that the Germans are the Lord's chosen people, that they are the most cultured, the best settlers, the best warriors.

If they were infinitely the best people, why should they not have the best things in the world?

In the light of the hatred for other peoples the Germans have fostered among themselves beginning with the Jews, I fear the results of a major war will be a heritage of hatred among the nations of Europe that will take a long time to abate.

And I feel too that the conditions of modern warfare must be more barbarous than anything seen since the Dark Ages. Civilian populations must bear the brunt formerly reserved for troops in the field.

Aircraft, both planes and dirigibles, and submarines must alter the conditions of war for all time. It is our ideal to fight in a sporting spirit. But I shan't be surprised to find it impossible to do so.

We are all well here. Hope you and yours are the same.

Arthur

Journal Entry Samuel Harper

January 16, 1912 (New York City)

"It's times like this you wonder if the telephone is really such a blessing." Jacques' voice sounded weary in my ear. As I held this extraordinary instrument and contemplated the unusual developments he was describing, I could see his usually buoyant features in my mind's eye, lines of fatigue about the eyes and mouth, the hair rumpled, the complexion more gray than its usual ruddy.

"What time did you receive this call?" I asked. "There's a clock next to the telephone. It was 2:30 a.m.," he groaned lugubriously. "Accept my sympathy of course," I said, "but I'm dying to learn what has happened." Jacques and I are two of the lucky quarter million New Yorkers who have Mr. Bell's miracle in our homes. Gone the days when Doyle and I had to employ the street urchins as messengers he amusingly dubbed "The Baker Street Irregulars."

"I think I know who it was, though he was deliberately speaking in such a way as to change his voice," Jacques began. "He told me he had something he knew I would be interested in, and I must meet him at once in Gramercy Park."

"You went, of course," I stated the obvious.

"Of course, but not without considerable misgiving," he responded. "It is not great amusement to meet one isn't quite certain who in utter darkness at 3 a.m. even in Gramercy Park."

I laughed at his little joke. "You say you think you know who it was?"

"Possibly a fellow who has earned a few dollars from me in the past as an informer," Jacques remarked, "works in the Coroner's Office and has been very helpful in the past."

"Why would he now choose to conceal his identity from you?" I asked.

"Good question," Jacques rejoined, "I can only speculate that he is aware of the powerful forces involved in the Fenster case. If that's correct one need feel no surprise he wants to remain unknown."

"Hmmm," I mused, "there's the additional possibility that someone in the hierarchy got the Coroner's Office to suppress evidence and your informer's job would be forfeit if they learned of his complicity with us."

"You astonish me Harper," Jacques said, mild surprise registering in his voice. "Have you already guessed what he drew me there to give me?"

"Not in the least," I said, "other than something pertinent to Rebecca Kopoloff's death and that but a wild shot."

"Closer to the mark than you might imagine," he continued. "There was a letter concealed in the girl's bosom and, are you settled in your chair? It was addressed to you."

"I am atingle with excitement, mon ami," I was wide awake and functioning at that exalted level of heightened perception that is the occasional great reward of my work. To be sure only rarely, but worth the waiting, the boredom and drudgery. "How soon can we meet to review this tidbit?"

"Don't you want to hear more about it right now?" Jacques temporized.

"Forgive me Futrelle, but what you say will only take time better spent reviewing the document itself," I said, "Where shall we meet?" It was agreed that we should employ the board room of the attorney's on 14th Street who do Futrelle's copyright work. It was 11:30 of a gray November morning when we settled down to review what I hoped might be an important new addition to our knowledge about the death of the lovely, young and quite tragic Jewess.

Jacques withdrew from his brief case a document he presented to me. "We can only have it for a brief time, so we have to record such details as interest us and return it to him before it's missed from the file."

"Just so," I responded as I withdrew the paper from the envelope in which it reposed. I observed at once that it was a fine, ivory colored vellum otherwise unmarked aside from the writing it bore, than by an embossed crest which I knew to be that of the Redwood family.

At 11:45 we were joined by Cornelia who, at my invitation, left her duties at the Fenster mansion to assist us. What a pleasure it was to see the look in her eyes when we greeted each other. A tiny detail that told so much about a developing relationship between us — a detail quickly interpreted by Futrelle with the tiniest knowing smile.

We sat, the three of us with the document on the table before us, at my left side Cornelia, and at my right Jacques. And what a curious document it was. It read:

"Dear Mr. Harper:

Emma has asked me to prepare this letter for you as she knows that when we meet you will ask me which are my favorite sections of scripture. So I have set them forth below in a list which you can take with you. These are set forth in the order they hold in my affections, my most favorite first, etc. though it was difficult to choose in many cases. Hope this responds to your request:

1. Prov. 5:8	2. Gen. 9:3	3. Ps. 139:21
4. Gen. 16:14	5. Hosea 14:1	6. Gen. 7:2
7. Gen. 32:11	8. Ps. 97:2	9. Gen. 1:2
10. Gen. 3:1	11. I Sam. 31:1	12. Ex. 1:5
13. Gen. 5:2	14. Num. 1:46	15. Gen. 8:16
16. Num. 2:2	17. Prov. 8:10	18. Jer. 1:11
19. Lev. 1:1	20. II Sam. 1:1	21. Gen. 4:12
22. Gen. 10:9	23. Sol. 2:14	24. II Sam. 1:9
25. Gen. 3:19	26. Prov. 8:18	27. Num. 4:40
28. Gen. 49:16	29. Gen. 2:1	30. Gen. 3:16
31. Prov. 8:31	32. Ex. 23:7	33. Titus 3:11
34. Rom. 11:1	35. Gen. 27:29	36. Gen. 29:17
37. Gen. 3:5	38. Num. 14:37	39. I Kings 2:1
40. Num. 6:2	41. II Sam. 1:11	42. Num. 15:23
43. Prov. 11:4	44. Num. 6:23	45. II Sam. 1:19
46. Ps. 139:1	47. Amos 3:9	48. Amos 6:1
49. Num. 34:1	50. Prov. 13:6	51. I Kings 1:1

52. Gen. 2:6	53. Josh. 14:1	54. Matt. 5:24
55. Jude 1:4	56. Job 31:35	57. Rev. 2:1
58. Jude 1:13	59. Num. 25:11	60. Jude 1:8
61. Judges 20:10	62. I Kings 1:12	63. Heb. 13:23
64. Matt. 5:31	65. Isa. 49:1	66. Ps. 141:1
67. Jer. 2:1	68. Num. 18.14	69. Hag. 2:18
70. Zech. 10:4	71. Hag. 1:5	72. Mal. 4:1
73. Zech. 6:13	74. Hag. 2:2	75. Hag. 2:16
76. Mic. 2:8	77. Zech. 2:7	78. Hag. 1:2
79. James 2:5	80. Mal. 3:7	81. Hag. 2:6
82. Hag. 1:3	83. Joel 1:6	84. Luke 1:2
85. Zech. 3:3	86. Hag. 2:21	87. Mal. 3:4
88. Luke 3:5	89. Prov. 9:8	90. I Sam. 18:4
91. Num. 9:10	92. II Sam. 1:25	93. I Kings 8:2
94. Ez. 7:1	95. Num. 18:15	96. Sol. 1:4
97. Gen. 5:2	98. Gen. 40:13	99. Gen. 19:32
100. Zech. 9:9	101. Rev. 2:19	102. Lam. 2:11
103. I Chron. 6:4		

Ask Emma to find it in her heart to forgive me.

R. Kopoloff"

"What do you make of it?", I said to both of them. Answers were a long time coming, but each was in character.

Jacques said, "I will contact Emma and see if she had been in touch with Rebecca. I will wager a week's wages she wasn't, but let us be thorough."

Cornelia's response was directed to the text itself. "Clearly this is a cipher — can be little doubt of that."

While I was already in agreement with her observation, I withheld any response to see how my American friend reacted to her remarks.

"How do you conclude that?" he asked, "looks like any other list of bible quotes to me."

Cornelia smiled and I joined her. "That's not possible Mr. Futrelle — Jacques," she said, "when we check these against the scriptures you will see that many of the sections cited are meaningless taken out of context."

Jacques eyes reflected his surprise at her erudition and his admiration for an ability he had already, though quite unwittingly, acknowledged himself not to possess.

"But there are questions in my mind too," she said, "how could a young Jewess whom we don't even know to have been religious conceive of the idea of a cipher based on the bible?"

"Emma may have something to contribute on that point," I said, "but I suspect we will discover that besides being bright enough to realize few people would suspect a cipher to be hidden in Holy Writ, that it was the only book available to her in the Redwood mansion which she could peruse at length without arousing the suspicion of her captors."

"Captors!" exclaimed Futrelle, "how have you two concluded she was a captive?"

"If we're correct," I said, "that it's a cipher, then it follows she was held against her will."

"I haven't yet accepted that it's a cipher," Jacques responded with some chagrin.

"That's obvious," I said, drawing deeply on my pipe and attempting to suppress a smile. "But you will admit that if we are correct on the one point, the other logically follows."

"I suppose," my Gallic friend grudgingly admitted to Cornelia's obvious amusement.

"I am struck," she said, "by the tragic circumstances of this poor girl's death. Though she may have occasioned the demise of my dear friend, I am sure she ended her life filled with terror and perhaps remorse. And who knows she may have only been an unwitting accomplice to Mr. Fenster's murder."

"I am struck," I said, "by the brilliance of her deception. She knew quite a number of hostile people had to be gulled before this message might come to my attention."

"How innocent it must have seemed," Cornelia observed, "for a young woman to be fervently consulting the Scriptures, especially in what her captors knew to be terror-filled circumstances, and how deeply she was in need of the comfort of Holy Writ. Yet," she went on, "trapped by their own irreligious natures into letting a message pass through their hands to give them the lie. For if they knew anything about the Bible they would know most of those passages are devoid of meaning and they would then suspect a trick."

"Got you there," Jacques verbally pounced, "the message would never be lying here before us now had not an informant smuggled it to us."

"Got you there," I pounced back, looking at Jacques with a victorious smile. "The fact the message was not destroyed forthwith is a tribute to her triumph. True, they did not deliver it to me for they probably had orders to suppress all evidence of whatever nature, but they did not destroy it as they surely should have, had they suspected a ruse. Unless I miss my guess, we will find a clue of the utmost importance to the identity of Fenster's murderer in this cipher."

Jacques departed our presence announcing his intention to call Emma Goldman. Cornelia and I transcribed the note so as to permit Jacques to return the original to his informant. I made a careful sketch of the crest embossed on the paper bearing this message from the departed Rebecca Kopoloff.

Jacques entered the oak paneled meeting room. "As we suspected," he said, "Emma had had no contact whatever with the girl and had no knowledge of her religious feelings. I concede it must be a cipher." He was taking it in good style and now was all readiness to get on with the work of breaking the cipher.

"But first," he said, "I must leave you long enough to return this message to my informant. I will be gone several hours, but we have permission to use

113

this room as long as we wish or until 6 p.m. when the firm closes."

Cornelia and I bid a temporary farewell to Jacques and armed with a King James Version Jacques had sent the office boy out to purchase, we sat down side by side, she calling the citations out and I looking them up. Then Cornelia transcribed them on a typewriter commandeered from the office manager of the firm of Jacques' attorneys.

How pleasant it was to be close to this lovely creature. Not all my thoughts were of the work at hand. And so we labored, enjoying each other's presence until Jacques' return at quarter to six in the evening.

"You were gone much longer than expected," I said to Futrelle.

"A minor inconvenience," he responded, "my contact couldn't break away immediately so I got to enjoy Gramercy Park, the nannies and les enfants terribles."

"What an unanticipated pleasure," I joshed. "Now I fear we must move the sight of our endeavors a chez Fenster. By the way did your informant reveal himself?"

"No," Jacques responded, "a street urchin appeared to take the envelope, gesturing toward the figure of a man a hundred or more yards away. I couldn't identify him to saye my soul from perdition."

"The heat is too great down at headquarters," I said, Jacques nodding agreement.

Cornelia, Jacques and I departed the 14th Street offices and made our way up town to continue our labors at the Fenster mansion with Cornelia brewing hot potions to keep us awake as we labored through the night hopefully to identify the killers of Rebecca Kopoloff and Isaac Fenster.

The cipher proved brilliantly simple when we finally broke it. But a good many hours were consumed attempting variations that all proved, in retrospect, much too labyrinthine.

Finally, at about 3:30 a.m. I ventured a guess that opened the problem up to solution. "What do we get, if we take the first letter of the first word in each citation?"

Cornelia called the letters off as Jacques transcribed them. I sipped my coffee smoking my pipe and fighting fatigue as I looked over the shoulder of bedraggled, perspiring Futrelle. Before our eyes the suicide message of Rebecca Kopoloff evolved as the moving finger on the wall of Nebuchadnezzar's chamber:

"REDWOOD CAN NAME GERMAN WHO HIRED TURK KILL FENSTER/ STOP WARN BALFOUR/ PLAN KILL ME/ CONFESSED THEFT FENSTER/ ASHAMED MY CRIME."

Our sense of triumph was subdued. Not merely because of the moving reaction of Cornelia to the sad revelations we had deciphered. She now realized that Isaac Fenster had forgiven Rebecca her transgressions. Could she do less? He had known his peril and still bore no enmity toward her who had betrayed his generous aid and his hospitality. It was entirely in keeping with the loving nature of her employer, and only rendered more poignant her sense of loss at his death.

It occurred to me, and I verbalized the fact, that only by killing herself could Rebecca Kopoloff hope this message would come to my attention. Her captors surely would not permit her to relay its contents and live. She had died by her own hand to expiate her guilt in connection with Fenster's death. This observation deepened Cornelia's sorrow, her sobs shaking her lovely frame. I was struck once again at the feeling of frustration over my inability to do much to comfort her just as I had felt as Tony suffered her fatal illness. And I knew at last that my love for Cornelia was every bit as deep as that I felt for Tony.

Journal Entry Samuel Harper

Dated January 25, 1912 (New York City)

He was unlike any man I'd ever met before. He was not imposing in any physical sense. But he was completely composed and what he said was with absolute conviction. He was not dogmatic and he did not hesitate to state when a point arose for which Mormon theology has no answer. His name is Joseph Benham and he is a fifth generation Mormon. By the time the evening was over I felt I had known him all my life. Cornelia said little but generously took copious notes in shorthand. (It is from these I have excerpted what I set forth.)

It was a cold November evening that intermittently brought cold wind bearing a driving snow and from time to time, the snow would cease and a hushed silence ensued during which the principal sound to be heard by pedestrians in the streets of Manhattan was the dripping of moisture from the eaves of the buildings to the street. Cornelia and I made our way from upper Fifth Avenue by cab to the flat of Brother Benham, as Cornelia referred to him and as I would before the evening ended, near Washington Square.

We dismissed the cab and walked the remaining two blocks to the address. The short walk gave us the opportunity to hold hands and to establish a greater feeling of one-ness before we met this man who was volunteering his precious time to help me.

"I hope," I said, "that Mr. Benham will understand how confused I am about my own feelings."

"He will Sam," she responded, "you will find him a most understanding person."

We knocked on the apartment door of Benham's third floor walk-up in a converted brownstone but two hundred yards from Washington Square. We were admitted to a comfortable but frugally appointed flat that was neat and functional. It also showed its owner to be little concerned with ostentatious display, indeed, its appointments were simple to the point of severity.

Mrs. Carrie Benham, a most attractive woman of, I should say mid-fifties, served us a warming cup of herb tea as we settled into easy chairs around a comforting wood fire in the living room fireplace. It was easy to feel completely at home with these unpretentious people. I especially appreciated the fact that nothing about the deportment of either Mr. or Mrs. Benham betrayed any assumptions about the relationship between Cornelia and me. It was clear from their attitude they regarded me as an individual seeking my own way subject to little outside influence in so important a matter.

This was, of course, not true. I recognized quite clearly that were I not so deeply in love with Cornelia, I could temporize indefinitely even about a subject as crucial as the eternal verities. It may sound supercilious to make such an admission, but I am too much a realist not to admit my own faults. No doubt existed in my mind that the primary reason for my being there was this wonderful woman's insistence that she would only marry in the

Temple. Nonetheless, I was still sincere in my desire to know more about the beliefs of the Mormons.

"I realize, Mr. Harper," Brother Benham began, "that several motivations bring you here. And I am in something of a quandary how to begin. Your needs to understand more about Isaac Fenster and his beliefs may supersede any direct interest of your own. I am not asserting this to be the case, but merely indicating to you I regard it as a possibility. As a consequence, may I suggest it might be more fruitful if I abandon our usual method and simply let you ask questions."

"You are most considerate," I replied, "but to respond I must ask what your usual method would be."

"That consists," he responded, "of a series of discussions in which we expose only the fundamentals. It is pretty basic stuff, designed as a primer, so to speak. Much of which Cornelia tells me you already understand."

I thought for a moment before responding, "I think we might proceed by my asking those things of greatest importance to my investigation of the Fenster murder and then let you determine how best to proceed with those matters beyond."

Cornelia gave an affirmative nod of her head indicating her agreement. "I am sure," she said, "we will end up on matters far removed from those covered in the basic discussions."

"I rather suspect you're right," Benham replied, smiling in Cornelia's direction.

I was about to ask permission to smoke my pipe but thought better of it and decided I must do without this usual comforting accompaniment to my contemplative moods.

"It is of the keenest interest to me how Fenster's embracing the gospel would impact his relationship with his fellow Jews, especially his father," I began.

"I am not competent," Benham responded, "to do more than expose some ideas that might bear directly on the point. Our founder Joseph Smith was asked once to state concisely what Mormons believe. He gave us, in responding, the Articles of Faith. We can discuss each of these at length later, but it occurs to me that most Jews to whom I have exposed the gospel find Article X to be of direct interest. That article speaks of our expecting the reunion of the twelve tribes of Israel. More especially it states that 'We believe in the literal gathering of Israel and in the restoration of the Ten Tribes; that Zion will be built upon this (the American) continent; that Christ will reign personally upon the earth; and, that the earth will be renewed and receive its paradisiacal glory.' Furthermore, Chapters 21 and 29 of third Nephi in the Book of Mormon state that the coming forth of the Book of Mormon shall be a sign that the covenant of the Father to restore Israel to the lands of their inheritance is beginning to be fulfilled. Likewise, Section 103, verse 17 of the Doctrine & Covenants states, in referring to members of the Church: For ye are the children of Israel, and of the seed of Abraham . . ."

"These are matters, surely, of great interest," I suggested, "and prompt many questions to come to my mind."

"Well then," said Benham, "let's dwell a while on this point and we'll see if we can answer your questions."

"As I'm sure you're aware, all the major Christian Churches have abandoned the expectation that the fulfillment of what is clearly mandated in the scriptures will take place regarding the gathering of Israel in the last days," I said, "this makes your church unique among Christian sects. But what does it mean really? Are Mormons of the belief they are of the twelve tribes?"

Benham did not hesitate. "Without question Sam, if I may be familiar. In fact, most Mormons have learned from which of the tribes their lineage derives when they requested and received their patriarchal blessing — a special blessing by which members learn many things specifically related to their personal mission and destiny here in mortality. My blessing tells me I am of the lineage of Ephraim. I suspect Cornelia's blessing says the same thing."

"Quite right Brother Benham," Cornelia said then looking at me, "Ephraim was one of Joseph's sons. It is upon the children of Ephraim that the responsibility lies for preparing the earth for the return of the Saviour."

"Then do I take it rightly," I asked, "that members of the Church from all the twelve tribes have been so advised in their blessings?"

"Theoretically possible," Joseph Benham said, "and I have heard of blessings conferred which related to Levi, Manasseh and Judah, but mostly to Ephraim."

"What has happened," I asked, "to the descendants of Reuben, Gad, Issacher, Benjamin, etc.?"

"A valid question," he responded, "and I can only speculate as to the answer. It is my surmise that only the principal line of inheritance is singled out in the blessing. We know that the twelve tribes intermarried extensively. They were commanded to do so and not to marry into the Gentile tribes. We use that term here to mean non-Israel although usually Mormons use the term Gentile to mean any non-Mormon. But since they intermarried extensively, it is practically certain we each of us has blood of all twelve tribes in our veins. The blessing, in singling out Ephraim or Manasseh or Judah, the three we see with great frequency, merely defines the primary responsibility of the person receiving the blessing. Ephraim is to prepare the world for the return of the Savior. Manasseh is the line to which the American Indians, the Samoans, Polynesians, the Maoris, the Japanese, the Chinese, etc. belong. Children of Judah are to proselytize amongst the Jews, etc."

"I needn't tell you, I'm sure," I said, "that Article X places the Mormon Church in a position diametrically opposite to that of all the other Christian Churches."

"Please be more explicit," Benham responded, "for there are a hundred ways I could make the same assertion."

"To be sure," I responded, "At the heart of the Holy Scriptures is a fundamental principle that has been rejected by the modern world as unacceptable. There is not a tree, a river, a city, a person mentioned in the Bible except as it bears some relationship to a people. That people are the progeny of Abraham, Isaac and Jacob whose name was changed to Israel. The people called Israel are in a special, covenant relationship with God the Father. The world has rejected, indeed the principal Christian Churches have led the way in rejecting, this concept of a Chosen People. To acknowledge and look to the fulfillment of Jaweh's promises is to reaffirm the core message of the Bible and that message has been deemed unacceptable by the modern world."

"There can be no doubt of what you say," Benham replied, "and let me just say, in passing, that the concept of a Chosen People cannot be truly understood if one accepts God as an impersonal, abstract force who set the universe in motion like winding up a clock, which thenceforward operated without any divine intercession. You must understand a personal God, the pre-mortal existence and the plan of salvation before the concept of a Chosen People becomes comprehensible."

"I will have to digest the content of your remarks to absorb them fully," I looked at Benham then at his wife and Cornelia who sat nearby attentively. "But I am beginning to see how great a breach exists between Mormons and other Christians. But I am of the opinion the gap between Mormons and Jews may not be so great."

"I think you may be both right and wrong," Benham said, "The idea of a Chosen People may not pose any difficulty for Jews, but it would be perhaps a greater hurdle to accept Christ as the messiah."

"Your point is well taken, and I quite agree that a sincere belief that Christ is not the Messiah must be a great difficulty to overcome," I glanced at Benham's placid countenance, "but Isaac Fenster had surmounted that difficulty. What does Mormon doctrine tell us about Isaac Fenster and his ability to accept Christ's divinity and the gospel as enunciated by Joseph Smith?"

Mrs. Benham spoke up. "Darling," she said, directing her remarks to her husband, "I think I see Mr. Harper's question." Then turning to me, "Our belief is that the blood of Israel is manifested by the readiness to accept the gospel and Christ as our savior. We believe that those possessing the blood of Israel are more readily able to accept Christ as the Messiah. This does not mean Christ is not still rejected by many Israelites amongst whom surely are many Jews."

"We come precisely to the point," I said with some vehemence. "Fenster's journal indicates he believed that many calling themselves Jews are not of the blood of Israel. In that he has considerable support from some of the findings of modern historians who point out that the Khazars, a modern racial strain of great importance amongst the Jews are only converts to the Judaic faith and conceivably have no Israelite blood whatever."

"There is no foundation of which I am aware for such a point of view in the writings of modern day prophets of our church. But perhaps more important is that such a belief is by no means excluded either. Many Mormons hold opinions on esoteric subjects of the type we are discussing that are neither supported nor excluded by the pronouncements of the general authorities of the Church," he paused thoughtfully. "And I must acknowledge too, that all who claim to accept the gospel as we profess it do not necessarily do so for the right reasons. I don't mean to disparage Brother Fenster, far be it

119

from me to judge. But he would not be the first to join an organization for the wrong reason. I can't do more than say that until the prophet enunciates revelation on the topic, he is entitled to his opinion. Until such time a man can not be faulted in any way for a belief about which the prophet has not declared doctrine."

"I begin to see Fenster within his Mormon framework," I said, "perhaps you will bear with me as I delineate some of his viewpoints so that you can gain a sense of his meaning and whether in your opinion, he breaches the tenets of revealed doctrine in any way."

"Don't hesitate to do so, but forgive me," Benham said, "if I find myself in over my head."

"Just so," I said as I collected my thoughts, "likewise, let me preface my remarks by saying don't hold Fenster responsible for the way I paraphrase his remarks and perhaps even mistakenly so."

Benham smiled and with a slight gesture of his hand both directed me to proceed and acknowledged his understanding.

"Fenster," I began, "apparently was greatly mystified by the ease with which he was able to accept Christ as the messiah. He describes with considerable power how he experienced what he called the witness of the Holy Spirit. He seems never to have doubted the rightness of his course from that point forward, no matter how deeply he regretted the breach that acceptance of Jesus created between himself and practically all those to whom we ordinarily look for understanding."

"A familiar story," Cornelia said. "Feelings frequently run as deep even in Christian families. I can confirm what Sam has observed from Brother Fenster's writings. There was a lack of closeness between Isaac and his parents and other family relatives that bordered on animosity."

Brother Benham and his wife shook their heads in sympathy with the difficulties of the deceased Fenster.

"Fenster apparently," I ventured, "became very nearly obsessed with the question of how he could be the odd ball of the family who became Christian. He had a sense of mission without doubt. That shows clearly in his journal. Still there is also apparently a great struggle to explain to himself why he was chosen for this 'unpopular calling' as he more often than not termed it." I paused and looked at my friends, yearning for my pipe.

"Even prior to joining the Mormon religion he was concerned about the question of who all the races might derive from that make up modern Jewry. He had traveled widely and he knew that the word 'Jew' has little racial meaning for there are those who call themselves Jews in every race and clime. It was a subject to which he devoted a great deal of study and about which he evolved decided opinions," I said and paused.

Sister Benham was the first to speak. "Utterly fascinating Mr. Harper. Do tell us what those opinions were."

"It is a topic not easily encapsulated," I said, "but his beginning point seems to have been Chapter 18 of the second book of Kings, verse 13: 'Now in the 14th year of King Hezekiah did Sennacherib King of Assyria come up against all the fenced cities of Judah, and took them.' That single verse and its identical confirmatory passage in Isaiah, not further elaborated by the scriptures, says a great deal. Sennacherib was the Assyrian king who succeeded Shalmanesar V who had already deported the Ten Tribes of the north to the area of the Caucasus. It led Fenster to the conclusion, a conclusion I find hard to dispute, that some part of Judah went into exile with the Ten Tribes. He thus reasoned that there are members of the tribe of Judah melded into Israel of the Ten Tribes and are racially indistinguishable from other Israelites." I paused, mentally taking a puff on my comforting pipe.

"At this point, Fenster apparently sought confirmation of his deductions from those unelaborated scriptural references in the findings of modern archaeology," I continued, "he went to London and lived there for over a year to be close to the archaeological evidence in the British Museum. I can't determine if he then came under the influence of the British-Israel group and was led to the archaeological confirmations so frequently cited by that group or whether the sequence was the other way around. At any rate he found in the museum a translation of a six-sided Assyrian cylinder which confirmed that two hundred thousand of the tribe of Judah went into captivity at the Assyrian's hand. It therefore appears that the tribe of Judah was richly represented amongst the exiled tribes." I paused to see if my companions were experiencing any difficulty following. Sensing none, I went on. "Fenster now was face to face with the question of who of the modern races is Israel-Judah? He apparently was deeply influenced by the British-Israel group in his studies from this point on. His journal makes clear he became convinced the Anglo-Saxons embrace much of modern Israel, which, I take it, causes no difficulty among Mormons, though, remember, he was not yet a Mormon and wouldn't become one for another five years. But having arrived at this point he was confronted with the necessity of ascertaining who are all those races who call themselves Jews other than those included, by his reasoning, in the Anglo-Saxon race, and more directly of interest to him since Fenster and all his family have a Nordic appearance, who is the 'assimilated Jew'?"

Benham raised his hand at this point. "I feel the need to pause here Sam," he smiled, "not only because I need clarification of the term 'assimilated Jew' but also to offer a refill of your tea cup."

Taking my refilled tea cup from Mrs. Benham with a smile of thanks, I addressed myself to Benham's question. "In modern usage the term 'assimilated Jew' begins from an assumption that the basic racial type we call a Jew has a dark complexion, wiry hair and a prominent nose. I generalize, of course, but the inherent assumption is that the assimilated Jew once embodied these physical traits which were lost over time by inter-marriage with persons of the Nordic type. He thus no longer looks like a 'Jew' but is assimilated. In other words, under the basic assumptions made in employing the term, the physical prototype is defined to be the 'Jew.' Fenster's concept turns the whole idea upside down." I sipped my tea. "Since he reasons that all twelve tribes were represented in the group deported by the Assyrians who then migrated into Europe and became Anglo-Saxons, it follows that there would be no racial traits manifested by members of the tribe of true Judah other than those we see in all Anglo-Saxons. The 'assimilated Jew' is not a person who began as a swarthy type whose traits were lost when he inter-married with Anglo-Saxons, although I suppose he would have conceded that in some cases this has undoubtedly occurred where prototypical 'Jews' married Nordic types but, in general, under Fenster's reasoning the 'assimilated Jew' is and always was an Anglo-Saxon!" I could see a look of perlexity on Benham's face.

"Who then," he queried, "is the man of the physical type we associate with the word 'Jew'?"

"A good question," I responded, "and I must say that Fenster wrestled with the same problem for years. Finally he was directed to the historical works of a man who, coincidentally, is an old friend of mine. Fenster read in manuscript form A HISTORY OF THE EASTERN ROMAN EMPIRE by James Bagnell Bury, which is due to be published soon and there he learned about the Khazar Empire. But the availability of the same information from other sources could have led him to the same conclusions earlier and probably did."

"Who were the Khazars?" asked Mrs. Benham.

"Khazaria, the nation of the Khazars was reduced to impotence by Genghis Khan about the 12th Century," I said, "But this people, thought to be of Turkish racial background, were of great influence in Eastern European affairs from the 7th Century until their fall. For our purposes, the important point is that under the leadership of the Khan, the Khazar Empire adopted Judaism some time about the time of Charlemagne's reign in Europe. And when the Khazar Empire was destroyed, many of the Khazars migrated to Poland and formed the cradle of Western Jewry. Prior to the eighth or ninth Century there never was a Khazar who was also a Jew. Now, the most influential racial group in modern Jewry is that of the Khazars."

"And Fenster, I assume, discovered all this?" Benham asked.

"Indeed he did," I acknowledged, "and his understanding that the Eastern Jew has no historical claim to the Holy Land was the sole reason he opposed the creation of a Jewish homeland in Palestine."

"But the British," Cornelia interjected, "by our understanding, true Israel, and the only ones with a valid claim to the Holy Land, are the very ones pushing to repatriate — I can see now the word is inaccurate — the 'Jews' to Palestine."

"You highlight," I smiled at her, "only two popular misconceptions about the situation. Think how long the Khazar-Jew has been castigated for his part in the crucifixion, when, in fact, there wasn't to be a Khazar-Jew for eight hundred years after Christ's death."

Benham looked to be deep in thought as he said, "A curious state of affairs that Fenster stumbled into."

"I regret to say," I commented, "he did not 'stumble into' them as you term it. He went out of his way to oppose the Zionist project in every way he could and to anyone who would listen, and in his heart, I have no doubt he believed himself to be working to spare the Khazar-Jews enormous pain and worse."

"Nonetheless, he must have become awfully unpopular," Benham offered, "first he becomes a Christian, then he preaches that the Jews are not

Israelites. Not a way to grow old peacefully."

"I like your way of understating things," I responded, "Fenster lived at the center of a boiling cauldron. Had he been a poor man he could have been dismissed as a crack-pot. But he was too wealthy and influential for that. In a dozen different ways he threatened the established order within and without the Jewish power structure as well as that of the banking world and his end was predictable by anyone privy to the facts."

"How sad," Mrs. Benham had a glisten of tears in her eyes as she spoke.

"Sad indeed," I offered, "this world can stand anything but the truth, I fear."

"Still Cornelia tells me," Benham said, "you don't think Fenster's insights about the Jews were his undoing."

"That's correct," my eyes locked with Benham's then with those of Cornelia. "It appears he got himself in the middle of a plot to frustrate Lord Balfour's plan for a Jewish homeland. It may be they intend to assassinate Balfour. But indications are this is a fairly straightforward effort by the Germans and the Turks to keep England from acquiring a base near Suez on Turkish territory which a Jewish homeland in Palestine would surely be. But let us get back to Mormon doctrine. You said the concept of a Chosen People only becomes comprehensible when an understanding is acquired of what I think you call the Plan of Salvation. Can we expand on this for a while?"

"Yes, indeed," said Benham, "I think that the most basic difference between Mormons and other Christians begins with the plan of salvation. We believe that Heavenly Father is a glorified man — a man who lived life as we are living it, in the flesh and subject to all of the trials of the flesh. 'As man is God once was; as God is man may be,' is the way one of our General Authorities stated it and his statement tells a lot about where we came from, why we're here and where we're going."

"I've told Sam about the Plan of Salvation," Cornelia said, "so he knows some of this."

"That's good," Benham remarked, "and if any of this seems superfluous, stop me."

"Not at all," I smiled. "Do go on."

"The concept of evolution," he gestured with his hand as though offering a gift, "has become fact in the minds of many both well-informed people and those less so. In my opinion, the greatest of many evils encompassed in this less than perfectly developed theory is that it burdens us with the idea of a God, if indeed he is conceded to exist at all, who wound up the elements like a clock, then went on vacation for eternity. There is no room for the supernatural, for a divinely-assisted destiny for mankind."

"I quite agree," I responded, "this is the most fundamental difference. It is startingly simple. Our father in heaven, the father of our spirit bodies is a man like you or I. Difficult for a modern person to accept but a comforting doctrine nonetheless."

Cornelia gestured to indicate her desire to speak. Benham and I turned in her direction. "The single most important discovery to me," she said, "when I was investigating the Church was this loving father-daughter relationship between my heavenly father and me."

"Alienation is bound to result," Mrs. Benham suggested, "when God is thought of as an impersonal force. What can we discern about or what allegiance owe to an inscrutable God?"

"We apparently," I said, "have no argument amongst us on this point. I too, as a person who knew very little of my father because he died when I was very young, find this concept not only totally acceptable as a theological matter but at a more personal level, very comforting."

"I understand," Benham said, "because the entire plan of salvation and the concept of a Chosen People flows quite naturally from the idea of a personal God, one who sent his children to earth with special missions by which they were to assist one another to return to his presence. I personally conclude that those who were chosen to come to earth as Israelites had prepared themselves well in the pre-mortal existence for the special role of responsibility all Israelites accepted before they came here."

"I await your developing this idea further," I said, fondling the bowl of my pipe in my jacket pocket.

"Let me digress for a moment," Benham said, "to point out another fundamental difference between Mormonism and other fundamentalist Christian sects. For the most part they believe the Bible to be the immutable word of God, complete and unchangable. We do not so believe. We know that many precious things have been lost from the Scriptures. In the Bible itself reference is made to nearly twenty books that are no longer in the canon as we know it. Otherwise the plan of salvation as revealed to the prophet Joseph Smith would be clearly set forth in the Bible. It is not, and further there are mistranslations. As a consequence we feel mankind could never recover the plan of salvation by himself and that the truth could only be restored to the earth by the direct intercession of the Father in sending a prophet."

"I take it then," I said, "that Joseph Smith himself was chosen in the pre-mortal existence to come to earth to be the instrument through whom Heavenly Father restored the plan of salvation to mankind, correct?"

"Exactly," Benham smiled, "you are getting the idea."

"It follows then," I offered, "that we each came to earth with our own peculiar mission, perhaps not quite so glorious, but nonetheless our own, correct?"

"Precisely," Sister Benham interjected with glee, "you're nearly ready for baptism."

"You're kind to say so," I laughed, ignoring the implication of her remark. "But do go on," I said, directing my gaze at Benham, "and show me the connection between the plan of salvation and the Chosen People."

"O.K.," Benham began, "the capacity for spiritual commitment with which we each come to earth is merely a reflection of how much growth we achieved in the pre-mortal existence. It follows that we all come to earth in different stages of development. This explains what many perceive to be an inequitable situation, but which really is completely just."

"Then if I follow what you're saying," I picked up his line of reasoning, "the degree of development in the pre-mortal existence results in some, like Joseph Smith, being called to higher missions than others. Therefore some come to earth as the Chosen People or Israel, correct?"

I saw by Benham's expression that I had understood the thrust of his remarks. "But is it just for the Chosen People to be hated by mankind for their chosenness when they came to assume a duty to help the rest of mankind find the truth?"

Benham gave a wry smile. "That's a new twist. Usually I am defending the concept of a Chosen People. But to respond to your question, you must recognize the principle of free agency operates in all that Heavenly Father does. In principle, we ratified every aspect of our present circumstances, perhaps not in detail but at least in general terms."

"How interesting," I remarked, "do you mean the suffragettes agreed to come to earth as women?"

Benham looked at his wife and roared with laughter. Cornelia looked at me with an impish grin.

"In general, we all, whatever our circumstances, accepted them as a pre-condition to our coming," Benham responded when he had brought his mirth under control.

"By implication," I both stated and asked, "you are describing a very sophisticated philosophy, one that I personally find worthy of a truly just God. Most people don't recognize that only our having accepted in advance our circumstance in this life could possibly justify the apparent inequities of life."

"There are no inequities," Benham said, "in actuality. We are all treated fairly and equally though Satan would keep us from understanding this prin-ciple, and we may not fully understand how the principle of justice operates on our behalf to achieve perfect equity until we are in the next world. I am reminded of a friend of mine who was born deformed. He railed against God in his heart over his condition, in effect, reproaching God for his defor-mity. One evening when he was especially down he got on his knees imploring assistance. He had opened to him an understanding of his condition, that he had understood before he came here that his condition would not only involve certain unusual hardships, but also would earn him special rewards which the rest of us won't receive. From that time forward he accepted his handicap and is today one of the most cheerful people I know."

"Two points," I said raising as many fingers, "Do I take it that we wanted to come to earth so badly we would accept any handicap to come, and last, explain the Mormon view of Satan for as you must know modern man leaves no role for Beelzebub any longer, just as evolution leaves no role for a God."

Benham looked pensive. "The answer to the first question is simply 'yes' we did want to come to earth so badly we would accept any conditions. To understand this fully it must be recognized that progression is a law of nature. We had progressed as far as we could in the pre-mortal existence. It was the next necessary step in our progress toward Godhood and we wanted to come very much."

"I must ponder this at my leisure for it belies the assertion we hear so often that children don't ask to be born." I said, "It makes perfect sense to me that we should eternally progress. It accords with all human experience and gives a valid motivation to so-called altruistic behavior. That makes perfect sense. What we do to advance the divine plan also accrues glory to us, still I will want to think about this principle a good deal more. Now let us talk about satan."

"Yes, an important point," Benham conceded. "Modern man in eliminating divine intercession in man's destiny — a logical result of accepting evolution and a mechanistic universe where all things run like a clock, all causes and effects flowing from having wound up this great clock, also eliminated the need for satan. We have a principle given to us by Joseph Smith: 'There must be opposition in all things.' That simply means that in a universe based on the principle of free agency, until we can accept the laws of the system voluntarily, we must find ourselves experiencing opposition. Satan was such a spirit. He craved Heavenly Father's glory prior to having earned it. Let me digress for a moment. Glory as we understand it is not worldly glory. It is the accumulated power from having lived righteous principles. And apparently it is a true source of energy. The prophet counseled us that we must prepare ourselves to dwell amidst everlasting burning. Heavenly Father's glory is so great Moses had to receive special protection to be able to stand in his presence on Mt. Sinai. But glory cannot be transferred and it must be earned. Further, there is but one way to earn it — by living the principles of the gospel. Satan apparently could not accept this. In the pre-mortal existence Heavenly Father asked for proposals." Benham paused, looking into the fire. He was silent for a moment before continuing. "We really are into much deeper material than may be good for you at this stage of things."

I demurred, "Perhaps, but so far you have only elaborated principles Cornelia and I have discussed previously."

"You've done well Cornelia," he said, looking and smiling at my beloved. He continued feeling, quite visibly, more relaxed. "Two plans were proposed by which Heavenly Father's spirit children should gain bodies, populate earth and live life in the flesh in their progress toward Godhood. The plan proposed by Jesus was dependent upon each of God's children having complete freedom to accept or reject the gospel. Alas, it involves the failure of many. Satan proposed a system denying free agency in which all would be saved. All humans who have ever lived or will live attended a congress in the pre-mortal world. We voted on both plans. Satan's plan was rejected, but it was approved by one-third of the spirits in attendance. Satan rebelled at the plan adopted and he and one-third the hosts of heaven were consigned to earth without bodies with the freedom to tempt mankind to follow Satan's plan instead of Heavenly Father's. They are not permitted to tempt man beyond his ability to resist unless, of course, his will to resist has been weakened by sin. Satan and his hosts so crave bodies themselves they can and do possess the bodies of humans. We see clear references to such instances in the scriptures such as the tale of the Gadarene swine." Benham heaved a sigh. "A long-winded response to a short question. But I feel your needs demand more detailed answers than most. Yes, we believe that satan lives and misleads many of

God's children hoping, ultimately to defeat totally the plan adopted at the congress in heaven."

"You have given me a lot to digest. But until I ruminate at length over it, I can't fault any aspect of it and perhaps not then." I was most pleased at the results we were achieving and time was moving on. It was already 10:30 p.m. I glanced at my watch. "Forgive me," I said, "for the way I am imposing upon your time, but before we adjourn for the evening may I ask one more question the answer to which is vitally important to me?"

"Of course, Sam," Benham said showing a pleased smile. "We are here to give you all the help we can. And have no concern for the time. Pray tell, what is this all-important query?"

"It relates," I began, "to the reference Fenster made in his journal to having received what he called the witness of the Holy Spirit that Jesus is the messiah. I have long believed in the principle of faith, largely by logic, however. I could see no way a truly just God could make salvation dependent upon how much intelligence each of us brought to earth or acquired after we got here. But I could not understand how a person acquires faith in practice. Will you elucidate for my benefit how Mormons view this problem?"

Benham arose from his seat. He crossed the room to a book case and brought a volume to me and handed me the book. "Here is your own copy of the Book of Mormon. You may have it with our best wishes. Please accept this little gift from Sister Benham and me. Also, won't you please look up in the book Chapter 10 of the Book of Moroni verses 3 to 5?"

I was moved by their generosity. I leafed through the volume until I found the verses he had named. I read aloud,

"Behold, I would exhort you that when ye shall read these things, if it be wisdom in God that ye should read them, that ye would remember how merciful the Lord hath been unto the children of men, from the creation of Adam even down unto the time that ye shall receive these things, and ponder it in your hearts.

And when ye shall receive these things, I would exhort you that ye would ask God, the Eternal Father, in the name of Christ, if these things are not true; and if ye shall ask with a sincere heart, with real intent, having faith in Christ, he will manifest the truth of it unto you, by the power of the Holy Ghost. And by the power of the Holy Ghost ye may know the truth of all things."

When I had finished, I looked up to Brother Benham who now was standing next to the fireplace one elbow on the mantle; I awaited his comment.

"This is the promise we are given, Mr. Harper, that if we will so live our lives as to reflect our sincere desire to know the truth, we will be granted the witness of the Holy Ghost and we shall know that which is true."

I pondered his response. "Your use of the word 'know' is fascinating. We most of us intuitively feel there is no magic to the recognition of 'truth.' One simply gets the facts into a particular array and voila! THE TRUTH! in capital letters. You lead me to wonder if Mormon doctrine requires us to conclude that the acquisition of knowledge in any field is dependent upon the witness of the Holy Spirit?" I gazed at him inquiringly.

"I know of no such doctrine," Benham said, "all we know is that we are promised the Holy Spirit will bear witness to our spirits when we sincerely desire to know the truth of the gospel."

"But the witness of the truth is achieved spirit to spirit," I said, "and comes after we demonstrate our willingness to live God's law."

"Yes, and I regard this," Benham said in confirmation, "as one of the most important of the prophet's revelations, second only to the restoration of the Holy Priesthood."

I digested this remark and looked at my watch. "Our time has flown and we have not even gotten to the Holy Priesthood. Would you consider holding another of these sessions on that topic alone?" I asked.

"At your convenience, Brother Harper," he said and smiled.

Cornelia and I thanked these wonderful people for their generosity and made our adieus. Our trip back up Fifth Avenue by cab was spent nearly in silence, but I held her hand and felt a great inner peace in her presence. At her door we kissed in a long and heady embrace. We said our goodbyes at midnight and I made my long way home to Brooklyn Heights pondering my future as the husband of Cornelia St. James.

Journal Entry of Cornelia St. James
January 26, 1912

It's good that you can't talk — journal — or I wouldn't dare confide in these your pages the things I do. Some day you will speak to my children and grandchildren (I hope), for Heavenly Father has promised me in my patriarchal blessing that I will one day have my own family. For now you must keep my confidences to yourself.

But a short time ago I was experiencing despair so deep I was ashamed to get on my knees to pray. After all, a person with faith should know that death, even of a person as wonderful as Mr. Fenster, is but an interruption, not an ending. It cannot be more than a few years until I will see him again in the Spirit World. But it is a mental exercise to repeat these assertions to one'self in the immediate grief of the loss of a loved one. With time we recover our ability to accept and the faith to be consoled.

What a deep man he was, Isaac Fenster. How gently he loved me out of the attitude of antipathy toward the Jews in which I was raised (as with most other people). But could he have done this had he not first overcome his own anti-semitism?

It takes a peculiar knowledge of the Divine Plan to comprehend the enormous depth of God's love for the Jews — both those called Jews in the Bible and the Khazar-Jew, a fairly recent convert to Judaism.

I shall never forget either his words or how he said them. "We shall be eons discharging our obligation to the jews for their role in the completion of the Plan of Salvation." And then he added, "Both the Jews who crucified him the first time, and those among us who reject his atoning sacrifice."

And seeing my incredulous stare, how gently he led me through the pathways of his reasoning.

This was the first I had ever learned of certain points of Mormon Doctrine. If this world, Mr. Fenster explained, is the only world evil enough to have crucified the Saviour, as Joseph Smith has taught us, are not all the worlds on which those who, like us, awaited the redemptive sacrifice of Christ indebted for the fact the crucifixion took place?

I had never known before that Mormons believe there are many other worlds on which humans like us were in need of redemption.

But then, how profound his next revelation.

"Since we cannot doubt that God loves the Jews as deeply as any of his other children, how earnestly must we pray for the understanding how their role could — can — be fulfilled and there yet be redemption possible for them."

Was it as simple as it seemed? Jesus pled for them (us) from the cross: "Father forgive them for they know not what they do."

Mr. Fenster did not believe — I do not believe — it is enough to say it was Satan's influence that overcame the pleading for Jesus that many so passionately undertook. We all, in some way not yet understood, are responsible for his suffering and death.

There had to be a Judas — there had to be the Jews, or the redemptive plan would have failed. We are all in their debt for their role in permitting the plan to unfold.

Had the Khazar not converted to Judaism, had he not perpetuated the concept of a Chosen People and the redemptive role yet to be fulfilled by that People, surely it would long ago have been forgotten and the Plan defeated.

It is not the least bit surprising that as converts the Khazars more zealously pursued Israel's redemptive function than the true Israelites did. Genuine, blood-Israel wanted and still wants to forget their covenant at Sinai.

Convert-Jews, the Khazars, as with many converts, were more zealous than those actually born to the covenant. In their zeal they have preserved the word's awareness of the Biblical prophecies of the coming denoument, the end of times, in spite of the world's unbelief — their nearly total attitude of derision toward Holy Writ. That is no insignificant undertaking and one for which the entire world, the entire universe, is indebted.

The Jews — both real and converted — will find their way back to Christ. And what a glorious reward awaits them for their special role in his mission.

And if we are all indebted to the Jews, I am indebted to Isaac Fenster for a deeper understanding of their vital role in the great unfolding of prophecy.

But now, what a strange turn of events! Now it seems it is Mr. Fenster's death itself which has brought about such an interesting change in my life. As though Heavenly Father has sent me this new support in the midst of my loss. Perhaps because of it!

How it has grieved my heart to see the anguish of Mr. Fenster's children at the loss of this wonderfully patient and kind father. They cling to me as though another loss — were I to be taken from them — would just destroy them. How I wish I might kiss away all their fears and sorrows.

To once again have my acquaintance with Sam Harper renewed has been something of a gift and a revelation. I now realize my feelings toward him the first time we interacted in the theft of Mr. Morgan's Sickert painting were not quite platonic.

How strange we are! We think we know so much more than we do. I would have sworn my reaction to him was nothing more than a degree of admiration for that intelligence he radiates.

Now I can see I suppressed something more. With this clear indication his interest in me is much more than professional, I can see I was attracted to him from the start.

Being married, even though it was unhappily, must have caused me to suppress my true feelings. It's well it did! I might have been tempted to some indiscretion otherwise. I should not have wished to have such a thing on my conscience, even if only a thought in my head, because Sam never manifested the slightest interest in me romantically then.

But now, what a joy to me to see that special light in his eyes that only appears when our eyes meet. I don't know what may come of it, but that I shall leave in Heavenly Father's hands. For now it is enough to know he loves me.

Journal Entry of Isaac Fenster

Dated June 1905

The anguish I have endured in becoming converted to the gospel was, I thought, as bad as anything could be. It appears I was wrong. Father seems more agonized by my action even than I was. It is strange and difficult beyond my worst anticipations. He has never manifested any piety whatever for Judaism, but his anguish is real and I am pained to have hurt him so, even though we've never been close. In fact, in seeing his pain, much akin to what I've felt so often at his distant, truly Prussian treatment, I feel close to him for the first time. Perhaps there is some good in even the worst things.

I believe it actually would have been much easier for him were he the most orthodox of Jews. Then, at least, there might have been a knowledge of the Talmud and the Torah and a piety for religious ideas. As it is, he reacts as though I have violated some deeply cherished concept and obviously I have, but since we know it is not any deep affection for Judaism itself, then what is it? What taboo have I transgressed?

It must be a deep racial pride in being a Jew. But even there I have only made things worse by attempting to share with him what I believe about the difference between the Khazar and the Jew.

Even if he understood, I wonder if it would make any difference in his eyes. He said, "Don't we all claim the title of 'Jew' and isn't that enough?" Or has the messianism of the Jews become the messianism of Jacob Fenster? After all, no individual, at least in modern times, has done more to finance and fulfill Jewish destiny. Does he believe himself a modern Moses for in a sense he is?

I have explained to him my theory that when the Assyrians deported the Ten Northern Tribes to the Caucasus it is indicated in II Kings 18:13 and Isaiah 36:1 that they also attacked Judah, the Ten Northern Tribes having broken away from Judah and Benjamin after the death of Solomon. Sennacherib's own records preserved in the British Museum indicate he deported over 200,000 members of the kingdom of Judah just as he did the Ten Northern Tribes.

Now if 200,000 of the tribes of Benjamin and Judah were commingled with the Ten in the Caucasus there is no reason to believe there are not members of these tribes commingled in the Anglo-Saxon peoples who LDS Church authorities instruct us, in our patriarchal blessings, represent Israel in the modern era and as I view it should be indistinguishable physically from them.

The Khazars, of course, so well personified by the Polish and Russian Jews are a race apart who adopted Judaism but remained physically identifiable as a distinct race from the Anglo-Saxons who embody true Israel.

Father was, I believe, before he closed his mind completely, close to comprehending my theory about what we call 'assimilated Jews,' those European Jews, quantitatively most represented in Germany, who appear as

Teutonic as any other Nordic just as father and I do. We know the root word from which the word German derives means genuine. This being the case doesn't the ever-present boast of the assimilated Jew: "I am a German Jew" have a new meaning? It becomes "I am a genuine Jew." As opposed to a false Jew?

Who would the false Jew be but the Khazar or convert to Judaism who, incidentally, was the enemy of the Goth in Scythia for centuries.

Therefore, Germany represents the nation where much of the blood of true Judah is, in my contemplation. Is there any support for such a position?

The Scriptures state that there will ever be a scion of Judah on the throne of Israel (Gen. 49:10) and we know that the Royal family of England, like the other crowned heads of Europe, are of German stock. The greatest source of strained relations between Victoria and her British subjects was the Germanism of Albert, Prince Consort. But surely she was as German as he and spoke as much German in the Royal Palace as ever she spoke English. And Victoria and Albert are both typical Anglo-Saxon physical types.

So, seating as it does a scion of Judah, the British throne thus supports the theory and confirms the Scriptures. Therefore, the 'assimilated Jews' are not assimilated at all but are simply people of what we regard as Anglo-Saxon blood who carried the religion of Judaism with them when deported by Sennacherib.

The unassimilated Jew, the Khazar, is not racially a member of Judah but descends from those who, much later, adopted the religion and the title of Jew.

It was not the Gentile who originated the term 'kike' but the 'assimilated Jew' who used it as a term of derision for the Eastern European or Khazar-Jew. And if we thought so badly of them why did we sponsor their flight from Russian oppression? There is a greater mystery here than meets the eye. Only Satan knows the answer and Heavenly Father himself.

Admittedly, I have been much influenced in my thinking by the historical research of J.B. Bury as reflected in his HISTORY OF THE EASTERN ROMAN EMPIRE but didn't the revelations of Joseph Smith and other high LDS Church authorities confirm these conclusions that the Anglo-Saxon nations contain much of the blood of Israel over and over as the result of direct revelations from Heavenly Father?

But why, if I am correct, have so few 'assimilated Jews' accepted Christ? I can see, perhaps, why a Khazar-Jew might resist accepting Christ but why wouldn't more true sons of Judah that is, assimilated Jews accept Christ? If they have the true blood of Abraham, Isaac and Jacob in their veins why wouldn't more accept? Perhaps it only remains for enough Jews to accept and preach the gospel to their own people and it is prophecied that the Jews will accept Christ in the end, but the work is surely proceeding slowly.

And what about the Khazar-Jew? Surely it would be easier for him to accept the Gospel to know he is not true Judah and therefore not responsible in any way for Christ's death. But is the challenge of facing the world without the concept of their chosenness too difficult?

My family, at least, have not mourned me as though dead which is the treatment orthodox Jews direct toward the son or daughter who turns Christian. And if the Khazar-Jew is not a true Jew what will be his role in the unfolding of the drama of the last days? Is he the Jew that it's prophecied will return to Jerusalem? Or is it the true Jew? Or is it both? I personally believe both. But only time will tell.

If I have resisted the Zionist idea of a homeland in Palestine it was in part my distaste for what I perceive will follow — Jews will be regarded as having a double allegiance and in time of trouble will be regarded as traitors to their homelands.

The idea of their chosenness is so deeply a part of the Khazar-Jew's personal dynamic that it surely will move them 'til the millenium, were we to have even the best of luck in recruiting numbers of them to the true gospel. But everything in the structure of Jewish life requires this concept of chosenness or that structure fails. All the authority of the Rabbi rests upon it and any challenge to it is a challenge to rabbinical power. So if we succeed in winning some to our beliefs surely most will persist in their erroneous belief and in their antagonism to Christ simply because it represents the path of least resistance.

But I personally can testify that only when the Jew accepts Christ can he be free of the anxieties felt by Jews everywhere. So it will come, soon or late, and may God be willing that I should have some small part in the work.

Of all the religions of mankind, none holds the promise of showing men how to live in the spirit of love with each other as does the Mormon faith. Acknowledge as it does that Israel is the chosen of God still it shows all men how to be adopted into the covenant. And it has avoided the grave error of past ages in that it has not debased the concept of a Chosen People into that of a superior people or an elite. That alone is proof to me the Church is true. Once baptized into the Church, if a man is not of true Israel blood, his blood is physically changed by the Holy Spirit to that of true Israel, such is our doctrine.

Surely my mission in life is to convert the Jew, but a difficult one it is and what a comfort to know I accepted it willingly in that life we lived before we came here.

The Jew is the man of destiny. He chose the role for himself or at least ratified it in the pre-mortal existence, and he must see his role to its conclusion on the plains of Armageddon.

Journal Entry Samuel Harper

January 31, 1912 (New York City)

"You heard the news about Nell?" Futrelle's inquiring eyes met mine. "Yes — a sad turn of events for her comeback." I puffed my pipe. "She seemed so certain that the White Star management had approved her idea."

Futrelle's expressive face showed resignation and mild cynicism. "You never know how even the best idea can be thrown off the track. I suspect the White Star people let the word out somehow and some powerful people felt it was not in keeping with their dignity."

"Dignity will have its day on the Titanic," I responded, "the ship is a veritable floating palace."

"Palace indeed," Futrelle responded, "you nearly can't get a first class ticket unless you belong to the Four Hundred."

"The Four Hundred will be well represented, as well as much of the British upper classes," I observed.

"Conspicuous waste and an unsinkable ship," Futrelle said to his glass of vichy water as we labored in my study over Fenster's journal.

· "Call me superstitious but I don't believe in tempting fate," I smiled, "deal me out when it comes to unsinkable ships."

"Pure promotion, a smart salesman dreamed up that one," said Jacques, "there's never going to be an unsinkable ship except in some advertisement."

"No harm really in putting folk's minds at rest, I suppose, but they would do better," I said, "to put enough lifeboats aboard to hold her entire compliment."

"There's a story angle!" Futrelle showed more life. "A disaster waiting to happen — new transatlantic luxury liner sinks with space for only half her passengers in the lifeboats."

"Not amusing," I snorted into my glass, "you could be perilously close to the truth some day."

"I suppose," Futrelle rejoined, "but if there was any reason to do so I would sail the Titanic without a fear."

"I too," I responded, "I suppose." But deep in both our minds the matter rested a trifle uneasily.

"The marvels of modern science inspire a religious ardor in people today." Futrelle shuffled his notes as he spoke. "The belief in progress is a philosophical touchstone — faith in progress is the only faith left to modern man. It is the only superstition permitted people who wish to be thought of as 'modern'."

"An exaggeration to be sure," I said, "but closer to the truth than not. All's well when science turns its power to peaceful purposes, but I can't forget the incredible efficiency with which science cuts bone and flesh when her skills are used for warfare. It was a brief and all-too-easily-forgotten skirmish, the Franco-Prussian War in '70, but it served notice that there is no glory left in warfare — not with modern artillery. The American Civil War said it, the Franco-Prussian War proved it. And now they have rapid-fire machine guns which can lay down a wall of firepower not one advancing soldier can survive."

"It was our last international war," said Jacques, "and forty years is a long time ago — perhaps we'll never have another."

"Perhaps," I puffed my pipe, "but don't count on it. War materiel is expensive. The nations of Europe have bankrupted themselves building their arms. It will prove politically easier to have those arms consumed in another war than to confess to the people that the Exchequer is empty."

"We are so bright and cheerful this evening," Futrelle smiled, "Let's do some work and leave off our Cassandra wailings."

"Let us indeed, Jacques," I said, "tell me what you've gleaned from Fenster's journal?"

"A remarkable document, to be sure, a Jew turned Christian — at least I think Mormons are Christians," Futrelle responded.

"Christians, yes, but they believe in what they call the 'restored gospel'. By their lights the gospel left the earth after the death of the last disciples and was only restored through the instrumentality of Joseph Smith their founder," I responded.

"I never cease to be amazed at your erudition," Futrelle said, "how did you learn that?"

"Research and a case I will tell you about some time and the fact that I was doing a little checking on Doyle," I said, "you will recall that Study in Scarlet, Doyle's first novel, was about Mormonism. I really wished to learn if Doyle's understanding of Mormon Doctrine was accurate. Accuracy — that's my penchant."

"Your conclusions?" Futrelle inquired.

"As usual, Conan Doyle was true to his motto — 'never spoil a good story by sticking to the facts'," I smiled. "I confess there are some perfectly remarkable aspects of this peculiarly American religion."

"Such as — ," Jacques inquired diffidently.

"An untutored boy reports a vision in which he sees the Father and the Son. He is led by an angel to a place in upstate New York where a set of gold plates are placed in his care. He deciphers the reformed Egyptian hieroglyphics and publishes the Book of Mormon, the story of a Hebrew people who emigrated to America prior to the time Jerusalem was captured by Babylon. At first they prosper here and give rise to the amazing cultures only now being discovered in Central and South America. Then they destroy themselves in internecine warfare." I observed his features for his reaction.

"An untutored youth deciphers reformed Egyptian hieroglyphics on plates delivered by an angel, — that takes some believing."

"Precisely the point," I exclaimed, "he could not have done it of his own power, nor could he even have dreamed up such a document, so you are faced with an immediate conundrum. He, like Christ, is either a charlatan and a fraud, or he is all he represents himself to be."

"You sound like a believer," Futrelle observed.

"Not at all," I objected, "but I clearly state the only alternatives. The truly interesting point of all this is how the book suggests we solve the conundrum."

"That would be what?" he queried.

"We are promised that if we will read the book prayerfully, with the sincere desire to know if it is true, that the Holy Spirit will cause us to know it is true. Now that's a remarkable promise — one unlike any I've ever heard before."

"Have you put it to the test?" Jacques asked.

"No I haven't," I said, "and I really don't know why not."

"Because you, like me and every other living soul today," Futrelle stated with some emotion, "don't truly want a religious commitment. We don't avoid such claims because we fear they're false, for we're egotistical enough to believe we will detect their falsehoods; we hesitate for fear it all may be true. Aye, there's the rub — what if they're true? Then we have no excuse for sitting passively any longer. We must act — we must declare ourselves for something, for — for goodness — there it is — goodness! And modern man no longer makes such commitments. Nor has the slightest desire to do so."

"Perhaps modern man deliberately complicates the problem to render it insoluble, ever increasing knowledge but never coming to an understanding of the truth. For some the quest is an end in itself, not intended to reach a conclusion," I said, "Do you believe in God?"

Futrelle accepted my question in all seriousness. "I did once. I haven't thought much about the problem recently."

"You and millions of others," I rejoined.

"A measure of truth in what you say," he conceded, "but Isaac Fenster didn't ignore the problem and he followed wherever his perception of the truth led him."

"That's true enough," I responded.

"And surely becoming a Mormon," Futrelle added, "must be tougher for a Jew than for anyone already calling himself a Christian."

"A surface observation," I commented, "perhaps misleadingly obvious. You will find it even more interesting how Mormons explain why one person accepts their gospel and another doesn't."

"I probably will," Jacques answered, "if you say so."

"They believe that lovers of truth accept the gospel because the true blood of Israel is in their veins," I responded.

"A truly Gothic concept," said Futrelle, his dark imagination hard at work, "but a Jew above all has the blood of Israel in his veins."

"I see you have not fully comprehended the remarkable nature of Fenster's journal," I said, "He had discovered that many, perhaps most of those we call Jews in the modern world have no Israelite blood at all."

"You are quite correct," Jacques admitted, "most of his notes on this point elude me completely."

"You are frank to admit it," I complimented him, "not one in a dozen would be so honest. I shall do my best to enlighten you, for I fear that we cannot understand the predicament of Isaac Fenster until this point is absolutely clear."

EDITOR'S NOTE: Here ensued a description of the role of the Khazar-Jew in modern Jewry as has been described adequately elsewhere.

Journal Entry of Samuel Harper

Dated March 15, 1912 (New York City)

Cornelia's exquisite profile delighted my heart as I gazed past her, toward Prospect Park, down from the modest prominence where we had spread our picnic blanket. On the park green below Leslie was frolicking with our Weimaraner Max. A precocious spring was smiling its sunny gaze upon us.

"It is a blessing Leslie has taken to you so well," I said.

"And Max," said she, laughing.

"Indeed," I chuckled, "but I was a lot more certain of Max than of Leslie."

"She is easy to love Sam. Children respond to what they feel radiating from us. If I were indifferent to her, her response would be indifference or worse." She paused. "She is the daughter I have longed for so long."

"It is one thing for a father alone to raise a son," I said, "It's quite a different proposition raising a daughter."

"It can be done," she conceded, "but it's not easy. It's tough enough with two parents."

"Amen to that," I snorted into my pipe, that old friend which now was making me so self-conscious, although not a word of remonstrance ever passed Cornelia's lips about my smoking. Thus do those who live a higher standard reproach us, without a word. So I was given more and more to sucking upon the pipe unlighted, and feeling vaguely unrequited. My failure, as yet, to conquer my Word of Wisdom problem was thus becoming an unavoidable topic, even if given no voice, whenever we pondered any topic related to marriage. It being impossible for me to marry in the Temple until I lived the Word of Wisdom, our relationship was narrowing down to a choice between Cornelia on one side, my pipe, coffee and alcoholic beverages on the other. And I confess to a slight feeling of resentment at being placed under the nagging pressure by my own sentiment for this lovely creature. But not once did she ever voice a word on the subject. Either I was voluntarily to make the choice or not at all. Still I temporized and looked for ways around this barrier.

"Would that I could obtain an understanding of why marriage in the Temple means so much to you," I ventured after some moments of silence.

Her response was slow in coming. "Your first marriage ended with the death of your wife. It was a happy marriage, honorably ended. My marriage ended with Tom's death. But it was not a happy situation and had Tom not died, I would probably have divorced him." She had an expression of ineffable sadness that pierced me to the core. "I didn't have the gospel then and I really didn't know why we were so unhappy together. Yes, he was weak and had a drinking problem, but those are symptoms not the problem itself. And now I realize that neither of us had clearly defined our life's goals. When I was baptized and accepted the gospel plan, my goals became clear to me. I wish to live my life so as to qualify to dwell for all eternity with my Heavenly Father. Marriage is difficult enough when two people share this goal with a commitment to assist each other to attain exaltation. But it can be a heaven on earth when two people see beyond each others frailties, the fading beauty, the diminishing powers and can see each other as they will be in the Celestial Kingdom. I found it impossible to live happily with Tom as we then were. I'm afraid to fail again at marriage Sam. My first marriage was a flop, and we were both to blame. I would not be fearful if I knew my husband and I were both committed to the principle of eternal marriage and the eternal family. You've told me yourself the hereafter could not be a heaven without Tony."

"I've been meaning to ask you about Tony," I said, "what room for her if you and I form an eternal marriage unit. Doesn't that exclude Tony?"

"Not necessarily," she responded somewhat diffidently. I waited some little time for her to continue.

"A man," she resumed, "can be sealed to more than one woman. You would, of course, have to have the necessary ordinances performed on her behalf and she would still have to accept voluntarily the eternal marriage state with you."

"Free agency once again," I said, "the touchstone of the universe."

"Precisely," Cornelia said, "to borrow your favorite word. All things must be given freely in God's system."

"Most attractive doctrine to me," I said.

"And to me," she responded, "but there is yet another reason I desire a celestial marriage. One you've not heard of."

"What will that be?" I asked.

"Perpetual increase, the opportunity to bear spirit children forever," she replied.

"I knew sooner or later this conversation would turn to sex," I said with a salacious grin.

"The greatest gift we have," she replied smiling, but to share the pleasure of sex forever, a man and wife must attain celestial glory."

"You begin to interest me considerably more," I remarked.

"I thought a Scorpio would find that irresistible," she teased.

"Mormonism begins to make much more sense already," I said with as straight a face as I could manage.

"In all seriousness," she said, "only a woman who has wanted children as badly as I have for so long, could truly understand how beautiful such a promise is."

"It's not a bad idea for a mere man either," I rejoined.

We fell silent for quite a while, a silence which finally I broke with a question. "How am I ever to gain a witness of the truth of these things? Attractive though they may seem, it means nothing if I have no conviction that they're true."

"It happens differently for each person," she responded, gazing at Leslie and Max playing on the green below. "The elements of the promise in Moroni 10:3 to 5 that Brother Benham called to your attention must all be present. We must desire to know the gospel's truth. We must pray for assistance. We must study, and last of all, we must live the commandments."

"Within that framework, I would have to conclude," I responded, "I am weakest in the desire to know the truth and in the area of prayer."

"Do you attempt to pray?" she asked, "for the desire can come in response to sincere prayer."

"I could use a cram course on prayer alone, I suspect," was my response, "for I am extremely uncomfortable getting on my knees to pray."

"I rather think women find it easier to pray than men do," she gazed directly into my eyes, "but my desire to acquire a testimony had little to do with prayer really. I wanted the gospel to be true so that I might be united beyond the grave with the parents I never knew. But we each achieve the desire in our own way."

Leslie and Max had tired of the intense activity in which they had engaged, or, at least Leslie did, as Max never tires. Now they were approaching us, Leslie smiling toward Cornelia and me, and Max imploring Leslie for more play by bounding about her and barking. Now as they approached, Max switched his attention from Leslie to me and dashed toward where I lay on the blanket, showing the excitement he invariably displays when he finds me lying on the floor, the instinctive response of a hunter feeling himself superior to his supine foe attempting to give me friendly nips about the head and shoulders. I grabbed him by the collar and wrestled him to the ground lying on top of him thumping him with the flat of my hand on his barrel chest, an intimacy he adores even after long usage. Rough housing Max is a game Leslie, Max and I delight in.

Suddenly Cornelia was upon my back pummeling me and laughing aloud. Just as suddenly Leslie was on Cornelia's back and I was struggling to support their weight and keep from crushing Max who was oblivious to his joyful peril, enjoying all the excitement. Thus, with laughter and shouts of hilarity did the four of us frolic until we were all fatigued. All but Max who, as I say, never tires.

"Daddy, I'm hungry," a not entirely novel remark from Leslie caused me to look at my watch. The noonday sun glinted on its face as I popped open the cover. "It's twelve thirty; I guess that's understandable, "let's have some lunch," I said, reaching for the picnic basket Cornelia had so generously prepared. I passed the container to Cornelia who accepted and began withdrawing from its depths plates and utensils, cold chicken and potato salad. Finally, she withdrew the piece de resistance, a large bone for Max well larded with scraps of meat. "You sure know the way to a dog's heart," I joshed.

"I couldn't show my face again," she laughed, "if I forgot old Max, right?"

"Right," shouted Leslie with glee and Max barked in anticipation of his repast. He lunged toward the bone as Cornelia placed it on the ground before him.

"Not the best-mannered dog in Brooklyn," I suggested.

"Merely the best," said Leslie. Max wagged his stubby tail as he attacked his lunch.

Thus did the four of us spend a sublimely happy day together in Prospect Park. I dropped Leslie off at the apartment in Mrs. Tumulty's care while I took Cornelia to Manhattan. By the time I returned home it was time for

Leslie to go to bed. I read to her from our friend Rudyard Kipling's KIM and she said her prayers. She climbed on my back for her horsy back ride, for which she is now nearly too old but who complains, and once deposited in her gayly decorated bed she accepted her ritual good night kiss. Then fixing me with the earnest gaze of an eight year old, she asked, "When will Cornelia come to live with us Daddy?"

"Would you like that very much?" I asked.

"Very, very much — please Daddy, get me Cornelia for a mommy."

I smiled and kissed her again, "We'll see," I said, "we'll see."

I closed her bedroom door and turned quietly and slowly, encountering the knowing smile of Mrs. Tumulty. "Yes," she said, in her Irish brogue, "I'm sure it'll not be long before little Leslie will have a mommy. Then you'll no longer be needing the likes of me." There was no bitterness in her remark, just gentle acceptance.

"Hush," I said to the sweet old Celt. "If you leave, it will be your own doing," I said, imitating her Irish lilt.

"What a dear you are Mr. Harper, I'll be going to bed myself," she said and turned toward her room.

"Goodnight Mrs. Tumulty, and pleasant dreams."

Journal Entry (continued) of Samuel Harper

Dated March 15, 1912 (New York City)

"It's a lovely fire," Cornelia remarked, her eyes gazing into the flames, but not really seeing the blaze that was licking the sides of three stout logs I had ignited upon our return to her apartment from our outing in Prospect Park. "Something hypnotic about fires," I responded, "the most primal of man's experiences. This we share with all of our ancestors back into pre-history."

I kneaded the muscles of her shoulders feeling her tensions slowly dissolve as my fingers pressed upon the various nerve centers. Her response was a series of soft sounds of pleasure that indicated how effective a therapy she found it to be.

"You're a magician Sherlock," she said, employing a monniker adopted not long after she learned of my connection with Doyle and our collaboration.

"Just a few tricks based on an understanding of human anatomy I picked up from Doyle," I responded. "I take it you're one Mormon who really believes in the laying on of hands," my amusement showing in my voice.

"Especially such skilled hands as yours," she complimented.

"I only work this well under inspiration," I remarked and smiled.

"Never lose it, darling," she purred.

We were silent for a short while, gazing with fascination at the flames leaping up the chimney, the noisy popping of the burning logs the only sound in the room.

"I shall never see a burning fire like this that I am not reminded of the pleasant times I spent as a youngster with Sir Henry, camping out at some archaeological dig or other. It was at such times he would tell me about my father," I said, "I relished every recollection."

"Some day you shall see him again, and all those you love just as I shall meet my own parents," she said wistfully, "isn't that a comforting bit of knowledge we are given?"

"Only one of many comforting concepts embraced in this gospel of yours. When you've lived as long as I have, the simpler things seem the most comforting." I responded. "Just the knowledge we shall see our dead in a happy place — what a beautiful thing as we each draw near the grave."

"Think of the millions," she said, "who lived and died in fear of eternal hell fire."

"A tragedy so monstrously large," I reflected aloud, "one has to believe in a devil to countenance anything so enormously evil. My father's and Sir Henry's good friend Frederick Maurice was hounded from his pulpit at Lincoln's Inn for declaring similar doctrine as recently as mid-century. He also believed it possible to acquire a knowledge of God and that eternity has nothing to do with time or indefinite duration. Sounds to me like he was close to the truth although his ideas were bitterly opposed by the orthodox."

"Bits of the truth are scattered all over the place," she said. "Plato believed that we have always existed, for instance, a doctrine not again recognized until Joseph Smith. When once we know the truth we can see that in every age the Holy Ghost has been at work preparing the world for Joseph's restoration of the fullness of the gospel. Luther declared his belief that the legitimate power of the priesthood left the earth with the death of the disciples."

"Isn't it amazing," I said, "how frequent the references in the Bible to the Holy Priesthood of God, yet no one until Joseph Smith made the declaration official that the priesthood was lost and could only be restored by God himself."

"Isn't it obvious why the established religions must oppose such doctrine," she asked, "the very legitimacy of their power is at stake."

"What power?" I remarked sardonically.

"The very point," she laughed adopting one of my phrases in perfect mimicry.

"You rascal," I shouted and tickled her. I came around from behind the sofa where I had been standing massaging her shoulders. We tussled for a moment on the sofa, tickling each other, hooting with laughter. She was amazingly strong. We rolled onto the floor in each other's arms. Finally we stopped our playful struggling. I could tell by the look in her eyes she longed for my kiss. I pressed my lips to hers, a glorious feeling of intimacy I had felt with no other woman since my wife's death.

"You kiss well — the same self assurance I feel about all you do," she said.

"You embarass me with such lavish praise," I said smiling.

She looked earnestly into my eyes. "I love you Sam — even if nothing comes of it — I love you."

"And I love you Cornelia — even if nothing comes of it," I said.

We each realized that our very real love wouldn't necessarily culminate at the altar. She was declaring her feelings and releasing me at the same time. I realized the genuineness both of her feeling for me and for the gospel. I was not being leveraged into a commitment to Mormonism. I was free to accept or reject it as I might her love. But even if I could not accept it, her love was freely expressed. I was grateful and relieved. I realized how my feelings for her would have been diminished had she attempted to use her love to pressure me to accept what I must intellectually ratify without coercion. I was now free to reason myself to a conclusion unswayed by her or my emotions. All my life I have resented being pressured to alter my conclusions for the sake of someone's feelings. The two were always separate compartments in my mind and many attachments I cherished had been lost over my detached analysis of feelings which others felt should nullify the facts.

We realized a wholly new and wonderful development in our relationship had taken place. Not long after, I sampled again her wonderful kiss at her apartment door and we parted, each aware the outcome of our relationship hung in the balance. But we were both willing to accept what God would decide about our future.

For the first time in my life, I thought, as I made my way home, I was willing to employ my intellect but to let the conclusion I reached come from another — the Holy Spirit. I was thankful for the promise in the Book of Moroni.

And I realized I would not willingly forego my minor vices unless I was satisfied intellectually there was an overriding reason to do so.

Excerpt from the Journal of Samuel Harper

Dated March 25, 1912 (New York City)

Sunday dawned under cloudy skys that gave way intermittently to rain. Having been notified by a cablegram from Doyle that my presence was needed in London to identify the body of John Netley, the driver of the hansom in which the Ripper slayings occurred who had just been killed by a kick from his horse which he was mistreating, this was to be our last time together prior to my departure with the Futrelles for England. Jacques and his wife needed a vacation and, in truth, Jacques did not want to miss the chance to acquire more 'grist for his mill'.

Cornelia and I had decided to attend services at her 'church', a mission of the L.D.S. Church in a poor section on the West Side of Manhattan near the North River on 52nd Street. We took a motor cab to the address and walked up a flight of stairs in a rundown building which 50 years ago was no longer new, its outside blackened by the foul atmosphere of the city.

Once inside, the gusting of the wind flung raindrops with great vigor against ancient windows that rattled against their sashes. These leaked and permitted intimations of the wind blowing outside to waft gently into the room. At times the gusting was forceful enough that the building creaked and moaned, occasionally shaking violently creating a feeling of the utmost impermanence.

Our fellow worshippers were few in number, not more than a dozen including Cornelia and me. They were a mixed lot, mostly in the rude Sunday get-up of the working class, men who brushed their forelocks with calloused hands when introduced, women fidgeting with tattered finery and out-of-style handbags. One or two might have had a measure of education. All were uniformly polite and possessed of a homely good will and honesty. Either manual laborers or clerks, mostly, and their spouses.

There was no piano or organ, but a few worn hymnbooks. Our 'exultant' celebration of the sacrament was intoned feebly and uncertainly by untrained and infrequently used voices. Our hymn JESUS CHRIST IS RISEN TODAY opened this humble service, myself being unable to make much of a contribution to the imperfectly pitched and tenuous sound because of my unfamiliarity with the words and the unavailability of a hymn book there being so few.

I confess that the site and the simple service and their extreme unlikeness to the sumptuousness and pomp evoked in the Anglican Church of my heritage was additionally depressing in weather already so. I was struck by the revelation that no matter how much I might, in theory, reject the lavish ceremonies of the established churches, there still is a basic need I feel for them.

How much, I asked myself, as the simple sacrament was passed, have we rejected Christ because of the humbleness of his origins and his message? But is there not in my case a special problem? Though as a rational matter I see the evils that have engrafted themselves upon all our customs by our having such a fondness for ostentation, wealth and status, can I live in this world which my only means of making a livelihood demands I live in, and yet subsist in utter simplicity?

No fine wines, no pipe, no after dinner brandy? At my age the simple pleasures are by no means simple. Do I really want to know the truth of this gospel if it entails such sacrifices? Are my reasons for not wanting to know if it is true the real reasons or simply rationalizations? I was confused and most unhappy.

A sense of being forced to re-examine my life was upon me and I have been comfortable too long in my petty (perhaps not quite petty) vices. But even more than the painful examination of my life being forced upon me by my love for this woman, I was impressed with a sense of futility. If I am to commit myself among other things to the Articles of Faith and therefore to the return of the Ten Tribes of Israel, is this not an invitation to re-enact the moral turmoil and agony of the Anglo-Saxons of the last 4,000 years? Christendom finally abandoned the imperative to proselytize the world. This imperative was amply justified by a religion whose founder could raise himself from the dead. All the attacks of the Higher Critics fail if Christ resurrected. And after 2,000 years of the Christian message much of mankind has convinced himself that Christ was but a man and did not rise from the dead.

Had this apostasy not happened, no other creed in the world could achieve any standing in Western eyes. How else this strange and ever increasing respect for the religions and philosophies of the East? A feeling among significant numbers of the upper classes of Anglo-Saxondom regards all the world's creeds as of equal value (perhaps not a great one either). What room for an archaic idea like that of a Chosen People? And if not a Chosen People then how to believe in the return of the Ten Tribes?

Love her as I do, I've been too long a widower to change my status readily especially at the pain of such soul-searching. I was aware half way through the simple service that our marriage could not be, certainly not soon, perhaps never. And this depressed me further.

With great difficulty because of the weather we managed to flag down a cab to take us to the Plaza for lunch after making our goodbyes to the simple folk in attendance. The gay music of the orchestra in the sumptuous Oak Room of New York's finest hotel as we were led to our table amongst a forest of palm frondes and a glittering crowd showing off their finery succeeded not at all to dispel my gloom.

It is not easy to tell a creature of great beauty in both spirit and body that, love her as you may, still the two of you cannot succeed at marriage given one's reservations and that you must therefore abandon the idea of a permanent relationship.

"Your service, quite oddly reminded me of one of my father's stories about Count Tolstoy." I could see in her eyes that my use of the term 'your service' had registered in her mind as a breach between us, a distancing of myself from her, rather than what she desired, a gesture bringing us closer together.

"I didn't know your father and Tolstoy were friends," she said, "perhaps you're aware Count Tolstoy studied Mormonism in some depth."

"Not surprising, he became fanatical on the subject of religion in his later years, studying many religions," I rejoined, realizing I was again hurting her by appearing to equate Mormonism with fanaticism. "Tolstoy took my father prisoner during the Crimean War. Father had been wounded in the Battle of Sebastopol. The Count saw his wounds were tended and nursed him back to health. During the last stages of father's convalescence, when he was up and around but not yet certified for any type of duty suitable to his rank, Tolstoy took him on a tour of the Crimea in the Count's off-duty hours. Tolstoy visited us on his trip to England in 1861 a month before my father died."

"How interesting," she said, "but why did our service remind you of him?"

"Because it was so simple, so devoid of all affectation and liturgy, and," I said, "that is precisely what Tolstoy advocated, that the religions of the world adopt. Regrettably his heart was ever in turmoil because those closest to him, his wife and children regarded his attitude as a form of mental illness, an inexplicable aberration. They preferred the glitter of Moscow society. Much of the world is like that — we profess simplicity with our lips, but can't really divorce ourselves from our desire for pomp and material display." I could see in her eyes that she understood where our conversation was leading, and the twinge of sadness I read there told me she knew what conclusion I had come to about our future.

"Mr. Fenster knew Count Tolstoy well," she said, "and I, in my duties, saw all of the correspondence that passed between them."

"Did you now?" My surprise reflected in my voice. "May I ask," my interest suddenly switching from our relationship to the matter of Fenster's death, "what things were of mutual interest to Fenster and the Count?"

"Very simple," she looked in my eyes, once again the sincere helper assisting me in my sleuthing, "Fenster first met Tolstoy through Andrew White who was a close friend of Mr. Fenster's father. Mr. White, as you know, became the U.S. Ambassador to Russia. Mr. Fenster's father was searching for someone to function as trustee in Russia disbursing large sums of money to assist Eastern European Jews who desired to emigrate to America. His father suggested he ask the help of Mr. White who recommended Count Tolstoy."

I looked into her lovely eyes. "A natural choice; Count Tolstoy was on his way to becoming the biggest man in Russia — in his own way more powerful than the Czar."

"A natural choice, of course." She leaned across the table her face close to mine and covered my hand with hers. In almost a pleading voice Cornelia spoke to me asking, really, if I might not change my mind, but saying, "The Count was well informed about Mormonism. After Mr. White's conversations with the Count on the topic, the Ambassador purchased the standard works of the Church for the University Library at Cornell."

"Yes," I said, "this may be true, but neither the Count nor Mr. White joined the Church." Our eyes were locked in a sad embrace.

A look of understanding came into her eyes. Now she comprehended the nature of the battle I was waging in the depths of my soul. There was no reproach in her gaze nor resentment. Just love and resignation, acceptance and, was I mistaken? — hope? She still hoped I might overcome my own difficulties and accept her faith.

We each had now accepted, at least, that our relationship could not culminate in marriage until much in my heart had changed. I was strangely pleased that she had not given up on me. But what could this strange elation mean?

"Doyle informs me that my solicitor in London recently received some effects from Count Tolstoy's widow. Apparently when the Count died last year there were some items he left to us, father being dead. I can't imagine what there will be — some useless odds and ends no doubt."

"Why didn't Myles claim them for you? Why the solicitor?" she asked.

"Myles could have had them as well as I might. He was offered them. He simply hadn't the room — or the interest," I replied.

"However trivial they may be," she remarked with considerable feeling, "I'm glad you want them."

"There is a melancholy reward to the son whose father dies early," I said, "Myles, being five critical years older than I, knew my father well. But he died before I enjoyed that opportunity. Consequently, Myles displays little interest in acquiring more of Father's effects than he already has, and I am able to hoard all the rest and to cherish every handwritten note in every margin. And I therefore, discovered the real man my father was, and in the process a good part of me."

Cherishing family as only one can who was raised by strangers, and this strong feeling further enhanced by the deep Mormon commitment to the family, her eyes glistened as she looked earnestly into mine. "Will you — some day," she pleaded, "show me the remembrances you have of your father?"

It seemed a simple enough request to grant and in the granting both to avoid a commitment of greater seriousness and yet to avoid terminating totally our relationship by a denial. Without speaking I agreed with a nod of my head. I stood and held her chair as we prepared to leave.

Our parting at her door was a tender one. "I shall write you from London," I said.

"Please do Sam," she said, "I shall wait for the mail impatiently."

I was pleased, strangely pleased that we had not terminated our relationship even though there seemed no chance of it leading to the Temple, where alone, her hand would be given in marriage.

Letter to Cornelia St. James
from Samuel Harper
Dated April 1, 1912 (London)

Dear Cornelia,

London has changed; would you believe there are over 400 cinemas here? I have just returned from Lincoln's Inn where my Solicitor has his offices. My first visit to Chancery Lane in ten years. It brought back many memories of a hundred different cases in which in one way or another I took part. I visited Mr. Barrett, the Solicitor who has handled my father's estate these many years. He must be, I suppose, about as old as my father would be were he alive, I would estimate 74 or 75 years, and he was most fond of my father. We went to Driver's, my favorite oyster bar, for lunch and I could see him watching my gestures and expressions with the smallest imaginable smile playing about the corners of his mouth. Perhaps I only imagine it, but he seems to be verifying any similarities with those of my father. He is a type from an earlier age who would be quite at home in the salon of his former law partners, the publishers John Murray & Co. (take your choice of either the elder Murray or the younger) holding fervent discussions with Lord Beaconsfield or his father Isaac Disraeli or even the lawyer and historian (also a Murray client) Sharon Turner who so influenced the works of Doyle's relative Sir Walter Scott and who persuaded Isaac Disraeli to have young Benjamin baptized a Christian thus laying the groundwork for his political career later. Or perhaps a contemporary of Disraeli, that iconoclastic American Herman Melville, also a Murray client.

John Murray & Co. were also my father's publishers and that of my guardian Sir Henry. Mr. Barrett loves to tell amusing anecdotes about that period. He tells of attempting to arrange an interview for Melville with Thomas Carlyle back in 1856 or 7. At the time Melville was long past the crest of his first successful romances and had registered poorly with his more recent efforts, but he had hoped that several of his more serious efforts might have come favorably to the attention of the old curmudgeon whose theory of the Hero he studied deeply and much admired. The interview, of course, was refused and Barrett tells how he consoled the crestfallen Melville by expressing the opinion that likely Her Majesty herself would have been refused. I'm sure that at that moment Melville's view of Carlyle was less than heroic.

My father, Sir Henry, etc. lived in the very last of the heroic age and its passing ushers in our era which, I fear, will seem lackluster by comparison. Will we see the era of the anti-hero or the non-hero? No Siegfried nor Ivanhoe? No Odin, Mahomet or Cromwell (Carlyle's favorites)? And what of that prototype of all heroes — the Messiah? What kind of world can come into existence if we no longer exalt the individual which has to be the inevitable result of the democratic ideal? The world has always cherished its priests, whom Carlyle ranked among the first line of heroes. And haven't we seen the role of the clergy diminish as democracy has become mankind's ideal? If all men are equal what room for a hero?

Perhaps Melville set the style in Moby Dick with the insensate animal as hero and evil Ahab as the anti-hero and the conscious I-character Ishmael the passive observer's role to which the individual is assigned. But there are layers upon layers of meaning in Melville who perceived quite clearly that without Christianity the Western world must falter and fall. Needless to say, Melville is a hero of mine.

Mr. Barrett delivered to me a somewhat battered package from Countess Tolstoy with newspapers printed in cyrillic characters showing through the holes in the outer wrappings. This, of course, contains the mementoes of my father bequeathed to Myles and me upon Count Tolstoy's death. I will finish this letter to you after I have examined its contents.

— — — — — — — — — — — — — — —

I am utterly astounded as you will be to learn of the contents of Count Tolstoy's package. The items it contains were few but were I the believer you are in Providence I would venture the guess their selection was Providential. There were some delightful tinted renderings by some Russian artist of scenes in the Crimea. On the back of each is a date and caption in father's hand telling of the places which I'm sure the Count and father visited while my father was recovering from the wounds he received in the Battle of Sebastopol. Why these should reach us so long after father's death I will only know (perhaps) after I have read the Countess' letter which I must first have translated as it is in Russian. Father and Tolstoy had to communicate in French their only common language. Neither understood the other's native tongue.

There was a packet of letters written over a number of years to the Count by father up to the time of his death. I am grateful for these. I will sharpen my French once again as I read them.

But the shocker of all the items were the last two, one a box which I recognized at once to be the distinctive case of a British decoration which I opened to find the Victoria Cross on its ribbon of claret. This ultimate decoration was posthumously awarded to and inscribed with the name of Robert Appleton who died in action at Sebastopol. Besides containing the Cross there was also a letter addressed to my father by a clergyman in Preston, Lancashire telling him that Appleton's sole survivor, an aged mother, died while he was in the service in the Crimea. Also enclosed with the clergyman's letter was a newspaper clipping from some unknown gazette describing Appleton's heroism in saving the life of his commanding officer Ellsworth Harper (my father).

The final item, to my utter bewilderment, is a Book of Mormon inscribed to Appleton by one John Taylor and given to him as a gift "in celebration of (his) baptism, confirmation and ordination to the Holy Priesthood — June 1st, 1840."

Inscribed on the next page in what I assume to be Appleton's own hand is the following:

"I was but 16 when the Mormon missionaries came to Preston.

149

Thier teaching caused much comoshun hereabouts. My parents being among those opposd I could not join for three years. But the sight of Brothers Kimball and Hyde (himself sick much of the time) entering the River Ribble through a hold in the ice in mid-Janry, five, ten maybe more times each day to baptize made a deep impreshun pon me. Folks in our country were suffring from starvation and hard times and were weak almost unto death in many cases. But I've seen friends and neighbors rise off what we took to be thier deathbeds to enter the icy waters of baptism, emurjing with no aparent harm, in fact, rejoicing, hale and hearty. Times were hard when the Brethren arrived and continud so, but something new and wondrful had entered our lives which comforted all our pains. The truth can fill even an empty stumuk. God has blessed us through the Brethren and those of us who accepted the Gospel are grateful.

How am I ever to repay these fine men and Heavenly Father for the great blessings they have given me?

Signed: ROB'T APPLETON

The citation with the medal states that Appleton among other heroic acts was instrumental in saving my father from death in an artillery barrage at Sebastopol.

Since I was conceived upon my father's return from the Crimea, I owe not only his life, but my own to Robert Appleton, VC who must have been one of an extremely small band of Mormon soldiers in the British Army since the war was in 1854 and the first missionaries to England preached the gospel in Britain no earlier than 1837 (the year Victoria became queen) and the entire Mormon population in England cannot have been large.

I know this story will be as moving to you as it is to me. A man who is nothing but a name to me, a name I heard for the first time today, sacrificed his own life that Father (and I) might live. I am filled with gratitude to this gallant man and to whatever it was about him that caused him to lay down his life for us. May his abode be in Heaven.

I love you Cornelia. I've never said or written those words to you before with as much feeling as I do now. I love you and your gospel and the wonderful man who embraced death that father might live and that I might embrace you.

I pledge you this: I will reread the Book of Mormon, this time with the sincere desire to know if it is true.

As you know, our departure is scheduled for April 10th from Southampton on the magnificent new liner Titanic. I long to hold you in my arms and the crossing time will seem endless until our embrace is a reality.

Love, Sam

Letter to Cornelia St. James
from Samuel Harper
Dated April 5, 1912 (London)

Dear Cornelia,

Last evening the true difficulty began. I rejected the wine with my dinner and the after dinner brandy with cigar. And I have not smoked a pipeful of tobacco in 48 hours, 32 minutes and 16 seconds! I exaggerate a little as to the difficulty of the undertaking, but only a little. Lucky Futrelle, he is the one who should be attempting to become a Mormon. He is allergic to alcohol and never smokes. An occasional cup of strong coffee to sacrifice would be very little to give up. But enough of the minor irritations along the pathway in the search for TRUTH.

As I have prepared myself for the specific task of attempting to determine if Joseph Smith is truly all he claimed to be, I have kept reminding myself of Thomas Carlyle's remark in his lecture on THE HERO AS PROPHET:

"The most precious gift that Heaven can give to the earth; a man of 'genius' as we call it; the Soul of a Man actually sent down from the skies with a Gods-Message to us."

Last night I prayed, or should say I tried to. I can't say that I experienced the enormous success of Joseph in that grove of trees in Palmyra. Has it ever struck you how overwhelmingly impressive it would be upon a young boy to succeed so richly at his first serious attempt at prayer? He kneels to pray, is nearly throttled by an unseen assailant and is delivered by the Savior himself. I have no testimony yet that this occurred, but assuming it did, it is easy to see why throughout all the trials he bore in his life including mobbings and martyrdom, he never denied the story of the vision.

A truly just, kind and loving God would give a man chosen for so difficult a task the reinforcement of a memory of so powerful an event to call upon when the going got rough.

And I am impressed with what I have read regarding the eight witnesses to whom Joseph showed the gold plates. Many apostatized but none ever denied what he had seen. To an expert in detection and the gathering of testimony this is impressive.

But I am even more impressed that the Book of Mormon was expressly intended for our day as promised in Isaiah (Isa. 29:13-14).

I had made a specific plan regarding the circumstances under which I would re-read the book. I planned to eat lightly (yesterday), to have no liquor, tobacco or coffee for we know these affect the senses even if they were not proscribed by the Word of Wisdom. I knelt and prayed that I might be filled with the desire to know if the book is true and asked for the witness of the Holy Ghost.

But as I arose from my knees I knocked the book from the table next to which I was kneeling. It fell to the floor and as it fell it opened. I thus picked it up already opened. I began to read exactly where it had by chance fallen open, remonstrating with myself for half-expecting what I regard as more superstition than a providential intervention in my learning process. Such occult happenings better suit Doyle than me. But I will tell you that whether accidental or providential, the place I began to read was well chosen for me and for our times. Perhaps I would have received the confirmation of the Holy Spirit in no other way. Only Heavenly Father knows. But receive it I did, for what I read made my bosom burn as my heart swelled and my eyes filled with tears.

The book fell open to Mosiah (Chs. 1 to 6) and I read the story of King Benjamin. Here was a king to my liking. Everything the British kings and other crowned heads of Europe are not. He took nothing from the people for his support but toiled in his own plot of ground like them for his sustenance. Subjected, as they were, to the uncertainties of striving for one's existence, he was at one with them in all things. He gave them holy service and counted himself blessed to have the opportunity to do so.

He honored his priesthood and was honored by them for the power from on high made available to them through his worthiness. His chosenness meant service only. Our kings have debased their chosenness into hauteur, elitism, license and privilege.

If ever a man was prepared to learn the message carried in these sections of Mosiah's message, it is I. I believe in the principle of priesthood, for I believe a truly just God would have to provide a means of projecting his power into men's lives. But how else to do this except by the interaction with our fellow men in exercising righteous power.

If not this, then a thunderbolt from on high every twelve minutes? It would make no sense to expect direct intervention on a constant basis and it would frustrate free will were it to happen. Above all else I've learned about Mormonism it is how important free will is regarded in the plan of salvation. All must be given voluntarily and nothing by coercion. Until mankind has learned this lesson there can be no paradise on earth.

Mankind taps the power from on high by living worthily as King Benjamin did and thus is a worthy conduit for God's power. It makes perfect sense but how unlike anything being taught by any of the other churches. And it has the simplicity I have come to associate with truth. In my experience, the truth is always simple.

Conversely, the minute the person serving as conduit for God's power fails through unrighteousness — that is — fails to be a worthy priesthood holder, the circuit is broken and the power of God can no longer flow through him.

Luke described rightly the feeling he experienced when he received the witness of the spirit (Luke 24:32). I felt the burning sensation I sought. And I now know how God saves even the unlearned, and understand the working principle of faith. Knowledge without this understanding is a trap. A trap into which I fell and have only recently, I hope, escaped.

I am grateful to you my love for your patience in not abandoning me when I rejected your beliefs for my worldly reasons. And the battle will be hard to overcome my worldly ways. But I can tell you that I am committed irrevocably to the fight.

Affectionately,

Sam

EDITOR'S NOTE: Reconstructed in June 1912 by Samuel Harper from entries in his journal and from his recollections. (London)

April 6, 1912

"My what a long time it's been," I exclaimed, as I opened the door of my suite at the Diogenes Club to admit Conan Doyle's gargantuan presence. His enormous frame filled the doorway, his great paw of a hand extended to take mine. With his right he clasped my extended digits and with his left he squeezed my shoulder firmly, his broad face expanded in an enormous and most heart-warming smile.

"Welcome home Sam; I see they assigned you the suite I asked for. I bring you the fondest regards of His Majesty King George V who asks me to say that he hopes you'll consider your exile at an end," Doyle paused, "and that you'll once again let Britain call herself your home!" He eyed me inquiringly.

"We shall see," I said, "express for me, if you will, my appreciation for his kind interest. I would like to have Leslie spend enough time to come to think of Britain as home. But there's Cornelia to think of now so let me just say 'we shall see'."

"As serious as that, eh?" he asked, "well it's time you found a wife."

"Speaking of wives, where's Jean?" I asked.

"The usual," he laughed, "she's presiding over the committee this year — you know — the flower show. I'm the first man with grounds for divorce against a hibiscus." He laughed his hearty Celtic best, his eyes twinkling and watering with merriment.

"You poor brute," I ridiculed, "just so long as she claims no grounds against you, you're all right."

"I've that to be thankful for, of course," he said, through his subsiding mirth.

We bantered back and forth as of old for another fifteen minutes. Finally, with all the small talk out of the way, I turned the topic to matters of greater seriousness.

"Are we going to identify the remains?" I asked. "If so let us head for the place as we are due back at 5:30 for cocktails and dinner with Futrelle and his wife and, I assume, Jean."

"Quite so, yes we are free to visit Netley, if such the carcass is, any time we wish," he said, "and no better time than right now."

153

In the street the doorman hailed a cab for us, Doyle directing the driver to go past Buckingham Palace on the way to Magdalen Hospital on Blackfriar's Road.

"Futrelle regrets not being able to be with us but has made me promise," I said, "to give him a thorough update on all that occurs."

"How much does he know or suspect?" Doyle asked.

"At first I refused to discuss the case at all with him," I said, "but with Fenster's murder that posture became untenable, unless I wished to cut him off completely, which I had no desire to do. I have since discovered that Roycroft Peel, who retained me in the Ripper case is his wife's cousin and told him pretty much everything. It really doesn't matter as long as he's discreet," I said, "which I assure you he is."

Doyle, deep in thought, only grunted in response. "Few cases we've ever been involved with — none really — ," he remarked, looking abstractedly out the window of the cab, "aroused so much interest or held such dangerous potential as this one. Fortunately, with Netley gone, assuming the body is his, the last direct witness to the Ripper killings is dead. I hope the danger to the throne passes with the blackguard."

The enormous bearskin busbies of the members of the Foot Guard standing at the position of Present Arms outside Buckingham Palace, which we were just then passing on our way to Magdalen Hospital caused me to feel a twinge and I realized how homesick I had been without knowing it, for the day to day pomp most British take for granted, since my departure so long ago.

"Surely you can't still believe there's any possibility the people would demand an end to the crown?" I asked.

"You didn't believe the protestations," Doyle remarked, "of those who insisted those poor harlots threatened the monarchy back in '88."

"Unworthy though some of its tenants have been," I answered, "I have never believed the British would dump the throne. An individual king might indeed be disposed of, the beheading of Charles I being as fine an example as any, but I've always felt the only one who could dictate that the crown must go — the common man — was as devoted as any and more than most to its perpetuance." I paused as a thought came to me, "Perhaps that's why I never could sympathize with Anderson, Warren, Gull, not to mention the Prime Minister, The Marquess of Salisbury himself and the whole Masonic lot who perpetrated or covered up the crimes from their positions of authority, in the Home Office or higher. They insisted the danger was to the crown, whereas it was only to their advantaged relationship to the Prince of Wales through their Masonic Brotherhood. I'm sure their fears were genuine enough too, that the Liberals might be returned to power which they regarded as an unmitigated disaster. Balfour told me that when his uncle, Salisbury became P.M. in '85 and called for the file on Turkey to determine the state of Britain's influence in Constantinople after five years of Gladstone's neglect he remarked in profound despair, 'they have just thrown it away into the sea, without getting anything whatever in exchange'."

"You may indeed be right," Doyle said, "but at the time revolution was in the air. Have you forgotten the Bloody Sunday Massacre in Trafalgar

Square, or the agitated state of the ordinary people over the land question after a decade of the fulminations of Henry George?"

"Surely not, but Macauley had it right when he said: "In England there is plenty of grumbling in bad years, and sometimes a little rioting, but it matters little, for here the sufferers are not the rulers. The supreme power is in the hands of a select class, deeply interested in the security of property and the maintenance of order." At this point in time," I said, "there's little to be gained in debating if the slayings were justified. Regardless of whether a threat to the crown existed or not, who can justify murder? Yes, it might embarass the Queen for the second in line to be linked to a homosexual brothel on Cleveland Street. It might even unseat her line if the Duke of Clarence's secret marriage to a Catholic and a commoner were known. But the throne has changed lines before as the Plantagenets, the Tudors and the Stuarts could tell you. The Duke of Clarence would have contracted a marriage years ago with Princess Helena d'Orleans, a Catholic and one of the hated Bourbons if he had had his simple-witted way. That would have created a constitutional crisis, but Britain would still have a king or queen, I'll wager."

We drove for a few moments in silence. "Why," I asked, "is the body still at the hospital where I assume they took Netley after the accident, instead of at the morgue? Or can I guess the answer?"

"I'm sure you can," Doyle said, "If it is Netley, they don't wish an entry in the official records of the morgue. Easy enough to understand why."

"Quite," I agreed, "You say the last witness is dead with Netley. Haven't you forgotten someone?" I asked.

"You mean Sickert, I suppose," Doyle responded. "He's a blabbermouth, of course, when in his cups, I'm told, he speaks of nothing else. And they did a stupid thing in organizing the effort to steal all the Sickert paintings in which he had sprinkled the clues to the slaying. He knew who the trollops were by sight and someone had to finger the poor creatures for the killer. He could not refuse to cooperate, or live with his conscience after he did. There can't be an art connoisseur anywhere who doesn't know that Gull loved grapes or that Masonic was involved after Sickert painted these clues into those purloined paintings. But with the challenge to the crown passed they assume, I'm told, the ramblings of a crazy painter will just be taken for so much rubbish. I suspect they're right too. If he gets too bad they'll just lock him up as they did Gull and Annie Crook and he won't be heard of again."

"All this in a constitutional monarchy," I remarked, more despairing than cynical.

"I suspect t'was ever thus," Doyle said as we approached Magdalen Hospital. "Please take the Emergency Entrance."

"Righto Guv'na," replied the cabbie. "Shall I white, sir?"

"No need," said Doyle, "we will be some time." Doyle paid the fare and dismissed the cab.

In truth we were not long. It took but a few minutes to be admitted to the hospital's cold room and in another thirty seconds I had seen what remained of the man who drove the carriage in which the unfortunate trollops had died who thought to blackmail the crown over the Duke of Clarence's strange liaison with Annie Crook, a common Irish Catholic girl whose child he sired and legitimized in a Roman Catholic ceremony at a time when anti-Catholic feeling still ran so high in England the Prince of Wales was refused his desire to visit the Pope on his trip to Italy.

Perhaps I imagined it, but his countenance in death seemed that of a man who lived in terror. Perhaps I only hoped this was true — that justice required some retribution not only for his part in the Ripper slayings, but also for his repeated attempts on the life of Annie Crook's daughter Alice Margaret. Perhaps her death was ordered as her mother's confinement had been, Annie spending thirty years of her life in various institutions for the mentally ill. Perhaps Netley, in an excess of zeal, took it upon himself to attempt to run the little girl down with his carriage, not once but twice, once in 1888 and again in '92. My network of informants, built up during the period I was retained by the Queen to work on the case, kept me advised of all such matters. I had it within my power, if I so desired, to know Sickert's every move and Alice Margaret became Sickert's ward first, and then his mistress.

"How much," I asked Doyle, as we boarded another cab to return to St. James, "do you think Balfour knew about the Ripper case?"

"Difficult to say, of course," he temporized. "As Salisbury's nephew and protege he should have learned about the case. But if he didn't then, I can't believe he doesn't know the whole story now. He would have had access to much of the evidence once he became Prime Minister. It wasn't the best kept secret among people at that level."

"I'm sure you're right," I said. "I must see Arthur while I'm here."

"About the Fenster case, of course," he acknowledged.

"Of course; he has to be advised of all we've learned, most especially the details of the plot on his life such as we know," I said. "Scotland Yard has already been alerted, of course."

"Arthur told me you're coming to see him while you're in town," Doyle said.

"Yes, and I suspect wisdom dictates I should see him alone," I said. "While he won't assume that I am solely privy to the facts I must disclose to him, the discretion with which we are treating the matter will seem compromised if you and Futrelle attend. Forgive me my bluntness, it is only appearances of which I speak. I know both of you to be the very soul of discretion."

It was clear he took no offense. "I think meeting alone with him would be wise," he said.

I was relieved at his acquiescence. "When," I asked, "did you see Arthur last?"

"We both attended," he responded, "a seance at Stead's a week or ten days ago. But we did not get to chat."

"Did you ever get to talk to him about J.B. Bury's book HISTORY OF THE EASTERN ROMAN EMPIRE?" I asked.

"I dropped him a note mentioning your suggestion," Doyle answered, "but he never responded. But I never thought he would."

"To be expected, really," I offered. "Arthur never answers his mail in the first place, but to do anything else would leave lying about, he wouldn't know where, what might become part of an embarassing record."

"So you won't discover until you meet with him," Doyle suggested, "what, if anything, he did about it."

"We will find he's done absolutely nothing," I said. "Arthur, though he terms himself a philosopher, is essentially not a man of ideas. You've read his works — not an original idea in the pile of it. He is an accommodator of ideas as he is an accommodator of political viewpoints. His concept of philosophy is to make people feel comfortable with utterly contradictory beliefs."

"What precisely does that mean?" Doyle asked.

"Balfour writes de-christianized philosophy for de-christianized Christians," I responded.

"Is that what that stuff is?" Doyle asked, a mischievous twinkle in his eye but a perfectly straight face. "I thought I was just too obtuse to comprehend . . ."

"Nothing to comprehend, once you understand his purposes," I said, ignoring his gentle ridicule. "The clergy perceived, if their parishoners didn't, that the complex of ideas embraced by the Enlightenment had gutted Christianity. Then science as we term it, buried the corpse. No man with the slightest claim to awareness believed the Scriptures to be more than a hollow shell. The only problem was the common man hadn't been informed. And while that old time religion still appealed to him, the philosophers had a problem."

"Enter the likes of Balfour," said Doyle, raising a gloved hand, the index finger extended.

The cab driver, at Doyle's direction had taken a circuitous route back to the club out Waterloo Road to the Strand, past Trafalgar Square to Pall Mall, St. James Street, Old and New Bond Streets to Oxford then past Orator's Corner in Hyde Park where we were now about to circle back to St. James Square. The gesticulating characters and the milling crowds were unchanged from my memories of them. My it was good to be home and I said as much to my old partner in crime detection.

"It's good to _have_ you _home_ Sam," he said, underlining the words by his emphasis. "It must all seem very different — so much has changed."

I pondered my response. "I think we've changed Arthur. Not London. Oh yes, there have been many changes, but mostly, speaking for myself anyway, mostly I seem different."

"Is that good or bad," he inquired.

"Both — bittersweet, so to speak. The passing of youth has its compensations, but nothing," I said, "half as good as youth itself. Paraphrasing an old maxim — I've been young and I've been old. Young is better."

"Of course," Doyle acknowledged, "but if you had it to do over, would you?"

"Not under any circumstances," I said, "how about you?"

We were greeted by the doorman at the Diogenes Club who opened the door to the cab to assist us. I paid the cab driver and tipped the doorman.

We were comfortably ensconced in the men's bar, our beverages in hand before Conan Doyle responded to my question.

"An enigma," said the voluble Irish-Scotsman, that life should move so fast, be so enjoyable in so many ways, and yet not cause us to wish to do it all over. The only people I know who admit to a desire to tarry are those who seem afraid to cross the veil. And it doesn't matter much how fortunate the person's life seems to have been. It's a rare individual, at least in my experience, that wants to do it over."

"You know," I said, "an American had some interesting things to say about death. He said:

'All men know that they must die . . . It is but reasonable to suppose that God would reveal something in reference to the matter . . .'

If we have any claim on our Heavenly Father for anything, it is for knowledge on this important subject."

"Seems reasonable enough," said Doyle, "but what enlightenment did he then offer on the subject? And who was he by the way?"

"It was the Mormon Prophet Joseph Smith and he taught his followers to have no fear of death," I said.

"I have much maligned the Mormons if such be true," Doyle said, "but what is Mormonism to you or me aside from the fact that long ago one of my novels was about them?"

"Cornelia is a Mormon," I said, "and I mean to marry her."

"Congratulations are in order here, I can see," he said extending his hand to be shaken, his broad Celtic countenance glorified in a smile. "But you are marrying more than Cornelia, are you not? You are also taking her beliefs. Is that the way of it with Mormons? It is with the Catholics — "

"She could marry a non-Mormon," I offered, "but she won't. She desires the most sacred form of marriage Mormonism offers — that in the Holy Temple. And this is not possible unless I too am a Mormon in the best standing."

"Is this why," he asked, "I see my old friend imbibing vichy water with a twist of lemon, who once let nothing below 100 proof touch his lips." He guffawed heartily.

I confess I was embarassed considerably. "The price I pay for the woman I love," I said sheepishly.

"Only a true romantic would ante up such a stern exactment!" he said smiling, but nonetheless admiringly.

"You're a better judge of that than I — romanticism is for writers," I suggested.

Turning serious again, "I fear I must," Doyle said, "qualify your point of view about Joseph Smith in the light of your current enamoured condition."

"And well you should," said I, "but by the strictest application of logic, the state of my heart has nothing whatever to do with the truth or falsehood of the gospel as revealed by these latter day prophets."

"What say they," he asked, "about our ability to contact the dead?"

"More than any other creed of which I have knowledge." I said, deliberately holding my response as short as possible so that he would be forced to elicit information which might offend him were it offered gratuitously.

"That's not very helpful," he commented, "do they acknowledge it to be possible? As you know, reference to such matters is a lacuna in other creeds."

"It is indeed possible," I responded, choosing my words most carefully, "but the dead at least those who died worthily, are only granted permission to contact the living when a very good purpose will be served, such as to console the grieving to enable those in pain to make constructive use of their lives once again."

Arthur's eyes clouded with the slightest mist of tears and I knew that grief over loss of his loved ones, his mother most especially, still wrought considerable pain in his sentimental Celtic heart. My own deep feelings for this enormous and thoroughly good man brought tears of empathy to my own eyes.

"Permission?" he asked, seizing upon the operative word which went to the very heart of spiritualism. "Why permission? What have they got that's better to do?"

I was elated at the question but contained my feelings. "The dead have much work to do in the spirit world learning the gospel and teaching it to others."

"Extraordinary doctrine," Doyle said, sipping his scotch. I slowly drew upon my perrier water.

"For all the charlatans," he said, "and Balfour, Stead and I have seen dozens of them, there have still been too many instances in which the psychic phenomenon was undeniable. How do you explain that?"

I thanked God he had drawn the question from his own lips. "Mormon doctrine is most explicit on the point, but you will not be happy with the answer," I said.

"As Noah Webster once said, 'Our wretched species is so made that those who walk on the well-trodden path always throw stones at those who are showing a new road.' I am quite able to handle anything," Doyle said, "you forget how I've been ridiculed for my beliefs."

"Satanic forces are free to tempt the living, and," I said, "can read the hearts of those seeking a sign, giving them signs deliberately intended to draw them deeper into satan's net."

"Were we not such good friends," Doyle said, "I would dismiss this satan rubbish out of hand. No man worthy of the description of enlightened even believes in satan!"

"Yet evil proliferates in the modern world that would make Caligula pale," I said. "I recently heard a poem which seems to express well my present feelings on the topic:

Men don't believe in the devil now as their
fathers used to do;
They've forced the door of the broadest creed
to let his majesty through.

The devil was fairly voted out, and of course
the devil is gone;
But simple people would like to know who
carries his business on."
"Man is his own devil," he responded, "and quite satanic enough."

"I don't wish to be drawn into contention," I said, "I can only tell you how I've become convinced there is a satan who leads a mighty legion of spirits as evil as himself."

"We might get somewhere," Doyle observed, a kindly tone replacing the slight edge of contention which colored his last few comments, "if you tell me that — why this system appeals to you, a thoroughly modern man by my lights. One I thought above such medieval concepts as satan."

I pondered how best to say what had to be said, how to be truthful to a dear friend and true to myself. "At my age," I began, "I no longer hold any illusions about how men make their most important decisions. They are made with the heart and not with the intellect. If I have made one error in this life over and over," I stopped briefly to lock eyes with my friend, "it is in thinking that reason could operate in some small percentage of cases to affect people's decisions. I now conclude that even I, when the final truth be known, base my decisions on what my emotional needs are."

"A major milestone in your development," he conceded.

"I'm a slow study," I laughed, "But having made what a sentient person like yourself must regard as a most rudimentary step forward, I concede the appeal of Mormonism to me is not primarily that it is the first body of doctrine to define the lineaments of deity in a way which makes sense, but that it satisfies a basic emotional need."

"The first sensible thing you've said about it so far," he joshed, "In what way may I ask?"

"It relates to this question of satan, but it begins with the nature of God the Father," I said. "When Joseph Smith had his first vision he saw the Father and the Son in the flesh. Not some abstract force, but a man like you and me, with a body and emotions and emotional needs like my own. This was the beginning of my conversion. Never really having known my father, I have yearned to know him. That I might know the father of my flesh in the life beyond this one satisfies a great need I feel. The doctrine that held this to be possible became credible if my Heavenly Father were a man of flesh and bones. Does that make sense?"

"Perfect sense to me," he conceded.

"Then how did we — did the world become misled into thinking there is no God?" I asked, "for an impersonal God with no traits we recognize is the same as no God at all."

"A not unacceptable position," Doyle said.

"But if there is no God," I suggested, "then certainly there's no need for satan, correct?"

"I guess I see the point, but where are you leading?" he asked.

"Precisely here," I responded, "if it follows that there is no God and no satan, which is essentially the world's attitude in spite of all protestations to

160

the contrary, for an unknowable God is no God at all, then once we recognize that God is a real person, the father of our spirit bodies as our earthly father is sire to our earthly bodies, we must logically accept the reality of satan and his power."

"You describe, I take it, the logical flip-flop," Doyle said, his countenance reflecting an inner light ignited, "your own conversion required, correct?"

"You've got it," I said, "No God — no satan metamorphosed into a highly personal God and a highly powerful satan."

"And it is to this satan we yield ourselves in spiritualism," I said almost remorsefully, meeting his eyes with mine. I could see that he comprehended what was said but had not accepted it.

"I am indeed happy our searching has led you to something you value," Doyle said, "I too have found something of value — Balfour, Stead and I and many others."

I thought it best not to mention how comparable to me spiritualism seemed to the practices of ancient Rome, when the priests attempted to divine the future from the twitching of a pigeon's entrails. That a former Prime Minister of the greatest nation on earth, one of that nation's leading publishers and its most famous author should be delving into the occult seemed to me the depth of decadence. But even our strong friendship might not withstand my giving expression to such feelings. "Is Balfour," I asked, "still attempting to contact his lost love May Lyttleton?"

"He never mentions the fact," said Doyle, "though there's no doubt in my mind you are right."

"We've known Arthur for so long," I said, "I didn't realize until I lived abroad how archetypical he is. In the eyes of those whose forebears left England to escape the system of hereditary privileges and powers, he exemplifies all that's wrong with England. On his visit in 1910 they asked me to be a part of the committee to welcome him. We were motoring up Fifth Ave. and Harry Connors, the New York Fire Commissioner proudly pointed out one of the many new skyscrapers going up, preening himself by the assertion the building is totally fireproof. To which Arthur responded, "What a pity! — can you imagine it?"

Laughing boisterously, his eyes twinkling, his great barrel-like body heaving, "How like Balfour!" Doyle said.

When he had regained control of himself Doyle said, "Can you ever forget Kipling's limerick about Balfour's most famous book, let's see how did it go — "The Foundations of Philosophic Doubt are based on this single premise — shall I be able to get out — to Wimbledon in time for tennis."

At which we both laughed uproariously. When our laughter had subsided I sipped my mineral water and Doyle his scotch.

"It is strange, is it not," I said, "how all who knew him best, totally misjudged the true potential of Balfour? Who of us who knew him at Eton and Cambridge would have believed he, of all of us, would go so far, even to become Prime Minister? In a world where appearances were everything, he was entirely wrong. He wore glasses — that was bad form; he liked music, something akin to effeminacy of which he is still suspected, he was languid in a world which only cherished the athletic, enthusiastic and dynamic. You name it and he did it — wrong."

"I didn't know him then, but I quite agree," Doyle allowed, "but the greatest error of all, we most fully misjudged his mettle. He perceived what none of the rest of us saw, that it was an age of extraordinary challenge to the Conservative way and that only by appearing to do something while doing nothing at all could he preserve things the way they were to a degree. He couldn't be moved, but most of all he coundn't be forced into an expression of opinion. It seems stupid, but it was deucedly clever. And that's how he bungled and survived his way to the top."

"Only in England with its system of hereditary privilege could a man so completely devoid of sympathy for others attain so much power," I said. "Do you remember Margot Tennant Asquith's story of the time she told Balfour he wouldn't care if we all dropped dead — to which Arthur said he would — if we all dropped dead at once?"

Doyle's hilarious reaction filled the room with the roar of his infectious laughter bringing the slightest smile to the face of Phipps, the utterly stoical bar waiter and startled expressions to the few old members about, either dozing over their copies of the Times or quietly sipping their drinks.

"Where Balfour is concerned," I said, "Hegel's words find perfect expression 'People and governments,' said the German philosopher, 'have never learned anything from history or acted upon principles deducible from it.' "

"You shall have your opportunity," Doyle said, "to tell Arthur that to his face."

"Quite right," I agreed, "The absent are never without fault, nor the present without excuse — if I can purloin an observation from Mr. Franklin."

"I recollect," said Doyle, "in one of your letters you referred to a remark of Ruskin that had achieved new meaning for you — do you recall?"

I plunged into my memory and started rummaging. "Doing is the great thing," I said, "For if resolutely, people do what is right, in time they come to like doing it. — Is that the one?"

"The very one," Doyle agreed, "you said it had assumed new meaning since your encounter with Mormon thought."

"I was deeply concerned," I responded, "that our search for eternal truth has apparently led us down such different paths. I was seeking an explanation why so many are delving into the occult, in effect, seeking a direct revelation of realities from the other side. You, Balfour and Stead are really only some of the grander individuals seeking, as it were, to grasp heaven by the throat. You have compatriots by the millions around the world who share your interest in spiritualism."

"True enough," the author responded, "but why do you and the rest of the world demean us for our efforts?"

"I can't say I know the answer," I replied, "but without question whatever it is lies at the heart of our differences. I mean no offense, but we are told in Matthew 12:39: 'It is a wicked and adulterous generation that seeketh a sign' and, surely, I know you belong in neither category but I think that passage means that many who do not live the commandments seek direct contact with the spirit world despite their unworthiness."

"No offense taken," Doyle said with a smile reflecting the genuineness of his sentiment, "but where does Ruskin come in?"

"Because I construe his meaning to have direct application," I answered, "to a passage in the Book of Mormon, the Book of Ether 12:12 — "For if there be no faith among the children of men God can do no miracle among them; wherefore he showed not himself until after their faith." It seems to me that spiritualism seeks a miracle as I define the term, and that those I see seeking miracles, if we believe the Book of Mormon, and I do, have not qualified by faith to receive the miracle they seek." I paused to see if my companion was attentive. "This line of thought caused Ruskin's remark to come to mind. Ruskin unconsciously was leading us to the secret of faith and of miracles. If we live the commandments, faith grows to the point we are given the sign we seek. Including conviction of the knowledge that our dead are in a better world than this one where we can one day join them. I mean we can come to have an unshakable testimony of these truths, not a mere mouthing of principles."

Doyle was most sober as I met his eyes. "You mean, I take it, that faith and obedience must precede the miracle?" His voice seemed tinged with the slightest twinge of remorse.

"I am inevitably drawn to this conclusion," I said.

"Then," he said, "I fear you must regard me as irrevocably doomed." He attempted without much success to deliver this remark jovially.

"You, like many good people," I said, "may depart this earth without embracing the gospel. An all-merciful Father will permit us to accept it in the spirit world."

"There is no hell in Mormon doctrine?" Doyle asked.

"Not as the world has been taught," I said, "Perhaps perpetual regret we did not so live our lives as to attain a greater degree of glory, but no pain or suffering — no fire and brimstone."

Doyle nearly finished his drink in a long draught. "There is much to be said for any religion which teaches there is no hell. I was years overcoming that fear enough to break out of Catholicism."

"Only one of the kindly qualities that one should expect from a loving Father," I suggested.

We finished our drinks. I settled the bar chit with the waiter and we went to our respective suites to dress for dinner. I was not optimistic that Doyle was at all likely to accept my religious point of view, but it was comforting to know he would sooner or later, either in this life or, as was more likely, the next.

163

Journal Entry of Arthur Conan Doyle

Dated April 7, 1912 (London)

Jean and I lay awake until nearly dawn conversing about many things. We arrived home about midnight after our evening out with Sam and Jacques and May Futrelle. Futrelle proved to be amusing good company and his wife, who writes also, is not only beautiful and well informed, but articulate also. Many writers can't converse worth a farthing, but she has an amusing and concise way of expressing herself that makes her a genuine delight.

Jean hasn't a jealous bone in her body or she might have been a bit put out over the fun May and I were having in our conversation. Jacques took it well too, but May and I got on especially well and I will look forward to entertaining them again some time, hopefully soon.

But most of the night, after Jean and I retired was devoted to my telling her of how I feel about the conversations Sam and I have had since he returned.

It really has caused me considerable soul searching, these discussions with Sam, coming as they do right on the heels of Harlan Pierpoint's unfavorable treatment of me in his recently published biography.

Jean could see how troubled I was and proved again by her understanding remarks how wonderful a thing it was for me to win her as my mate.

"Sam, I am sure," she said, "desires only the best for you as he sees things. But Harlan betrayed your confidence in getting you to cooperate with him on his book and then ridiculing you."

I am sure she's right on both counts, but Harlan's comment that my interest in spiritualism is merely the ultimate manifestation of a materialistic outlook — an insistence that all things be verified by the senses — is only too close to what Sam is saying in a nicer, different way. But Harlan hopes to sell his book at my expense capitalizing on my celebrity. Sam at least is sincerely interested in the state of my soul.

"How are they at all alike?" she asked and I must say it required a bit of patience on my part not to be a little short with her, out of temper as I was, and I had to make allowances, for religion and metaphysics really are not her strong suit.

Neither Sam nor Harlan grew up as Roman Catholics, or they would know how the souls of little children are harrowed up by the threats of devils and hell-fire employed by the nuns and priests to coerce the unruly. And I was definitely one of the unruly.

Most assuredly I agree with the attitude reflected in W.T. Stead's comment to our fellow writer Sir Wm. Robertson Nicoll when he said: "It is shameful that a Christian journalist should refuse to study the only proof of Christianity that can be offered to the human mind." And Stead is a kindly and very unselfish son of a Congregational minister.

But have I really succumbed to a materialistic outlook? Yes, I love the things the wealth I have accumulated can buy, and I have justified this attitude as something the world has owed me for the squalor and deprivation of my childhood. But I have so thoroughly deluded myself in thinking myself to be otherworldly — to be, in a sense, an ascetic, a mystic? If this be true, I have most thoroughly been misled in my own evaluation of myself. Is our insistence that the truth of Christianity is verifiable by the senses, as spiritualism holds, the ultimate form of materialism as Pierpoint asserts?

I have stood forthrightly for the spirit of helping my fellow man. The enormous expenses I incurred defending and seeing to the acquittal of Gorman of the baseless charges brought against him of mutilating horses proves my willingness to do a good turn to others. I seek no honor or reward for such actions of which there have been many. But though I believe in righteous action, in the fatherhood of God and the brotherhood of man, still I have no faith in religion as such.

I have no doubt that the fatalism of the East leads to no place good for mankind. An Asiatic is not moved to do anything at all to help though a thousand a day perish of starvation before his very eyes.

And only Christianity espouses the action to assist one another the world must see in order to progress. But while logic dictates one must be true and the other false, why am I unconvinced?

And how can I believe so completely in the survival of the spirit after the death of the body with at best the tenuous proof I've seen in spiritualism? Does this not require an act of faith?

Why do I demand free will for myself and yet curse God for a chaotic world in which all selfishly seek their own free will even to steal and murder?

And why do I reject Sam's argument that there is both a God and a devil? Has the devil himself deceived me into thinking there is no devil?

I am reminded of the words of Descartes who, above all, spearheaded the challenge of the Enlightenment which brought on the downfall of Christianity: "I am supposing there exists a very powerful, and if I may so speak, malignant being, who employs all his powers and skill in deceiving me." If Descartes, the intellectual father of Spinoza, who was the father of Biblical Criticism, suspected he was misled by satan, how can I be so sure no such being exists?

At least Sam's refuge in Mormonism gives us one thing in common — a belief in eternal progression — although Sam is convinced that spiritualism is the devil's counterfeit of the true 'plan of salvation' as they term it.

My creed is as well defined as his and startlingly similar to it:
1. The Fatherhood of God,
2. The brotherhood of man,
3. The survival after death of personality,
4. Communion with the dead,
5. Personal responsibility,
6. Compensation and retribution, and
7. Eternal progression in a series of cycles or spheres to that highest sphere wherein Christ dwells.

But where we part most sharply is over the ages-old issue of knowledge versus faith. The Manichean heresy, the Gnostic tradition, of occult knowledge, only achieved by the initiates in a secret order, for that is what we believers in spiritualism are, opposing those whose faith leads them to a conviction of the truth.

For the very first time, someone, my good friend Sam, has brought to me a description of what faith is and how it works.

The witness of the Holy Spirit, he calls it, that the Plan of Salvation is true. And this witness only can come <u>after</u> our desire to acquire it and our having lived the commandments to prove that desire.

In all my years as a Catholic with all their prattling about faith, I never heard anything that even vaguely approached an answer to the question — What is faith and how does it work?

Now Sam gives a most concise and believable one, but in its simplicity lies an obstacle as great or greater than my past ignorance. For to release the lock and to be admitted through the door of faith I must sincerely desire to know the Gospel — Sam's — the Mormon Gospel — the Plan of Salvation is true. Is this not a hurdle as great or greater than any?

How do I acquire the desire to know its truth? This is the most troubling enigma of them all. And here I sit immobilized by my own lack of desire.

I am discovering as King Arthur, the man after whom I am named discovered, and as every man undoubtedly has learned from Adam to now that — "The war is with oneself." And who is the hero in the battle with oneself? Obviously, the spirit must triumph over the flesh. How real the comment of Jesus thus becomes: "The spirit is willing, but the flesh is weak."

The light of dawn had started to appear in the East before I stopped verbalizing my thoughts and Jean was making velvety little sounds the closest thing to a snore her ladylike nature permits, before I finally turned my thoughts toward sleep and quickly dozed off, leaving the serious thoughts which were so troubling to me to another day.

Journal Entry of Samuel Harper

Dated June 1912 (New York City)

Journal entry covering a meeting in London on April 7, 1912 with Sir Henry Rawlings.

"In those days we were all what would now be called amateur linguists but it was Sir Wm. Jones, while serving in India as a Judge," said Sir Henry, "who first recognized the affinity between Sanskrit and Latin and Greek. That was something of a bombshell, of course, but he also indicated his belief there were similarities between Greco-Latin and Indian mythology. Now that was more striking still."

I looked from Sir Henry's benign countenance to the vigorously burning logs in the fireplace in the oak-paneled study of his lovely home on Belgrave Square. "That touched off," I finally offered, "an argument that hasn't ended yet, did it not?"

"Quite," he smiled, "in fact, argument is a mild word for the uproar he occasioned. At the time a Sanskrit scholar Theodor Benfey, a German Jew himself, suggested that Jones might have gone a step further even to compare Sanskrit, Latin and Greek to Hebrew. A German philologist Friedrich von Adelung advanced the theory of an original common language for all of these, that began at the same time as the human race, in Kashmir where he placed the Biblical Garden of Eden."

"How did the matter become so intensely controversial?" I asked.

"An interesting question, of course, because scholars love to think of themselves as the soul of objectivity. Unfortunately, most of the disputants shed more heat than light, I fear." Sir Henry took a sip of his brandy and I of my soda and lemon.

"It was," he said, "another 30 years, about 1818, before a German philologist Franz Bopp proved the structural affinities and gave us a truly scientific verification of Jones' hypothesis. But it was not long before that Sanskrit pioneer Karl Wilhelm von Schlegel united the ideas of race and language and succeeded in galvanizing German youth with the idea of an Aryan race. There was no anti-semitism associated with the Aryan idea at the time. In fact, Schlegel married the daughter of Moses Mendelsohn, one of Europe's most distinguished Jews."

"Schlegel was no linguist," I asked, "or scientist was he?"

"Quite right," Sir Henry said, "he had studied Sanskrit, but he only united two ideas that probably, in our race-conscious era, would sooner or later have found their way together. Remember, the Scriptures were under attack and the Biblical origins in the minds of many, especially the Germans, were discredited. So people were free to speculate about such things. And any apparently scientific explanation could find a hearing and an enthusiastic following."

"It hasn't diminished has it?" I asked.

"No indeed," he responded, "and, of course, the Aryan myth of the Germans then became associated with the anti-semitism of most German intellectuals. But I'm a bit ahead of myself. 'Everything,' Schlegel declared, 'absolutely everything, is of Indian origin.' But that was totally unacceptable to Britons."

"I can imagine several dozen reasons," I said, smiling, "why that concept didn't sit well here."

"Of course," Sir Henry chuckled, "Believers, and there were many, that the British are Hebrews, that is, the Lost Ten Tribes, were certain Schlegel must be wrong. They never dreamed that the flow of Israelites from the Holy Land which had been under way a long time before either the Assyrian conquest of Samaria or the Babylonian conquest of Jerusalem, might have seen Israelites carrying Hebrew language and customs across India as far as China and the islands of the Pacific. It was, of course, possible the Aryan culture of India was of Hebrew origin but I'm not aware that anyone made such a suggestion. One reason this idea had little currency perhaps was because with the advent of those ideas advanced by geologist Sir Charles Lyell whose suggestion of long, totally undisturbed periods of a static geological state, even though we now know that no such period has existed, still it then was enough to give Darwin's theory of evolution which required this long period of stasis in which his primeval stew could brew the first cell, an intellectual climate in which it could be accepted. But Darwin it was whose theories led men to speculate that people of such early origins must have been too backward to have been able to travel so far. But more potent, I think," said my former guardian, "was that anti-semitism was so strong among all Europeans and Britons, that, confusing as they did the prototypical Jew and the Ten Lost Tribes, they were unable to accept the hated Jew as the origin of our 'glorious' race."

"Don't you think," I suggested, "that our colonial position in India, justified as it was by our belief in the superiority of our Christian culture to that of India also obscured the issue in British minds? People today are ignorant of the incredible turmoil that occurred in India when Britain outlawed the barbaric practices of slavery and suttee."

Sir Henry looked at me with the amused little twist of his moustached lips revealing his deep enjoyment of our discussion. I was happy to give him the opportunity to resume his role of teacher and father he had not experienced for so long.

"Without a doubt," he said, "Gladstone was only one of the more prominent Englishmen who rejected out of hand the Mother India concept. How could our backward Indian wards and we be sons of the same progenitors? It was too obviously impossible."

He took a sip of his brandy fingering the cuff link in his immaculate shirt cuffs, taking a piece of lint off his dinner jacket. "The German Orientalist Heinrich von Klaproth originated the term 'Indo-Europeans' which has continued in use to this day," Sir Henry said gazing pensively into the fire. "Ultimately," he said, 'linguistics, racial anthropology, anti-semitism and world politics became mixed into a witches' brew that was decidedly unscientific. It was — and is — for the most part pure speculation which has yet to be confirmed."

"It was," I suggested, "this unpalatable combination that kept me, I think, from giving more serious consideration to your desires for me to follow a career in archaeology."

Sir Henry showed me, by the way in which his eyes avoided mine, welling slightly with tears, that the hurt of my refusal was still present. "We must each," he said with a sigh and a long pause, "follow our personal lights."

"I thought my reasons at the time were sound," I said, "the choice was difficult because I loved working with you, but I had lost or really never found a conviction that the Scriptures were true. You recall the Higher Critics claimed, and we young people believed, that the Hebrews had not even possessed the ability to write, which cast the accuracy, even the authorship of the various books of the Bible under a cloud."

"You were very young," Sir Henry said. "We older people demanded proof for all the hypotheses of the Higher Critics, proof they were never able to produce. And finally, when archaeology had done its work, their speculations were proven wrong. Also we were proud Englishmen whose divine mission was to Christianize the world. We were not about to accept any casual postulation, especially when it so conveniently attacked British power all of which was justified by the Scriptural mandate we knew we possessed. We rejected all such claims by the Germans and their home-grown British lackeys believing it to be satanic. In fact, I so believe it to be still."

"I have no trouble believing it now myself," I offered. "And as you say, we know modern archaeology has proven the speculation of the Higher Critics to be false. Much thanks to you and your colleagues." He looked at me fondly, our eyes meeting, the only sound in the room the crackling fire and the ticking clock on the mantle.

"How interesting," he said, seemingly attempting to avoid what appeared to be looming as an emotional, perhaps even tearful exchange between us. "Tell me how this change came about."

"Two reasons, really," I responded. "We have known for a long time as you surely will concede, that while much of the Germanic languages can be found to originate in the Indo-European, still about a third of the words are regarded to be of unknown origin. I am now convinced that a linguist friend of mine, an American, has conclusively demonstrated that the origins of that one-third previously of unknown source is Hebrew. Further, he has demonstrated the changes took place within the time frame we know the Ten Lost Tribes were advancing into Europe from the area of their exile by the Assyrians in ancient Scythia."

"You feel then," Sir Henry interjected, "that your friend has demonstrated the Anglo-Saxons to be of Israel origin?"

"Let us say that, taken with the other indicia we have," I responded, "that this is now conclusive. Remember that the other evidence we possess was already powerful. This I should admit, is evidence I either didn't accept or was ignorant of when I was younger."

"What other evidence?" asked Sir Henry.

"British heraldry abounds with Israelite symbols, of course, and the Assyrian artifacts identify the Scythians as Israelites as you better than anyone alive can attest. Perhaps the most powerful evidence, by my lights," I responded, "is the longstanding conviction of the Anglo-Saxons themselves that they are Israel. The Puritans believed it though by Cromwell's time they were only a minority probably. In Charlemagne's time a majority didn't question it. Only a tiny minority now so believe, but their numbers are not important, since so many are ignorant of the facts."

"How," Sir Henry asked, "does the fact the Anglo-Saxons are Israelites alter your thinking?"

"Quite simply," I smiled as I answered, "because if we are able to identify Israel in the modern world we have irresistible proof that the Scriptures are true."

"I think I follow," my surrogate father said, "but are you saying that identifying the Israel people gives us a means of determining if the Biblical prophecies have indeed been fulfilled as to what would occur to Israel?"

"Precisely," I responded. "There can be little doubt in my mind that the prophecies have been fulfilled where, and only where, the Ango-Saxons are concerned."

"But Sam," Sir Henry asked, "why is it necessary to prove the Anglo-Saxon is Israel by linguistics or any other means? You need only read the Scriptures to know that."

"That is true, Sir Henry, only," I said, "if you have a conviction the Scriptures are divinely inspired to begin with such as you and my father possessed. As a young man when, for instance, you asked me to join your team, I had no such conviction. Time had to pass and I had to learn new things and experience new things."

"Surely," he observed, "it can't only be the accumulation of this kind of evidence that changed your mind, can it?"

"I'm afraid you're right," I admitted. "Once I thought only rationality could bring me to a religious conviction. I must either have a certain conviction of facts or no faith was possible."

"And that changed?" he asked.

"Yes and no," I answered. "Once I satisfied myself there was a rational basis to believe the Scriptures are the divinely inspired book you and father believed them to be, I still had a problem."

"A problem?" he inquired.

"A very big problem," I said. "If the Scriptures are true then no church can be true which does not profess as one of its central principles that the Israel of the Bible are to serve a pivotal role in the final unfolding of events. No church of which I was aware so held. In fact, all the churches of my acquaintance attempted to ignore it as though they found the idea of a Chosen People to be most embarassing. As I did when I was young."

"And embarassing it surely is," said Sir Henry.

"A hot potato the major creeds wish would go away," I said. "But then I discovered a creed that recognizes Israel's role in the evolution of God's plan and showed me how the concept of a Chosen People does not conflict with the idea of a supremely just God — which was my problem when I was young."

170

"They must certainly be grossly unpopular on that account," the old man observed.

"Not really," I rejoined, "they have not distorted chosen to mean elite or privileged, in fact, they make no point at all of the issue as far as non-members are concerned."

"What group can you be referring to?" Sir Henry asked.

"It is the Mormons," I said.

"You've become a Mormon?" he asked, an amazed expression on his countenance.

"I am about to," I submitted.

"The Mormons believe the Anglo-Saxon to be Israel?" he asked.

"Yes, though they make no fetish of it," I responded, "one of their Articles of Faith proclaims their expectation of the gathering of Israel. Also each member can obtain a blessing in which he will be advised from which of the twelve tribes his heritage descends."

"I've never known much of this sect," he conceded.

"Nor I," I concurred, "until I was forced to acquaint myself with their beliefs in connection with a murder case I worked on."

Sir Henry looked at me with a fatherly smile upon his face. "I can see," he said, "that much good has come of your choice of a profession though I seriously doubted it ever would."

"I'm happy you understand," I said.

"I'm happy for you," said Sir Henry shaking my hand and toasting me with his brandy snifter.

I gestured my thanks for his sentiments with my glass.

Later that evening as we parted at the front door of his Georgian mansion I looked at him smiling, wondering when next we might see each other, in this life or the next? "Incidently," I said, "Adelung was right according to Joseph Smith the Mormon prophet."

Sir Henry said quizzically, "You mean the Adamic language is the true root stock?"

"Exactly," I smiled.

"There is something more to your new religion than I would have guessed," he observed, "it will bear some looking into." He shook my hand as we made our farewells. "Incidently," he said, "are you aware that you travel on the Titanic in the august company of one of the finest works to come out of ancient Persia?"

"You mean," I asked, "the precious copy of THE RUBAIYAT they're shipping to New York?"

"None other," said Sir Henry, "much wealth there will be in that company, but few things more precious by scholarly standards or, I dare say, those of the materialistic-minded."

It was a clear and lovely night in Mayfair as we parted.

I wondered as I returned afoot to my room at the club, enjoying a lovely spring evening stroll through St. James, when next Sir Henry and I might meet.

Excerpt from Journal of Samuel Harper

Dated April 20, 1912

(Excerpt from journal in which Samuel Harper recorded his visit to the Titanic with Arthur Conan Doyle April 8, 1912, prior to the ship's maiden voyage.)

"Do you recall how, as boys, we used to enrage the women of the neighborhood dancing with their dresses which froze on the clothesline in the cold winter wind?" Doyle asked his rhetorical question with tears of mirth rolling down his face.

"You may have done in Edinburgh," I said, "but by the time you were of an age to be pulling your boyhood pranks, I was camping out at some dig or other in the Levant with Sir Henry. Mine was not a typical British boyhood."

"Quite so," agreed the huge bewhiskered walrus Doyle, "who else do I know who read Sanskrit at age ten."

"Eight," I corrected.

"Yes, eight," he conceded, drinking his champagne. "I think it was Sir Henry's influence, reverential as he was toward the Scriptures that was decisive in your coming to a religion like Mormonism which reveres the Scriptures."

"Perhaps so," I allowed, "but as a young man I would have laughed at you had you predicted I would one day embrace a creed so Scripture-oriented and so uncompromising. Remember we knew Darwin had unseated the Bible for all time."

"I believe it yet," said Doyle. He surveyed my suite on the starboard side of B Deck in the most luxurious section of the Titanic's first class.

"Haven't we come a long way from the trying times of our youth?" he said, waving his champagne glass over this opulence.

"I begin to wonder how far really," I said. "The journey back to our beginnings seems both long and short. When other boys were primping in front of their mirrors, worrying if that pimple would burst before Saturday so as not to be too embarassing on their date with true love, I was black as a native and blonde as a Viking from the searing sun and winds of Persia. I knew with what extraordinary effort and devotion we were wrenching the secrets of the past from the face of the earth in those God-forsaken places. And our omnipresent guide was Sir Henry and his lodestone, the Bible."

Doyle and I had obtained permission from Bruce Ismay, Managing Director of the White Star Line and a dear friend of ours to board the ship a day early to bring to my suite the last of my secret files which Doyle had graciously offered to store for me in the haste of my original departure. Five innocuous looking large boxes were now locked into the armoire in my suite.

"Ismay will be traveling with you," Doyle said, "to comfort the princes of industry traveling on Titanic's maiden voyage as will Stead and a number of other friends of ours."

"So I understand," I responded, "I shall be sure to give Ismay your regards and my thanks."

"Please do so," said Doyle, "it was kind of him to accommodate us, though I fear your taking the last of your files means you've made up your mind not to return to Blighty."

"I shall spend protracted periods here," I said. "I've made application to enter Leslie at Mrs. Finch's school in the fall. But I fear I am now both a man without a country and a citizen of two. My business is too lucrative to abandon, even if I wished to do so which I don't, and yet it won't run itself. Besides — truth be known — England, with its highly structured social mores no longer fits me. I never did much hold for the social amenities. In America you can ignore stuffy convention if you choose to. I've grown to like that."

"The breezy way of Americans is contagious," said Doyle, "I've been most pleased each time I've toured the U.S. But I've never wanted to live there."

"You've never been forced to stay long enough to get used to it," I said. "It takes a while."

"Quite so," agreed Doyle. "Every new place takes getting used to. It's making your mind up that you must do it. I didn't have to stay, but you did."

"You've got it right," I said, "I knew I had to stay. I had to make the best of it and the best of America is very good. Strangely — I feel about re-entering the married state a bit the way I did leaving for America."

"At our age," Doyle smiled an understanding smile, "marriage is not a panacea, but a perilous voyage, which we would have known the first time if we were smarter."

I quietly laughed in agreement. "I don't think I would have the slightest problem with marriage alone. But involving as this marriage does a new religion — well that compounds the problem. It is a genuine challenge. Rather like the rites of passage of the Gnostics*. For the first time things seem to make perfect sense, spiritually speaking, but not one whit easier, nonetheless."

Doyle looked perplexed. "I am afraid you lost me at the last turn."

"Let's see if I can clarify my thinking for myself as well as you." I said. "Let's take a simple analogy. You now know that salvation requires you to lift three hundred pounds. The outlines of the job are fixed and clear. But an enormous amount of self-discipline and application will be required even though you have defined with absolute precision what your goal is."

"The goal definition of which you speak," Doyle replied pensively, "pre-supposes a conviction of the truth of one's beliefs approaching the dogmatic." This last was said warily, very low-keyed so as not to offend.

"The adjective 'dogmatic' is meaningful to ex-Roman Catholics," I said, also wishing to avoid offense. "It has little or no meaning to Mormons. This is a creed in which people either gain their own testimony of its truth or not. Once done, all things are either given freely by way of compliance, or not at all."

"And have you," Doyle asked, "a conviction of that truth?"

"I do — I have known of its truth almost from the first time I became fully aware of certain points," I said, "though I have temporized because compliance is, to say the least, a gross inconvenience."

*Ancient heretics whose rites involve degrees of special, occult knowledge and trial.

"You sound very mysterious," said Doyle.

"I don't mean to," I replied, "But conversion has not been easy. Nor is it easy to tell you concisely the precise steps in my coming to accept it."

"I have all the time in the world," the great Celt smiled.

"You may regret that invitation." I laughed, taking the champagne bottle out of the ice bucket to refill his glass. He lifted his glass in my direction by way of a gesture of thanks. I toasted him in return with my glass of soda.

"I have had to search my soul for reasons why, in spite of my great yearning to marry Cornelia, for I am sure our life together will be pleasant, I have felt so reluctant to abandon my petty vices — my pipe, coffee and liquor. Yes, I enjoy them." I said, "but not to the point they could reasonably be weighed in the balance with my desire to take Cornelia to wife."

"You fascinate me," Doyle complimented.

"It was not until I became fully acquainted with the facts of the Fenster case that I understood the problem I was facing and how cowardly I've been in the past in dealing with this problem, to the hurt of some people I deeply love," I said.

"That will be Cornelia?" he asked.

"Not at all — Sir Henry," I said.

"I am hopelessly lost." Doyle raised his hands in the air in a gesture of helplessness.

"It will be clear in but a moment," I said. "When the Fenster case revealed to me that Mormons believe in the gathering of the Tribes of Israel, I was face to face with an issue I had confronted as a young man — the implications of which were too unpleasant for me to handle."

"That seems a bit overly dramatic," my friend said. "Don't you overstate a bit."

"Not a bit," I countered. "My father and Sir Henry and other precious souls too numerous to mention knew what it meant to the Anglo-Saxon and to the whole world if Israel could be indentified among the modern nations."

"You left out a piece," said Doyle. "Do you mean that Mormons believe the Anglo-Saxon to be Israel in the modern world?"

"Sorry to leave you at sea," I apologized. "Quite right. Is my point becoming clear?"

"Not yet," Doyle responded, "but I'm getting close I think. You mean that if the Anglo-Saxon is Israel, the Mormons are alone among modern churches in so believing?"

"True enough," I said, "but not only that. They have embraced the belief upon which all other churches can be said to have apostasized. The very point I had resolved years ago a church must embrace to be the true church; one without which I could not accept it as true. Of course, I now came to realize I was engaged in self-deception — believing no such church existed I had employed the point to avoid a commitment. Now I was faced with having to commit however reluctantly since I have long regarded this point as the primary doctrinal point the true church must embrace."

"Mighty strong language, podner," said my friend imitating a Western drawl.

"But true nonetheless," I insisted. "The entire eighteenth and nineteenth centuries were nothing if not a battle between two intellectual groups — one insisting the Scriptures are true and that they will be literally fulfilled. And those who debunked them as mere folk myths."

"You are better able to make such a statement than I," he replied.

"And that is why we have trod different pathways in search of religious truth." I suggested.

"Perhaps," he conceded, "but that seems a poor reason, standing alone, to join so demanding a creed."

"I haven't made the point clear," I responded. "If we are able to identify Israel in the modern world, we then have a means of proving if the Scriptures are a divine document."

"How so?" he asked, "here you must take my hand and proceed very slowly. Unlike you I have little understanding of the Bible really."

"That's your Catholic background," I suggested, "The Bible is the story of the origins of Israel, where the family originated and where it is to end up. And of Israel's or Jacob's covenant to be a Holy Priesthood unto Jehovah. The prophets told all that had befallen and would befall this people. If you once identify Israel in the modern world you can ascertain if those prophecies have been fulfilled."

"You are saying then that the Anglo-Saxons fulfill these prophecies?" Doyle asked.

"Without question," I responded.

"But what's so new about that?" Doyle queried. "For centuries the world has listened to the arguments pro and con on that subject. That is, until the Christian churches, as you complain so vociferously, abandoned the fight and tacitly agreed among themselves to deemphasize that aspect of Holy Writ."

"The General Benson and Stone of Scone case, right?" I asked.

"I get your point," Doyle conceded, "but there's a gap in your logic."

"What's that?" I asked.

"There is no proof, in the secular sense, that the Anglo-Saxons are Israel," he sagaciously observed, "thus we are back to square one, with every man having his own opinion or none whatever on the topic."

"Not entirely true, but let's delay taking up the question of proof. Enter Joseph Smith," I said, "to show us that each Mormon can know from which of the twelve tribes he descends in the form of what Mormons call a patriarchal blessing."

"But that's no proof," Doyle said, "to any non-Mormon."

"True enough," I said, "but perhaps to Sir Henry and surely to my father it would be enough. They knew the Scriptures to be true and it followed the Anglo-Saxon must be Israel because they alone fulfill the prophecies. And I have finally decided from my own researches that they were right. I arrived at my conclusions differently and independently and only after years of effort. They first believed the Scriptures to be true, and were confirmed in this opinion by all they discovered in their archaeological pursuits. I came to this result after my own analysis of similarities between the Germanic languages and Hebrew. But having decided we are Israel, it followed in my mind, that

175

no church which ignored our Israel identity could be true. But when I was young, at the time Sir Henry attempted to influence me to join him and make archaeology my career, I could not handle the dichotomy with which he so casually lived. I didn't concede that the British are Israel, but I knew he did and yet he ignored, I felt, the implications such a belief required."

"But aren't you judging him and, in a sense, your father who shared his belief?" Doyle asked.

"Not now," I said, "but surely did then — a callow youth not worthy to carry their satchel of tools."

"You are now sitting in judgment on yourself," he said, "once again too harshly."

"You may be right," I said, "and I've explained to Sir Henry how I felt. Since Mormons know they will be reunited with their dead, I should not let my regrets about my father oppress me. I have not progressed enough spiritually to be free entirely of such feelings."

"Perhaps you will," Doyle consoled, "but let's get back to Israel in the modern world."

"To me, this is the key issue of the ages," I said, "all the problems of mankind pale into insignificance by comparison."

"If I follow you, you are averring," Doyle looked at me for confirmation, "that an issue the world has ridiculed into non-existence is about to take center stage in world events to the consternation of all."

"If Balfour has his way it surely will," I said.

"He has a way of getting his way," Doyle offered.

"It shall occur or not as some power greater than ours decides," I said, "but I must do what my reason tells me is necessary."

"I agree, but I still am in the dark about some points," Doyle said.

"Such as?" I asked.

"First, do you abandon your usually cautious approach toward evidence?" Doyle asked, "in asserting that you are certain the Anglo-Saxon is Israel?"

"It will be difficult for you to judge for yourself," I said, "because you have to be a linguist to understand. But I begin poorly. Let me back up a step. Most of those you encounter who have written anything in support of the hypothesis that the Anglo-Saxon peoples embrace modern Israel, have sought their evidence from such sources as the Israelite symbols in the heraldry of the Anglo-Saxon which simply abound, or from such artifacts as the Hebrew tombstones in the Crimea. And these support such a conclusion but don't prove it. Sharon Turner in his HISTORY OF THE ANGLO-SAXONS sought out the ancient records of our forefathers and concluded what has been amply demonstrated since Turner's time, that our forebears were called Scythians. The records of the ancient Assyrians confirm that the Scythians and Israel were the same people but the evidence has been so sparse as to seem to be much less than irresistible. I know that I have driven more than one believer in the British-Israel hypothesis to distraction when I insisted his case wouldn't stand up in a courtroom. But such was my conviction for many years, as it was at the time I so gravely injured Sir Henry's feelings when I refused his offer to train me in his footsteps."

"But you speak," said Doyle, "as though you now possess what you regard as conclusive evidence."

"Yes I think such proof is now possible. I also think," I said, "that even the proof that exists without my more recent discoveries is more than that for which I've seen any number of men hung, contrary to my clever assertions as a young man. Even at the time I refused to join Sir Henry's team I think I may really have believed the evidence, but couldn't accept it — I must have, the principal complaint I held against his generation was that they believed the Scriptures but ignored the special role of the white man in the Biblical schema. And that role I felt to be inconsistent with what could be the work of a truly just God. I didn't believe infinite justice would permit a Chosen People which I regarded as obviously unjust to all other races."

"This is a most complicated thing," Doyle said in such a way it was clear I hadn't explained much.

"Let me take a new approach," I said, "Scholars for over a century have been unable to establish the origins of about one-third of the words in German which are agreed not to be of the same Indo-European derivation as the rest. Also certain changes known to have taken place in German in the pre-Christian era have been a mystery. My researches have uncovered the efforts of a Mormon linguist who has demonstrated that these changes are directly related to an influx of Hebrew speaking people into Europe. The changes began at the same approximate time we know the Israelites deported by the Assyrians to the Caucasus were advancing into Europe."

"In other words," Doyle asked, "you regard this additional evidence as conclusive proof of the Israelitish origin of the Anglo-Saxon?"

"The scales were already heavily tilted in that direction," I responded, "by the heraldic evidence, the research in the ancient manuscripts best exemplified by the works of Turner and the thousands of facts indicating the ancient belief existed among the Anglo-Saxons themselves of their Israelitish origin. None of that was of such a nature as to satisfy the scientific community nor me as a young man. But this evidence will, I think conclusively establish the proposition."

"I doubt any of this will have much meaning for the layman." Doyle ventured.

"Ideas rule the world. Contrary to what heroes and politicians may believe. Sooner or later," I said, "all human actions are framed by the ideation of scholars."

"I see now," commented Doyle, "why you lament Balfour's lack of ideas."

"I am too harsh in saying he has no ideas," I said. "He merely received the ideas of his era and did his best to manipulate them. The problem is those ideas are about to be unseated."

"But it will take years," Doyle said, "for anything as esoteric and complicated as this to become of general understanding."

"Tom Huxley said 'It is the customary fate of new truth to begin as heresies and end as superstition.' but however long it takes," I responded, "truth will out. And if Balfour has his way, it will happen much sooner by pressure of the warfare it will precipitate to displace the Palestinians to make way for Eastern Jewry."

"A bloody truth it well might be," Doyle said.

We finished our drinks, a decidedly somber mood prevailing, and headed for the gangplank where we had to thread our way through heavy traffic of seamen bringing provisions aboard the Titanic from the pier. We finally were able to flag a cab for the not inconsiderable ride back to London from South-ampton. I was relieved my files were safely aboard, and not likely to be lost in the bustle at dockside tomorrow.

Excerpt from Journal of Samuel Harper
Dated June 1912

(Transcribed from shorthand notes made in London and mailed to New York prior to his departure from England – April 9, 1912)

"How's your backhand Arthur?" I asked by way of reviving a very old tennis joke between us. In truth, the Earl of Balfour hasn't a shot worthy of the name, but that's the joke, and he takes it very well when I kid him about it.

"Nothing less than superb," he responded smiling and looking at me with a mirthful twinkle in his eye that says he doesn't give a damn for the opinion of any man about his poor tennis or anything else. "Doyle told me of your coming visit. Are you staying at your usual digs at the Diogenes Club?"

"As usual — when I return to Blighty," I responded, "Doyle and I had dinner together last evening. Your name was taken in vain once or twice."

"I dare say," he smiled, "how have you enjoyed your visit thus far? Does your future hold any plans to return your base of operations to Blighty as you so irreverently term our fair islands?"

"I confess to being in something of a quandary on the point," I responded, "His Majesty's invitation to return, which Doyle was kind enough to convey, opens a pleasant prospect and a tempting one. But, realistically, it poses some practical difficulties."

"Such as?" he asked with what seemed like genuine sincerety though, knowing him as I do, I expected he probably was planning to think of something else during my response.

"First is the fact I have a lucrative business in New York that demands my presence," I said, somewhat impressed at the fact he seemed genuinely to pay attention to my answer. "Second, I am about to re-marry and to an American who might or might not approve."

"Congratulations are certainly in order," he said, reaching for the velvet covered cord next to his desk that serves to summon his butler. In a moment this venerable institution who for unnumbered years has been in service at 4 Carleton Gardens, Balfour's sumptuous Mayfair residence in London's fasionable West End made his appearance, tea tray in hand and proceeded to serve us.

"How are you Harlow?" I asked, "it's been a long time."

"Indeed it has sir — I'm fine thank you," he rejoined mildly, "I trust you're well."

, And so we passed the first half hour of our visit almost as though there was little of consequence to be covered. But when our tea was finished and the butler had collected his tray and departed, Arthur turned to me and handed me a piece of paper from the pocket of his jacket. It proved to be a message from the Chief Inspector of Scotland Yard as follows:

HAVE RECEIVED ADVICE IN THE FORM OF A DIPLOMATIC CIPHER THAT THE NEW YORK CONSULATE HAS BEEN NOTIFIED BY THE CHIEF OF POLICE OF THAT CITY THAT

THEY HAVE APPREHENDED A TURKISH TERRORIST WHO HAS CONFESSED TO THE MURDER OF ISAAC FENSTER, WEALTHY WALL STREET BANKER, UNDER INTENSIVE INTERROGATION HE HAS REVEALED THAT FENSTER WAS KILLED AS PART OF A PLAN BY PERSONS ASSUMED TO BE PAID AGENTS OF THE GERMAN GOVERNMENT. FENSTER APPARENTLY UNCOVERED A PLOT TO KILL THE EARL OF BALFOUR TO ABORT EFFORTS BY BALFOUR TO MOBILIZE THE POWER OF THE BRITISH CROWN BEHIND THE MOVE TO CREATE A JEWISH HOMELAND IN PALESTINE. ADVISE ALL STEPS NECESSARY TO PROTECT BALFOUR.

I looked up from reading this message into the cool eyes of this man who earned the name "Bloody Balfour" as Minister for Ireland during the tenure as Prime Minister of his uncle the Marquess of Salisbury. Salisbury, who was also Prime Minister during the Ripper slayings, and who certainly was privy to all the facts related to that case, in appointing Balfour had probably caused him to become the subject of more scorn and hatred than any man before or since. As such his life had been threatened dozens of times. Such threats had come to have little meaning for him, and as a man who despises adulation, while appearing to crave it, he could scarcely care less that some unnamed parties might be seeking his life or that they disagreed with his policies.

His approach to the problem was direct. "Tell me," he said, "about Isaac Fenster."

"He was," I responded, "one of the most wealthy and powerful men on Wall Street, the son of Jacob Fenster who was the lead underwriter in the American financing of Japanese bond offerings and is cordially despised by the Russians as a consequence. An anti-Zionist, he has actively opposed the idea of a Jewish homeland on somewhat different grounds than other assimilated Jews. He was killed by slashing in a simulation of the Masonic ritual, the throat, breast and belly being cut from left to right, precisely as was done in the Ripper slayings. I have been involved in the case since its inception, and, while many had motives to kill Fenster, I cannot determine any on the part of the Masons." I finished these remarks and awaited his comments.

Balfour looked out the window into his lovely garden before saying absent mindedly, "Some chaps will undertake anything if asked to do so by the right people. We found that out. We thought Gull would have the whores certified insane and locked up. But he took it upon himself to execute the poor bitches." Then turning back to me and to the present he said, "Someone may have wished to blame the Masons and so followed the ritual. Tell me why Fenster opposed the idea of a Palestinian homeland for Jewry."

I mustered my thoughts as I pondered how to begin. "He was a Jew who converted to Mormonism. He was a good friend of J.B. Bury and knew of the Khazar make-up of Eastern Jewry. And he believed the Khazars who are only converts to Judaism have no historical claim to the Holy Land. Further, while he believed in prophecy and the fulfillment of the prediction of Israel's ultimate return to the Holy Land, since he was convinced the Khazar-Jews who would go to Palestine, none of the assimilated Jews desiring to do so, would only be going to their death, since they have no valid claim to the area, he opposed the ideas of the Zionists vigorously. He died, I might add, with your name on his lips."

"Did he now?" Balfour asked.

"I was present," I said, "as he breathed his last. 'Balfour will die — if you don't warn him' were his last words. I can only conclude he discovered the plot to which the New York Police refer in the diplomatic cipher you just showed me."

"Do you recall," Balfour asked, "that the Ripper slayings all followed the Masonic ritual?"

"Of course," I responded, wondering to myself if he could think that I was ignorant of the fact both Balfour and his uncle the Marquess of Salisbury were Masonic members themselves, "you know the circumstances surrounding my exile. No one knows more about those killings than I."

"Quite so," he said, "You will recall then that those responsible for the slayings attempted to blame the Jews. Remember that close to the scene of one of the slayings the inscription was found: 'The Juwes are the men who will not be blamed for nothing.' I believe the only reason Fenster was slain in a simulated appearance of a Masonic ritual probably was to attempt to blame the Masons just as the Masons, you and I know, who committed the Ripper slayings attempted to blame the Jews. Be all that as it may," he concluded, "Fenster died for reasons more important than the fact he unearthed a German plot to kill me."

"I am fascinated — please proceed," I said.

"What I say must, of necessity, go no further," he cautioned.

"I fully understand," I said in agreement.

"The Germans in killing Fenster and in attempting to kill me," he said, his voice several levels of volume softer to add emphasis and seriousness to his words, "are merely sending a signal to his Majesty's government that the policy of a Jewish homeland in Palestine is regarded by the Germans as cause for the utmost concern, even war."

"Can be no doubt of that," I agreed, "but they cannot believe even killing you would alter basic British policy — or could they be so naive as to think you alone support that policy regarding the Jews and that your removal would bring about any change?"

"Anti-semitism," said the former Prime Minister, "is more virulent in Germany than here and Lord knows it is not negligible here. They too seek to solidify the masses behind their pre-determined intention to go to war with us. Even I, who am most identified with this project have lost no love for the Jews. The King himself shoved the old patriarch of the Sassoon family down the stairs when that venerable Jew attempted to touch, however gently, the Royal person, an act not believed by anyone to be entirely motivated by Royal pride."

"Have you read Bury's book," I asked, "as Doyle mentioned to me he suggested?"

"Of course not," he responded, a disdainful expression and one of mild amusement at my naivete on his countenance. "The only reality worthy of consideration is the belief of the British people that the Jews are Israel and that in adopting a policy to repatriate the Jews to the Holy Land they believe we fulfill the Scriptural prophecies."

"But you know," I rejoined, "as does all the world, that Turkey, the sick man of Europe, must fall. We are bound to get our share when that happens. Why not claim our portion as conquerors alone with no other justification?"

"Not so fast," he cautioned, "a major war will result if we attempt to dismember that sick and tottering Ottoman Empire. That's why Fenster died and why they threaten me. Germany is warning us that a move to take Turkish territory anywhere will mean total war. So, in a sense, if we want Turkish territory in the eastern Mediterranean to protect Suez, we must be prepared to fight a major war."

"But," I asked, "is such a war not inevitable? Isn't it really only a matter of when we decide to fight Germany and her allies who surely will include the Turks?"

"You have it right," he said, "Germany must either be stopped or she will dominate the civilized world. Technologically she has outstripped us already. All the nations of Europe, including Germany, have bankrupted themselves building their war potential. And politicians will prefer war to admitting they have bankrupted their peoples. So it behooves us to make sure we are not on the losing side, for only the winner can recoup his losses through reparations."

"Can we really hope to win such a war," I asked, "in the traditional sense? Modern weaponry makes a mockery of the notion that anyone can win."

"The public don't know that," Balfour replied, "and we must deal with the reality of their understanding. Rapid fire weaponry, heavy artillery, tanks and aircraft have totally altered the consequences of war. Europe can be utterly destroyed in a prolonged war — and though I would hope it might be a short war, we must be prepared for a long one."

"You still have not made a cogent case for your policy," I said, "toward a Jewish homeland."

"I have, but you haven't thought enough about the realities," he said, "of how modern nations wage and finance war."

"If we are, indeed, bankrupt," I suggested, "I don't see how we can afford to go to war at all."

"Now you're on the right track," Balfour commented cryptically, lying back in his comfortable chair in the languid pose only he can assume.

"So what you are saying, if I read you rightly," I spoke my thoughts aloud, "is that creation of a Jewish homeland is one of the conditions upon which we shall be able to finance the war against Germany?"

"You said that," he replied, "I have no comment. But let's say you're nearly at a point of complete understanding. No one in his right mind, however, would bet on our chances to win a war with the powers aligned as they surely will be — England, France and Russia against Germany, Austria and Turkey. That would have to end in stalemate. So make your own guess as to the remaining condition to be fulfilled before we can be assured of the aid of the bankers who, as you well know, never bet on anything but a sure thing?"

"That will be," I responded my heart filled with dismay, "that my adopted country must be committed to wage war at Britain's side."

"Rest assured we have such a commitment no matter how the next American election turns out — Knowledge maketh a bloody entrance, does it not?" Balfour remarked.

"So, in truth," I offered, "your beliefs, one way or the other, about the Jews are irrelevant."

"True," he smiled, "how else could an old anti-semite like me be chosen for the job?"

"I see," was my dispirited reply, "But why," I asked, "would we agree to fight at Russia's side, she being the nation most hated by the Jews."

"Remember," he said slyly, "Russia is the only major nation which has not permitted the creation of a central bank in private hands. I suspect her days as a major power are numbered unless things in Russia change radically and quickly. Jacob Fenster himself warned the Czar when he financed Japan in her war against Russia."

"International finance pursues its aims," I offered, "disguised as the fulfillment of prophecy."

"Something like that," Balfour responded, "but would you have us preside over the dissolution of the British Empire? We cannot let Germany establish hegemony over the world."

"Hmmmm," I responded non-committally.

"I will, of course, deny all of this," the Earl of Balfour said only half smiling, "if you repeat it and," his face turning serious, "I would be careful if I were you, as to your personal safety."

I took my leave of Balfour shortly thereafter, hailing a cab for the journey back to my club. As I pondered our conversation, I realized that his amazing frankness in disclosing all that had been revealed to me could, indeed, must, be construed as an indication of how dangerous and important the knowledge was for which Isaac Fenster died which I now possessed, perhaps to my peril.

Upon my return to the Club, the doorman handed me a note as I entered, advising me that two visitors awaited my return in the dark oak-paneled Drawing Room. I asked their names.

"A Mr. Clawson and a Mrs. Corbett, Mr. Harper," he responded.

I went directly there, but a short distance from the lobby, the doorman at my elbow, to point out these visitors to me as their names were utterly unknown to me. Gesturing in the direction of the (only) two people in the great chamber, the doorman withdrew. I walked toward these two people who sat next to the great Norman fireplace where brisk flames dispelled the chill of the room. They arose as I approached, the man tall, dark-haired though greying at the temples, perhaps 65 years old with a hardy moustache and beard; the woman dark-haired about thirty, trim and quite attractive. They smiled in a friendly fashion.

"I am Rudger Clawson, Mr. Harper and this is Mrs. Corbett," said he, "we bring you the greetings of Joseph Benham whom you will probably remember, a friend of Mrs. St. James in New York."

"I do indeed remember," I replied, "and to what fortunate circumstance do I owe the pleasure of this surprise visit?" I asked.

"Mr. Benham sent me a cable advising me of your visit and of your plan to return to America on the Titanic," he replied, "I am here to offer you my services, should you desire them and to make a request."

"I shall demur for the moment on the kind offer of your services," I said, "but pray tell what request can I possibly grant?"

"No great difficulty, I hope," he smiled. "I am hoping you can occasionally look in on Mrs. Corbett who is also ticketed on the Titanic. She will be on C Deck and she is traveling alone. Mr. Benham speaks highly of you — I hope you might consider acting as, shall we say, a shepherd to see her home to America safely, to her husband and three children."

"I should be delighted to render whatever simple services I might," I answered, turning my eyes from Mr. Clawson to Mrs. Corbett. "Where is your home Mrs. Corbett and what brings you to London?"

She smiled most attractively and said, "Provo, Utah is home and I have been studying obstetrics at Charing Cross Hospital. I am returning to my family as soon as we dock in New York."

"You have quite a long train trip," I suggested, "even after your ocean journey."

"That's true," she agreed, "and I have been away from my family so long, the trip can't pass fast enough even though I love to travel whether by boat, train or whatever."

"Consider me at your service," I said, "such as my humble abilities permit."

"You're very kind," Mr. Clawson said, as Mrs. Corbett smiled by way of ratifying my new role as her informal protector.

"Mr. Benham wasn't wrong about you," said Mr. Clawson, "you are very kind to help."

"Not at all," I said somewhat embarassed. Then to avoid further compliments, "Tell me what brings you to England Elder Clawson?"

"Mr. Clawson is an Apostle," said Mrs. Corbett, "and is in charge of the church's missionary efforts in Europe, based in Liverpool."

"Did Brother Benham tell you," I asked, "that I am investigating the Church?"

"Yes he did," said Mr. Clawson, "and I sincerely hope you will receive a witness of the Holy Spirit that the gospel is true."

"That I have already," I commented. "I have received the witness of the Holy Spirit that the Book of Mormon is true. But now I have a request to make of you."

"Anything I have it in my power to grant," said Elder Clawson.

"I wish to have you exercise your Priesthood power to tell me if I should be baptized and confirmed immediately or wait until I return to New York."

A strange expression danced across his features and was gone as rapidly as it came.

"Let me ponder the question," he said, "and I shall give you a response presently."

"Do I recall correctly," he asked, "that you are engaged to marry Sister St. James?"

"That's approximately true," I laughed, slightly embarassed, "though we have not yet formalized that arrangement. I plan to do so immediately upon my return to New York."

There returned to his features that fleeting expression of strangeness I knew not how to interpret. I waited for his comment which was slow coming. Finally, he looked at me directly.

"Brother Harper," he said, "I feel very strongly that you should be baptized and confirmed before your departure and the sooner the better."

Astonished by the urgency implicit in his reply, I hesitated to respond, but immediately felt peaceful about the decision to proceed at once.

"When do you return to Liverpool?" I asked.

"I am scheduled on a train at 10 p.m. this evening," he said, "When does your schedule allow you the time?" he asked.

"They have a pool here in the Club," I said, "if you can trouble yourself right now."

And thus it was, to the astonishment of several bathers in the swimming pool of the Diogenes Club, to my considerable embarassment, and while Irene Corbett waited in the Drawing Room (where first I concluded there must be faith in a truly just God's plan) that Apostle Rudger Clawson performed my baptism and confirmation.

After having received these ordinances I felt much closer to my beloved and at peace with the most serious undertaking of my life. I saw Elder Clawson and Mrs. Corbett to the lobby where I arranged to pick her up at her hotel the day of our departure to take her to the ship at Southampton.

Elder Clawson turned toward the door, about to leave. Then he paused and turned back to face me. "I hear you and Mrs. Corbett will be traveling in the company of a man who has rendered singularly important service to the work of the L.D.S. Church here in England."

"Who will that be?" I inquired.

"W.T. Stead," he responded to my amazement.

"A very old friend," I said, then asked, "how did he render this great service?"

"A while back," Elder Clawson responded, "a great hue was raised here in the sensational press with its objective to have legislation enacted by Parliament to prohibit our missionary effort here, charging we were inducing young girls to leave England for Utah to become polygamous wives."

"And Stead intervened?" I asked.

"Yes, he wrote a letter to the London Daily Express which was published just a year ago," Clawson replied, "which shamed the clergymen leading the movement into abandoning their agitation. And his great reputation brought into action the public's desire for fair play to our great advantage. Mr. Stead has been a good friend to God's work here. In fact, without his aid the work could have received an incalculably bad reversal for years."

185

"You have given me much to think about," I said as I finally bid them goodbye.

I returned to the Drawing Room long enough to write Cornelia a letter giving her the good news of my formal membership in the Church which I requested the doorman to post for me. Then I retired feeling at peace with myself and my decision. I slept soundly and awoke early thinking of my future and of the vast changes under way in my life.

It was with feelings of both consternation and a strange sense of detachment that I read the copy of the Times left outside my room at the club. A news item had great meaning for me and for Doyle whom I phoned at once. The drowsiness in his voice was dispelled instantaneously at what he heard. "BALFOUR ESCAPES DEATH AS UNKNOWN ASSAILANT SLAIN BY SCOTLAND YARD," I said, reading the headline.

"Precisely what we expected," said Doyle, "and for once, Balfour took another's advice and, just incidentally, saved his own life."

"An interesting point to all this," I said, "is that, according to the newspaper report, the Turks did not use either a German or a middle-easterner. About what you'd expect since they would wish to conceal the true background of the attack. Apparently the gunman broke into Balfour's study having gained access from the garden. The man assigned by Scotland Yard to protect Balfour intercepted him, but only just."

But it was Doyle's turn to surprise. "You will be interested to know," he said, "that my sources tell me of an important event disclosed in the diplomatic cipher received from New York yesterday by cable."

"What would that be?" I asked.

"It is reported," Doyle said, his voice lowered conspiratorially, "that Michael Redwood died in a fall from his Wall Street office."

"My word!" was my surprised and not too original response, "Do you suppose he was pushed?"

"I fear we'll never know," Doyle responded pensively, "but it looks suspiciously to me as though the Germans are attempting to tidy up the loose ends."

"That being the case," I responded, "Balfour had best watch himself as they may not stop until they've done him in. I recommend you warn him to exercise the utmost care."

"That I shall surely do," said my good friend, "though I'm sure Scotland Yard has already given him the same advice."

Doyle and I abbreviated our telephone conversation and each completed his preparations for the trip to Southampton, my friend having agreed to drive me and Mrs. Corbett to the ship.

Editor's note:
Reconstructed in June 1912 by Samuel Harper

The day of Titanic's departure I had escorted Mrs. Corbett by taxi to the ship and saw her safely to her stateroom on C Deck. We were now four days at sea in an uneventful trip, my first few days having been spent with old friends who were making the voyage also, such as W.T. Stead, Sir Cosmo Duff Gordon, the Countess of Rothes, Bruce Ismay, etc.

Now Futrelle and I were meeting as planned for the first time since our coming aboard. "How's the wife, Jacques?" I enquired of my companion as we settled into our chairs around a bridge table in the First Class Smoking Room. A mild swell occasionally could be detected as the chandeliers appeared to sway ever so slightly, above the oaken elegance of the salon, but for the most part the sea was smooth as glass, the ship as steady as the Hotel Claridge. The Titanic was making about 26 knots through pitch black seas under a gloriously starry sky. The air was cold, about 40 degrees and the sea was even colder this April night at 32 degrees, the freezing temperature of fresh water. Coming in from the promenade deck passengers were grateful for the warmth of the salon. Unknown to us, Bruce Ismay and the captain had decided to ignore iceberg warnings in an attempt to set a new speed record which would make travelling on the new ship more attractive to the line's wealthy patrons.

It was 9 p.m. Greenwich time April 14, 1912 and Jacques had just put his wife to bed after receiving her complaint of a headache. "She'll be fine in the morning," he said, "nothing serious. She's still unwinding from all the rushing about to the shops she visited in London."

A white-coated young waiter took our orders, departed for the bar and returned in a trice with two glasses of vichy water.

"Not drinking?" Jacques enquired.

"Is this not a fluid you see me quaffing?" I smiled

"You know what I mean. When did you go on the wagon?" he pressed.

"Let's say I've developed an allergy," I responded.

"Not likely," he murmured into his glass. "That's my department."

After a contemplative pause he said, "I think I hear wedding bells." His countenance lightened in a knowing grin.

"Oh shut up," I said, feigning irritation. "I think I know why White Star turned Nellie's project down," I said, attempting to change the subject.

"Let me be the first to congratulate you," he continued, amused at my embarassment. "She's much too good for you, but I'll never say so."

"You just did, you ass," I chided.

"Quite so, but that's our secret," he laughed, "I mean I'll never tell her."

"Terribly kind of you," I rejoined deciding to return his ribbing kind for kind. "Now don't you wish to hear my theory of why Nellie's idea was scotched?"

"Of course, mon ami, do proceed," he gestured expansively to direct me to continue, a broad grin on his Gallic face signifying his pleasure at the 'good

187

news' he had manufactured of an upcoming marriage.

"Now if you've quite finished," I tucked my waistcoat down and arranged my tie. "If you were more observant, you too would have perceived that the Marconi shack is like Grand Central Station. Any attempt to communicate dispatches by a reporter would hopelessly bog down the system."

"You're quite right," he said, "in fact, I contributed to the confusion myself sending a wireless message to my daughter which should become a valuable souvenir some day."

"Everyone else has the same idea," I said, "those poor wireless operators never get to leave their stations. There's only two of them and the key is never silent."

"I don't think they could interrupt the love and kisses messages even to transmit a distress signal," Futrelle exaggerated.

"A vogue, a new bauble to this jaded crowd, like a thousand other marvels of science we've seen in the last fifty years," I said, "but in a way different from all the rest. It was the death knell of the Empire when the telegraph was extended to India, but what a difference it makes to know we can communicate from this watery blackness if we have to."

"I'm interested in your comments about the demise of the Empire," Jacques said, his expression asking me to develop the idea.

"Very simple," I said, gesturing, glass in hand. "From 1865 it was possible to communicate with Downing Street, and from that time the swashbucklers like Clive and Hastings and the rest could no longer act first and explain later, which was how we acquired so many of our possessions. Once the timid politicians, who always worried about the budget, could moderate the activities of the buccaneers we were through."

"You exaggerate for effect, right?" Futrelle enquired.

"Not much," I responded, "I dare say you haven't pondered as I have how differently problems are handled when men feel compelled to review in advance every contemplated maneuver with the timid politicians. Not much that isn't lacklustre can come of it. In fact, instantaneous communications was one of the greatest contributing forces that brought to an end the era of the Hero. By definition the Hero is he who acts alone, out of touch with all the comfort-loving nannies back home. An Alexander or Philip — ."

"Are you perhaps," he asked, "describing the reasons you selected your own profession for the autonomy you possess?"

"An interesting question that I shall contemplate at length before responding," I said, sipping my vichy water. "But ponder, if you will, how the star of the hero-athlete has risen as that of the hero-military commander in the field has been eclipsed."

"Your theory seems to have answer for a question never posed," he joshed.

"Only your obtuseness to blame," I returned his gentle sarcasm, "The athlete is the man who must function without interference. We send him out to win. Only within the most narrow limits can we circumscribe his actions. In the split second that elapses from the time the ball leaves the pitcher's hand the coach cannot order the batter to strike the ball. The batter either reads it as a good throw and implements his decision autonomously or not at all."

"Athletes are not the only heroes, surely," he countered, picking away at my theory.

"Of course not. Even those men of mystery, the archaeologists are heroes for the same reason, they must act on their own and take the consequences," I said, "and others too if we attempted to enumerate them. But what a qualitative difference between the heroism of a Drake or a Nelson and that of Jim Jeffries or Sir Flinders Petrie*," I said, "to name but a few."

"I think I begin to see your point," he said unconvincingly.

I could see he was bored with my theorizing. I sipped my drink falling silent to permit him to turn the conversation to topics of greater interest to himself.

"What case did you have reference to," he said, "back in Southampton when you told Doyle and me you had never revealed the facts of your most exotic adventure?"

"I knew you'd ask that question before we reached New York," I grinned.

"Of course you did," he responded pettishly. "Who's being an ass now?"

"Tut tut, my child," I chided, "an old man is entitled to his whimsy."

"Why refer to the case at all," he asked, "if not to bait me?"

"My way of repaying you and Doyle," I said, "for the ribbing I received at your not too gentle hands. I'll bet five to one Conan Doyle hasn't had a good night's sleep since I made the remark."

"Well I haven't lost any sleep over it," Futrelle said.

"But you haven't the trained sensibilities of Doyle," I suggested, "Arthur won't rest until he digs it out of me."

"Neither will I," Jacques threatened half seriously, "so you might as well level with me."

"An interesting Americanism — level with me," I temporized.

"Cut the crap," he bullied.

"Mind your language, there are ladies present," I mocked a horrified expression looking about the salon though there was no one within fifty feet of our table.

"Have it your way, but I'll get it out of you if it's the last thing I do," Futrelle said, visibly disappointed.

"Now if you're sufficiently chastened," I said, "maybe you'll be perfectly silent and I'll tell you a bedtime story."

"Yes daddy, I'll be good," he smiled, razing the gloomy facade that besat his features.

I pondered the elements of the story I was about to begin. "In 1878 Sir Henry Rawlings was selected by the Queen, as head of the Royal Commission to represent Her Majesty's government at the Paris Exhibition. He was kind enough to ask me to go along as his assistant. I was nineteen at the time and still uncertain of what to do with myself. It was an ideal opportunity to delay a decision as to my future, and to make a little money while having some excitement in the City of Light. Also, Sir Henry and I had not spent any

*Famous archaeologist.

189

great amount of time together since my youthful years when we used to camp out at the archaeological digs he was laboring on."

"Quite an opportunity at that," Futrelle acknowledged.

"It was to prove most extraordinary, and quite decisive in the way it affected my decision as to the career I would pursue," I said, "There was a period of eight weeks for which we were committed. At the beginning, a stretch of about three weeks we were running around putting out fires for twenty-four hours a day getting ready for the opening. Then, after the exhibition was under way, just when I thought I would have much my own way of leisure time, Sir Henry asked me to join him for dinner with a decidedly conspiratorial air about him."

"The plot thickens," Jacques contributed.

"Quit sounding like a writer," I said. "Sir Henry had a sumptuous repast set for us in our suite at the Hotel de l'Europe, and over the brandy and cigars he described an assignment he'd been given by Prime Minister Disraeli with which he desired my assistance."

"Nothing minor I'm sure?" Futrelle interjected.

"Even now I can't answer that," I said. "That's one of the reasons why it represents my weirdest case. But let me tell it my own way."

"Of course, forgive my interruption," Jacques said solicitously.

"For years I had suspected that Sir Henry had made a secret pledge to my father to attempt to influence me," I said, "to adopt my father's and Sir Henry's profession of archaeology."

"Any concrete evidence of that?" he asked.

"A few shreds," I said, "mostly a feeling, but his request that I accompany him to Paris took on a new meaning when I learned of this assignment from the Prime Minister."

"This suspense is killing me," Futrelle exaggerated.

"In due course, old boy," I paused, longing for my pipe. "It appears that Disraeli spent the year 1842 in Paris where he was favored considerably by Louis Napoleon and took a deep interest in things French, especially matters relating to the overthrow of the monarchy and the Revolution. Seems he learned from the future President that, prior to the Revolution, in the niches of the exterior of the Cathedral of Notre Dame there were statues of the Kings of Judah that were torn down by the revolutionary regime, who desired to desecrate both the crown and the Church. It was Disraeli's desire to discover what had become of those statues."

"What on earth for?" Futrelle enquired.

"Let me tell it in the sequence I think best," I said.

"Sorry," he said penitently, "please ignore the intrusion."

"Of course," I remarked, "I can only guess the answer, but let me tell the story before I tell you what I theorize about that. We were, in effect, given the assignment to develop a case whose evidence had been lost for nearly one hundred years. I asked Sir Henry how the P. M. could possibly expect us to succeed.

"What is archaeology," Sir Henry, knowing I was considering a career in crime detection, asked me, "but detective work as to events hundreds, even thousands of years in the past. He has given us an assignment that is neither pure archaeology nor crime detection, but has aspects of both."

Sir Henry then took me quite by surprise when he said, "I am placing this assignment entirely in your hands — I shall be available to render such assistance as you may request — but I should like to see how far you can go on your own. Truth be told," he continued, "I have some matters of personal interest to the Crown that will keep me pretty busy. But I shall make myself available, no matter what, if you so request."

He could see my dumbfounded condition. "Come, come Sam," he consoled, "I won't let you be embarrassed in any way. If you fail, which you very well may — it's an extraordinarily difficult assignment — I shall say that I failed. And if you succeed," he said wafting a huge cloud of cigar smoke into the air, "I shall see you get full credit."

"He awaited my response. There being none, he quickly added, "What I would have given for this kind of an adventure at your age."

Finally I found my voice. "But I don't know where to begin — "

"You've seen us operate often enough in the field," he said, "but what got us to the site of a particular dig?"

"Research," I said, furiously plumbing the depths of my memory to recollect scenes from my childhood and youth, "the Scriptures, inscriptions from other antiquities . . ." "Precisely," he smiled congratulatorily, "I would suggest the same approach here." He leaned forward to add more brandy to our snifters from the decanter on the coffee table before us.

"None for me, sir," I said placing my fingers over my glass.

"Are you sure?" he urged.

"Quite, Sir Henry." I was deep into the problem he had assigned me. "I shall need a street map of Paris in 1790."

"Not a bad beginning. In the Holy Land we had only the Bible and unfortunately," he laughed, "it contained no street maps."

"I shall need to determine the number of statues and their approximate weight and size," I verbalized my thoughts, pulling a three by five card from the breast pocket of my shirt to make notes.

"Where will you seek that type of information?" he asked.

"The Louvre, the library at the Sorbonne, who knows? I won't know until I do the research." I looked to Sir Henry for affirmation.

"Quite right," he agreed. "I think you'll have a jolly time of it Sam, and do your father proud. He was like a terrier after a bone, my boy, and he never quit. Maybe you inherited some of that. I think so." He looked inquiringly at me.

"You be the judge of that later," I said.

"You'll do well, Sam," he smiled, "I can see that already. By the way, how's your French?"

"Improving rapidly," I laughed, "by the time this assignment is finished, should be parfait."

"Assurement, mon fils," he responded.

"That's how it all began Jacques, and I shan't bore you with all the details. I have a complete dossier on the case in New York which you can peruse at your leisure. I must say for a young man I did rather well and," I conceded, "was rather lucky."

"Where did you find the statues," Futrelle asked, "for I assume you found them."

"Indeed I did," I answered, "and thought at the time I likely would get at least a DSO for my efforts."

"But where?" he insisted.

"I was able to determine from the family journals of the Duke of Orleans that the statues while badly damaged, had not been utterly destroyed. The Duke's attitude toward the crown was a strange one. He and many others used the pledge of secrecy of his Masonic brethren to conceal his conspiratorial activities against his cousin Louis the Fourteenth, and while he conspired with opponents to the crown hoping to bring himself to power, like many another in that period, he hedged his bets," I said. "Apparently, he intended, if necessary and appropriate, to produce the statues, which were inextricably tied to the question of legitimacy of the throne, to demonstrate his loyalty if Bourbon rule was restored other than through his line. Not so strangely, he chose the vaults of a Jewish banking house in which to hide the relics. The vault was sealed with brick and mortar, a great deal of time passed and all was nearly forgotten."

Futrelle and I sipped our vichy water.

"Fortunately the Jewish bankers, today we would liken them more to gold coin dealers, in whose vault he stored the statues, had good reason to wish to assist the crown if restored. Indeed, their circumstances were incalculably damaged by the fall of the throne as they had been financial counselors to the King. They too, kept good family journals, and I was able to ascertain that they received the statuary, though the particular volume of the journals needed was missing," I said to Futrelle, "a clue that the particular volume must contain important, perhaps dangerous information.

"You found it, of course?" Jacques asked.

"Mortared into the wall of a chateau in Provence purchased by the Jewish family many years after the establishment of the Republic." I said, "Isn't it interesting that nearly a century later they still guarded their precious secret."

"What Jewish family?" Jacques asked.

"A secret of state," I said raising my hand in a sign that he was trespassing.

"Of course," he said meekly.

"Still, the big trick was finding where that old vault lay in modern Paris," I said.

"I'll say," agreed Jacques, "were there maps and were they any good?"

"Yes, they existed, but I can't claim credit for finding them," I said, "but then I didn't try very hard either."

"Why's that?" Futrelle questioned.

"It really wasn't necessary. But I'm ahead of myself. By the time I found the missing journal of the Orleans family," I said, "it was apparent to me the preservation of the statues of the kings of Judah was vitally important to the people involved, but it was also guilty knowledge. Should they be caught, it meant the guillotine, for the Reign of Terror was on."

"Only someone with a lot at stake would run the risks involved, I reasoned." Futrelle was following intently. "I was certain the journals of the Jewish family would reveal the location of the vault, but I failed to reckon with the fact that the sector of Paris in which it was located had long since been rebuilt, new streets, new numbers, etc. Where, in an area of several hundred acres was one to find the vault? Finally, lady luck came to my rescue, also I owe a great deal to that great American naval hero John Paul Jones."

"John Paul Jones!" exclaimed Futrelle, "impossible; Jones died shortly after the French Revolution began."

"1792 to be exact," I said, "but in case you're unaware, his body was preserved in alcohol and buried in Paris. A quest was begun in 1845 which ultimately led to the site of his interment in a section of Paris which had been razed and rebuilt."

"You mean that in finding the burial site of Jones they located the vault with the statues?" Futrelle asked, attempting to anticipate the story.

"Not precisely, but close enough," I said. "In the search for Jones' burial place they had unearthed the precise maps I needed to locate the quarters of the Jewish bankers and their vault. So in a very real sense I owed my success to the fame of an American naval hero."

"But now la piece de resistance — what did the Prime Minister make of your perfectly spectacular feat?" asked Futrelle.

"I haven't told you yet the techniques by which we entered the vault," I said.

"A detail I can manufacture at will," Futrelle said.

"There you go again. It's all mere grist for your mill, isn't it?" I chided.

He was flustered momentarily. "Of course not, please tell me how you dug up the vault."

"You're right," I said, "it is a mere detail to you. I guess that's why I'm a detective and not a writer."

"I see your point," he said, slightly chagrined, "do go on."

"Not at all, you're quite right, it's not important. The important thing is that I had found the statues, had met on cordial terms the most influential people in France in doing so, and now I wished my reward," I said.

"I take it you were to be disappointed?" Futrelle asked.

"Disappointed and much enlightened as to the ways of those in power," I said.

"Disraeli was not impressed?" Jacques enquired.

"Not favorably," I said, "duly impressed yes, with my sleuthing, but there was a purpose in his request that was not subserved, through no fault of mine."

"What was that?" he asked.

"Disraeli assumed that statues of the kings of Judah would look like Jews. I shall never forget the startled expression on the old man's countenance when he inspected the photographs I had taken of the remnants of those ancient rulers."

"He thought they'd look like Jews?" Futrelle queried.

"Exactly, and when each one had a perfect Frankish or Norman appearance not the least unlike that of the Anglo-Saxon," I said, "he could not conceal his disappointment. He ordered the entire matter closed, demanded secrecy and to this day those remnants remain buried in a musty vault far below the streets of Paris."

"There went your DSO," Jacques said.

"A DSO was too much to expect of course, but like the silly young man I was, always looking for the main chance to make my reputation, I was buried too, in a mood of deepest indigo," I said.

"Quite understandable," I said, "but in the light of facts made known to me years later, I suspect he was planning to announce the find with a great flourish hoping to tap the sympathies of the western European communities in support of the creation of a Jewish homeland in Palestine."

"It seems there's another story lurking here somewhere," he stated as much as asked.

"True but one which likewise remains a secret of state." I said. "As disappointed as I was at being denied the recognition I thought, perhaps innocently and naively, my services deserved, I gained a great deal from that case."

"Thus Sam Harper, the world's foremost consultant on crime detection?" Jacques offered.

"Precisely," I said. "That case so exhilarated me, my choice of a career was clear from that time on."

"How did Sir Henry like that?" he asked.

"He took it well, but I could see clearly he was disappointed." I said. "He felt my talents should be employed to enlighten the world as to the glories of the past. He regarded it as an inferior choice to spend my life devoted to crime."

"Was it crime that interested you?" Futrelle asked.

"Not crime — justice," I said, "and why I shall never know. Justice, and the pleasure of pitting my intelligence against the evidence. There's a great ego satisfaction in the work you know."

"Of course," Futrelle agreed, "not unlike the intellectual stimulus of plotting an exciting detective story."

"I suppose," I said, "at any rate you've dragged out of me my most exotic, and in a way, my most important case — and I must retire." I brought you a copy of the excerpt from my journal for the period so you can see how I reacted at the time."

"I'm ready for bed too, but I shall read this before shutting off my light," he said.

We toasted each other with the dregs of our glasses of vichy water, shook hands and retired the salon. Futrelle's wife was fast asleep when he crawled into bed, but he took a few minutes before retiring to read the entry in the journal of Sam Harper dated Nov. 11, 1878:

"Sir Henry regards the Paris project as an unqualified success. I must say I do also. He has received many congratulatory letters from the high and mighty since our return, one from Her Majesty herself. There is no doubt that he acquitted himself extremely well. And he has both privately acknowledged his gratitude for my assistance, and is preparing a letter for the record which I may keep in my files for the future.

"But the experience was not without its unhappy side. My suspicions were confirmed, although I was never in doubt, that Sir Henry desires me to train with him to become an archaeologist and I felt forced to turn him down. Worse yet, the reasons I felt forced to give him, visibly devastated this wonderful man who is like a father to me. Yet in being true to myself, there was no way to avoid hurting him. How long is it now that I have pondered the response I would give him when he asked the inevitable question, seeking a way to tell him kindly what I knew was certain to wound.

"Sir Henry, my father, aye an entire generation have lived on their spiritual capital, not recognizing their balance was dropping to zero, leaving nothing for those coming along behind. They have accepted the Scriptures as an infallible guide, at least where translated correctly, but they have ignored the Bible's most fundamental message. This I am unable to do. Either the Scriptures are true in this vital matter or they are false. They have picked them over like garments on a bargain counter, taken what they wished, and ignored the rest.

"But to me, what they choose to ignore is neither susceptible of being ignored, nor acceptable to reason. The core message I read in Holy Writ is that God chose a single family to be his holy priesthood nation. This is to say that God is not infinitely just, for if he were, all men would be treated equally.

"Sir Henry thinks my becoming a private consulting detective is unworthy of me. He doesn't feel the pleasure it gives me to serve the cause of justice. A goodly dollop of snobbery in his attitude and concern that I might not make a living at it, but he only wishes the best for me as he sees things.

"Often have I heard him complain that the younger breed of archaeologists coming up regard the Bible as 'anthropologically interesting'. That is to say, a mere folk record evidencing a metamorphosis of the religious beliefs of the Habiru (Hebrews) one of which was the idea of their chosenness. "Pietistic they call me — all of us," says Sir Henry, "who believe the Scriptures to be a divine work." I did not say it, but he knew when we finished our talk that I am one of 'them' and it hurt him deeply.

"I am not sure there is a God. But if there is, he must be just, the very essence of justice. And in my book, that rules out the idea of a Chosen People. All the churches agree with this conclusion, they just haven't the guts to say so. So they simply ignore this part of the Bible and think they can keep the rest. It simply won't wash and the rest of the world knows it.

"I could limp through life indefinitely with no strong conviction about religion. It was Sir Henry's misfortune to force me to define and reveal my feelings.

"If the Scriptures were true, there would have to be a Chosen People and no religion which embraces the Bible but ignores this fact can be true. Fortunately for me, I don't have to try to answer these embarassing questions. Perhaps some day, but not now. My only regret is how badly I've hurt the feelings of a kind, gentle and true friend."

Futrelle placed the notes on the deck beside his bed and turned out the reading light at the head of the bed. In but a short while he was, as I had for a few minutes been, deeply asleep in the cradled protection of what seemed the most secure ship plying the darkling waters of the North Atlantic.

195

Written in 1921 at the Request of the Editor by Samuel Harper Employing Notes Committed to Writing in June 1912

The death of a great ship involves a vast and kaleidoscopic series of impressions of events so shocking and of such terror they are etched upon the memory too vividly ever to be erased. The people aboard the Titanic were first made aware that something extraordinary was taking place when she veered sharply to the port side in her attempt to avoid the iceberg which caused her death.

To a minority, those playing cards in the salons, drinks went sliding to starboard, spilling their contents as they went. But most, like myself, already retired for the night, were gently rolled in their beds by the heeling over of the ship.

My head being close to the starboard exterior skin of the ship which, seventy-five feet below was being sliced by the ice like a loaf of bread, I was aware that a most serious, perhaps fatal collision had occurred. Since my porthole was ajar to let the cool night air into my stateroom, chunks of ice were forced through the port and thrown onto the deck as the ship brushed the side of the berg. I was thus aware at once that we had collided with an iceberg.

Being somewhat familiar with the rules of modern seamanship, I am aware that it is better to meet a berg head-on than to risk striking a glancing blow. A head-on encounter might crush a few forward compartments causing damage and loss of life, but the ship will likely remain afloat. A glancing blow can lay open a wound which is fatal in that it penetrates so many compartments there is insufficient residual bouyancy to save the ship. And there was no doubt in my mind from the long, grinding sound that I heard that the brush with the berg might indeed have inflicted a mortal wound.

I knew I must determine at once how severely the Titanic was damaged. Yet my frame of mind was such, having been comtemplating religious matters so seriously for a considerable period of time prior to that fatal night, that I felt the first thing to be done was to pray. I prayed not so much for deliverance if our ship's troubles proved fatal, but that I might die bravely if such were to be my fate and that, God willing, I might live to see Cornelia again.

And I arose from my knees after my hasty prayer determined to survive if human determination and ingenuity might turn the task. I dressed at once making a special effort to select the warmest clothing I had and wherever possible garments made of wool which can retain warmth and bouyancy even when wet. Having checked the weather before retiring I was aware that the air temperature was close to freezing and the water temperature almost certainly at or below the 32' which will turn fresh water to ice. The brine of the North Atlantic likely being between 28 and 30 degrees fahrenheit. In such water even the most rugged individual can die of hypothermia in fifteen minutes or less.

The thought occurred to me that the most likely method of withstanding water temperatures of such severity was to fortify the system with a considerable amount of alcohol. I was making a mental note to visit the first class salon when I remembered a package that had been sent to me as a going away present in care of the ship by the Chief Inspector of Scotland Yard. It looked suspiciously as though it might shelter a bottle of the Chief's favorite brandy.

I rummaged about in my baggage until I found the package. Shaking it revealed it to contain a beverage. A quick tearing off of the wrappings disclosed that my hunch was right. I glanced at my watch. It was 11:45 p.m. Sunday April 14, 1912. I took my first draught of brandy at once, and determined to imbibe small amounts steadily as long as the bottle lasted. Then I went to the stateroom next door to rouse Jacques and Mrs. Futrelle.

It was my intention to see them up to the lifeboats, if information might confirm my guess that the ship was sinking, and then to go down to second class country to locate Mrs. Corbett who I knew to be traveling alone and who would be in need of help.

Jacques, who like any true journalist seemed to ferret out intelligence almost by osmosis, knew already the ship was sinking. From where, I cannot say, but I didn't take time to ask him. He was already dressed and was shouting directives to his wife in the adjoining bedroom suggesting her warmest clothing, life jacket, etc.

As I stood talking with Jacques we both were suddenly aware of how silent the ship had become. The clothes in the closets no longer swayed and the steady, rhythmic vibration of the engines was gone. I am sure the sudden silence of the ship woke more people than did the thunderous noise of ice penetrating her vitals. Topside, I could hear the deafening roar of steam being blown off which was no longer being employed to drive her engines. And slowly doors along the passageway were opening while passengers could be heard enquiring of the stewards in the companionways what had happened.

Aware as Jacques and I were that there were only 20 lifeboats aboard, enough for 800 on a ship bearing 2200 people, we conversed within a framework of understanding that Mrs. Futrelle could be saved, but that he and I likely must take to the water.

"Can you tolerate a draught of brandy?" I asked offering my bottle.

"A small one and I will vomit," he said, "and a large one I will be unconscious in ten minutes."

"Better unconscious than to freeze to death," I said in utter seriousness.

"I shall have to take my chances," he said.

That was the last of our discussion on the subject and when I left Jacques and Mrs. Futrelle at the boat deck while he waited to put his beloved May into boat number seven, the first boat put over Titanic's side, that was the last I saw of him in this life. But I can tell you I know he died a brave man's death. I long to shake his hand when next we meet.

Only a half hour had elapsed since the crash, but by now, 12:10 a.m. by my watch, She was already down somewhat by the bow and everyone on R.M.S. Titanic knew she was headed for the bottom. The ways in which a great mass of people react to disaster are as varied as the personalities and circumstances of the people themselves.

As I walked past the open door of the stateroom of an elderly gentleman in first class whom I had seen being pushed about the lower promenade in a wheelchair by his husky manservant, and who was rumored on the never-to-be-verified grapevine of the ship to have terminal cancer, I heard the easily recognized report of a 45 caliber pistol and saw the top of his head flash into the air and spatter the ceiling of his stateroom. That was the first of at least six suicides I saw that night, and a number of shootings as crewmen stopped several onslaughts by groups of men who attempted to rush the lifeboats.

But in a long, terror-filled night that saw fifteen hundred or more people die in innumerable violent ways, the emotional impact of any single death was totally lost. Like men in war, the enormity of the tragedy and the desire simply to survive insulate the emotions from the dread and revulsion that would overwhelm the feelings at seeing a single violent occurrence in other circumstances.

But some impressions forever remain. I can never forget certain trivial details. The breeze, becoming later a strong wind, blowing up from below in every passageway out of the bowels of the ship where she was taking water so fast it forced the air out of the flooding compartments in a steady gail. This wind of death moaned about us without surcease and bore the scent of fresh paint and other odors of newness one would expect on a ship making its maiden voyage.

Acts of heroism and cowardice were so common as to be scarcely worthy of notice. As I moved past the first class reading room on my way below to find Mrs. Corbett I saw W.T. Stead sitting quietly with a book and a glass of scotch. I asked if he shouldn't don his lifebelt. He looked slowly up from his book which looked like a well-worn copy of the Scriptures and said "At last the great adventure — I shall shortly see my loved ones — why postpone what must happen soon or late?" His expression was one of complete peace and resignation. I waved a silent goodbye and left. Quiet partings such as this were occurring everywhere, as well as hysterics and craven fear from those who one would have hoped would have faced their end fearlessly.

Also striking was the seemingly unlimited ability of some people to ignore reality. Many refused to enter the boats for fear of the long drop into the inky blackness below, in spite of the certain knowledge that to remain meant an excruciatingly painful death. They had, perhaps, deluded themselves into thinking the ship might yet be saved. But in my experience some people have an impenetrable ability to ignore bad news. On that night it really didn't matter; brave or cowardly, intelligent or stupid, blindly hopeful or realistically resigned, all met the same fate.

In spite of the dramatic circumstances, I couldn't help being amused at the extraordinary and varied garbs people thought fitting. One man appeared in white tie and tails, prepared to meet his end as a gentleman. A number of the first class women were fully decked out in finery and jewels, but most people showed the state of disarray in which the wounding of the ship found them. Many had only nightgowns and bathrobes. One woman had nothing on whatever but a sable coat.

Some had the presence of mind to attempt to dress to meet the bitter cold of a clear starry April night in mid-Atlantic, but had not come prepared for such an occurrence as this. The efforts to make do with what was at hand were sometimes ludicrous in the extreme. One man had tied a silk evening scarf under and around his chin, covering his ears, circling over the top of a fedora hat protecting his bald head. A black chesterfield coat was buttoned over his bulky life jacket. I believe every suit of long underwear on the ship was pressed into service that night.

In the companionway outside my stateroom two first class ladies had beset the Purser Mr. McElroy demanding he go to the ship's safe to retrieve their jewels before they embarked the life boats. I added to his stout resistance when I commented softly "Ladies you'll be lucky to escape with your lives this night — go to the life boats and pray you survive." With that they left off their demands and McElroy disappeared down the companionway toward the bridge.

I heard an acquaintance, General Grace, remark to the squash racquet professional as they passed each other, "I think we best cancel our game for 7:30 tomorrow." To which the casual reply with a smile, "As you wish." The court was already under 30 feet of water.

But as I went below leaving first class country, attitudes clearly changed, and the very British atmosphere of stiff upper lip and upcoming death met with a quip on one's lips, gave way to different modes of thought and behavior. More realism and less braggadocio obtained here. And the stolid virtues of the British middle class seemed to rule. Parents were to be seen dressing their children warmly and comforting the tears of the fearful. Words of warning of the bitter cold and the probability of separation of husbands from wives were exchanged to prepare the children for the frightful scene they knew would take place on the boat deck above. One child refused to leave without her teddy bear and her understanding parents wasted precious moments until the all-important possession was found.

Once located they made their way through the throngs toward the ladders (stairways) leading topside. In second class much cockney was to be heard and the heavy dialects of the provinces. The solid core of the British working people travel second class. I was suddenly very proud of my countrymen as I observed their unflappability in the face of great danger and, for many, certain death.

Outside Mrs. Corbett's empty stateroom, by merest chance, I found a steward who advised me she had gone down to steerage class to deliver a Middle Eastern woman's baby. My admiration for her courage and self-sacrifice was considerable.

I asked the steward to unlock the gate at the end of the passageway leading below to the third class country. This he did with a strange look on his face and a glance at my garb which announced to him my first class status. And as quickly as he let me through he relocked the gates and departed attempting to arrest the progress of a number of steerage class young men and women who had escaped their prison below decks on this great sinking community grave while he let me through. I was pleased some had escaped and immediately turned to some strapping young bucks nearby and told them to break down the gate and head topside. They needed no other encouragement and soon were gone, a group of older steerage people following the example of their boldness, while acting as though they felt what they were doing was either illegal or sinful. For the most part, those in third class seemed to accept without cavil the idea that first and second class passengers claimed by perfect right first chance at the lifeboats. Such attitudes died with the Titanic.

I was making my way aft on E Deck amidst crowds of third class people in a babble of five or six languages other than English. Most were surprisingly quiet, many were praying, but there was no panic. Strangely, there seemed an air of resignation and the necessity to wait until those in authority directed them where to go and what to do. Some young folks even seemed to be enjoying the excitement. But the older people recognized the seriousness of the situation and sought their solace praying, rosary beads and books of Scripture and prayer books being fervently employed by many.

I stopped an officer making his way forward to ask if he knew where the woman was having her baby. He directed me to the Engineer's Mess on the port side of E Deck opposite the engine room casing where I found a miniature hospital set up since there was plenty of hot water handy.

A Middle Eastern woman, Mrs. Sarkies, perhaps twenty years old, was stoicly giving birth to her first child under the gentle but firm direction of Irene Corbett who had tied a handkerchief over her face as a sanitary mask. I was grateful to have had experience in delivering my own daughter who was born before the doctor could arrive. I was thus able to be of some small assistance to Mrs. Corbett as the birth progressed.

The great achievement, of course, was to maintain an air of total calm in such distressing circumstances so that the young mother might not delay the delivery by her own emotional tension. Remarkably, this was done, complete credit for the controlled, peaceful atmosphere being due to the superb professionalism of the midwife, Irene Corbett. And there amidst the death of so many was born a child, a son, who, should he survive, which did not then seem too likely, would be known as long as he lived as the child born as a great ship died.

But no sooner had the child been born and hastily cleaned up, than it was necessary to get both mother and child into some kind of shape that they could make the trip to the boat deck, hopefully before the last of the lifeboats had left. It was now 1:35 a.m.

As incredible as it may seem, that young woman got up off the mess table that had served as her birthing place, and walked with minimal assistance from me, while Mrs. Corbett carried the baby wrapped in makeshift clothing composed of mess linens, all of this within 15 minutes of the birth of her son.

It took us perhaps twenty minutes to make the journey from E Deck to the boat deck. The Titanic was now well down by the head and the companionways and stairways represented an enormous challenge. Within but a few more minutes it would be impossible to use the stairways as they would be pitched at an angle too steep to be usable. But by holding the railings we were able to get our patient and her child to the boat deck.

The night air was growing colder by the minute and I guessed it to be well below freezing as we emerged under the starry canopy above the boat deck. With as much gentleness as the haste of the emergency permitted we shepherded Mrs. Sarkies and her baby to collapsible boat D now in the davits from which boat No. 2 had departed. It was already very full and ready to depart. This was the last remaining lifeboat in which anyone might escape the watery plunge Titanic would shortly take to her grave on the ocean floor 12,000 feet below. Officer Lightoller, a fine officer, was in charge of loading this boat and only with the greatest difficulty did I manage to persuade him to permit the new mother and her child to find place in the overcrowded boat. Even Mrs. Corbett was denied a place. And so it was that at 2:05 a.m. collapsible boat D left the ship loaded with sixty or more people and one newly born baby, the last boat to leave R.M.S. Titanic.

Now with the last of the boats gone, a great calm seemed to descend over the ship. The power seemed to be failing and the ship's lights which miraculously functioned to the very last, were glowing slightly red as the emergency power generators began to lose power. I thought of the valiant men below decks who would go to their graves in order to insure that the lights did not fail. Many who would survive owed their lives to these unsung heroes.

I led Mrs. Corbett up the sharply pitched boat deck to the ladder down through the promenade decks to the bridge deck and then to the poop deck on the aftermost part of the ship. This was second class country but all such distinctions were waived as those still aboard fled to what clearly would be the last part of the ship to go under.

It required a great effort to force our way through the struggling bodies of those who, like us, were fighting gravity as the deck pitched ever higher toward the perpendicular. A steady roar from below decks as everything loose fell forward and downward, smashing as it went, together with an ever rising wail as people began jumping from the ship, rendered all conversation impossible.

Hundreds jumped a hundred or more feet from the fan tail to the calm blackness of the sea, striking debris as they reached the water. The screams of anguish of the injured were punctuated by the dull thuds of the bodies of those who either were knocked unconscious or killed as they struck the deadly wreckage that so profusely littered the surface of the sea. I reasoned that there was but one way to avoid a similar fate and that was to ride the ship down in her final plunge.

I now was able to avoid pitching forward toward the sea only with the utmost effort as I held the poop deck railing, my left arm around Mrs. Corbett's waist as my left hand clutched the rail beyond her, the ship moving ever faster to the perpendicular position in which she would make her last plunge.

I had long since consumed the last of my bottle of brandy having offered a share to Mrs. Corbett who steadfastly refused to partake. All my persuasion was insufficient to obtain her consent to fortify herself against the freezing water that awaited us.

I now made the attempt to shout my final words of counsel and farewell to her. But my words were lost as with a profound shudder the ship gave up her boilers, these mammoth masses of steel breaking loose from their moorings as they plunged downward, bursting through the bow of the ship as though it were so much paper.

Amidst the deafening roar which continuously rumbled from the ship in her death throes, I saw this brave woman's lips move in forming the words "God help you Mr. Harper. Tell my family I love them." To which I replied "God bless you Mrs. Corbett," as the ship made its final plunge. Beyond all my efforts to hold on to this valiant woman, the shock of immersion in that frigid water, like a thousand knives thrust into my body, made any such effort impossible.

By the time I floated to the surface after the ship was gone from beneath us, she was gone and search for her as I might in the inky blackness, I could not find a trace of her.

I was in the water perhaps an hour when Fifth Officer Lowe came by in a lifeboat under his command in search of survivors and picked me up. Fortified as I was by a quart of fine French brandy, the two hours we waited until we were picked up by the Carpathia were not as stressful as those of most the Titanic's survivors, but they were filled with regrets that I could not have done more to save this brave woman who passed up her own chance to board a lifeboat to deliver the baby of a woman in distress. I thought too of the sad duty that lay ahead of advising her family of the brave way in which she died. The one comforting thought was that my arrival in New York would bring me close once again to my beloved.

Regrettably, the woman and her child to serve whom Mrs. Corbett occasioned her own death were never recorded amongst the survivors of the Titanic. It appears they froze to death and their bodies were thrown overboard to make room in the badly overcrowded lifeboat.

Excerpt from Diary of May Futrelle

Dated April 15, 1913

It was just a year ago that everything changed so drastically for us. I will, of course, never be able to forget that horrible night, though for the last year I have had quite deliberately to force the events of that night out of my mind. But I record these things now in the hope that by writing them down they will bother me less and that I might be able to get on with my life without my beloved Jacques.

It is a terrible thing to lose a loved one in a tragedy at sea. Consigning a mate to the grave has an appropriate finality to it. There is an open wound left not to have the opportunity to see him buried in a place that I can visit and where I can ultimately join him. For weeks I had nightmares in which Jacques' body was struck at sea by a ghostly ship and hurled high in the air, coming back to earth to land upon me. I could see a look of terror upon his face in detail that was quite unreal as no such clarity would be possible from such a distance, his body being hurled a hundred feet or more by the force of the bow wave of the ship. And how could I witness this and still be standing on dry land when the body came back down? But such unreal things happen in dreams amidst a pervasive atmosphere of dread.

Try as I might to forget the night the Titanic sank, and sometimes I go for days at a time without reliving some part of that evil night, still things happen which unavoidably bring it all back.

The other evening I was having an aperitif with Eloise at the Taft. The orchestra was playing lively music for a few couples dancing. I was paying no attention to the music as Eloise and I gossiped. Suddenly I felt a terrible chill and a feeling of dread for no apparent reason. I paused in mid-sentence wondering what was wrong. Then I realized that the last time I had heard the song the band was playing was that night.

A week ago that same feeling of awful loss was brought on by the scent of flaming brandy in a chafing dish at Delmonico's. Jacques and I had crepes suzette on the Titanic that night which they flamed next to our table. Such things involve dark memories irresistibly and there is no defense possible. I know now there will never be a way totally to escape that night. Time may help, but no complete release.

Much as we loved each other, there are still regrets. We needn't have been on that ship at all. Our trip to London was more a frolic than a necessity. Yes, we justified it on the basis that Jacques needed to stay close to Sam Harper as the Ripper case came to a close. But that was merely a flimsy excuse for a trip we took really more as a lark. But how can such thoughts possibly help or change the unchangeable?

I remember being struck by the awesome beauty of the starry firmament in the vault of the night sky as Sam and Jacques and I arrived on the boat deck. It was below freezing and there was an eerie sense of unreality in the way we and the others moved about. It simply was not possible the ship was sinking. And yet that immense floating palace was already pitched downward toward the bow, and slightly to the right. I believed Jacques' insistent assurances that she was heading for the bottom.

Sam left us quickly to see to the safety of the Corbett woman he had pledged to watch over. And Jacques was pushing me toward the lifeboat suspended over the inky blackness, rocking unsteadily as they loaded the passengers. It was more frightening to step over the void between the ship and that swaying lifeboat than to stay with the sinking ship.

I pulled back and clung to Jacques, clenching the lapels of his overcoat. It wasn't until Jacques shouted in my ear that one of us had to live for the sake of our little daughter back in New York that I knew I had to leave him in spite of my fear of that long step from the side of the ship to that swaying boat.

Still he had to shout again. This time — "For God's sake go!" — then he half lifted, half threw me across the black gap of night over the ocean 70 feet below. Then I was in the boat, only half full of men, women and children from first class and the boat dropped in jerky motions first the bow being higher, then the stern, toward the frigid water below. Finally the boat cut loose from the falls and we drifted slowly away from the Titanic, brightly lit from bow to stern, looking more like a carnival fairway than the crypt it would soon become.

The officer in charge of our boat asserted his authority with more deference to the aristocrats in our group than was conducive to the discipline that would be needed before the night gave way to dawn.

The boat had places for 40 people comfortably but there were only 22 of us ten of whom were men from first class, including Bruce Ismay the President of the White Star Line. Only later did we learn that Captain Smith and the designer of the ship both elected to perish with the ship rather than board the lifeboats. Ismay, I am told, has lived as a recluse the past year in shame over his actions which the press almost without exception came to characterize as cowardice. In fact, no man who survived the sinking is delivered from the need to defend his honor just to be alive.

Of course, anyone who first went down with the ship, as Sam did, and then was picked up and saved has claim to the role of genuine hero, but there are precious few of them.

It became clear at once there would be a conflict between those of us who wished to stay close to the ship to save whomever we might, and those who wished to move off to a considerable distance from the ship.

At first the justification to move off was based on the argument that we would be sucked under as the ship went down. Finally, however, the true reason was voiced openly. To attempt to save anyone, there were so many more aboard the Titanic than there were places for in the boats, that we would endanger ourselves. For those of us whose loved ones would soon be drowning in that freezing water, it was dismaying in the exreme. It seemed worth risking our own lives to save as many as could be accommodated in the boats.

I've since learned that the reaction of the people in our boat was, with one or two exceptions, the universal one, all the boats having sought their own safety rather than to attempt to save those in the water. For weeks, ships plying the North Atlantic trade routes were discovering bodies of those who died when the Titanic went down. Unhappily, Jacques' was not among them. Considering how many women in the boats left husbands aboard as I did, I find this attitude utterly perplexing. Is it possible there were none in the boats who felt as I did that we should stand by close to the sinking ship to help whomever we might?

Sam Harper was lucky enough to have been picked up by one of the few boats that ventured back into the area when the ship went down. Most of the boats stood off at a considerable distance, well beyond the range of any swimmer in that cold water no matter how strong his skills. By the time they ventured back, most who took to the water were already dead from cold. In 28 degree water no one could survive longer than a few minutes.

Even dry as we were and well clothed, the night was bitterly cold and how anyone survived once he immersed himself is more than I can understand, even if he was lucky enough to be picked up. And, of course, many — most didn't survive. Only Sam's foresight in fortifying himself with copious amounts of brandy saved him, no doubt.

Shocked as we were by our appalling circumstances, we still were aware of the rapidly declining prospects of those aboard as the ship pitched steadily forward approaching the vertical attitude in which it would make its final plunge.

We didn't know for sure if anyone in the world knew of our plight or how soon, if ever, help might come. And with all our frustrations, the worst of all, the lights of that ship sitting such a short distance away unmoving. It was, of course, the CALIFORNIA whose radioman had even intercepted Titanic's S.O.S. and whose lookouts saw our lights, but whose Captain didn't rouse himself from his sleep when notified repeatedly by his crewmen that our ship's flares were spotted. Not ten miles away she sat, able to have reached us in time to save all aboard.

We in the boat, standing off at a distance of perhaps 500 yards, could still hear much of what went on aboard. Someone was throwing deck chairs into the water to which swimmers might cling, no doubt to await rescue. This was a mixed blessing if any at all. When the passengers began jumping from the ship after the departure of the last of the boats, many jumpers struck this flotsam to their serious injury or death.

To the very last Titanic's lights were lit although toward the end they were more red than yellow as the power began to fail. But as the stern of the ship rose ever higher, a steady roar, a succession of bumping, grinding, thunderous sounds grew ever louder as everything in the ship fell from its place and slid forward. The hissing steam, as the funnels one by one submerged mingled with the cacophony of sounds from inside the hull and the crys of anguish of those on the decks or in the water.

Finally, the sounds of the forlorn humans aboard dominated all others in my impressions as great numbers began jumping from various parts of the ship. A wail of such piercing and poignant intensity rose from the Titanic as she made her final plunge, that all of us in our boat sobbed and cried aloud in sympathy for those dying before our eyes.

And still we waited before we began rowing back to the site of the sinking. With astonishing speed all sounds from those who took to the sea were extinguished. It took fifteen minutes or more to row back to her last position, but no sound betrayed that anyone was still alive, all having frozen to death or drowned in but a few minutes from the time they entered the waters.

I knew then there was no hope that Jacques had survived. I didn't really care if we were rescued or not. But the ultimate irony was the way the newspapers, upon our arrival broadcast perfectly incredible stories depicting the first class men in the boats as heroes. This, of course, lasted but a day until we were able to tell the truth and then deserved ignominy descended upon them. But seeing the men who survived by boarding the lifeboats with the women and children described in more appropriate terms did nothing to return our loved ones to us, and merely deepened the sense of utter devastation, disillusion and despair which descended upon us. For now my daughter and I live from day to day awaiting the healing hands of time to mitigate our pain and I have nothing left of Jacques except the memory of his love, a few mementoes and his writings — more, as I count my blessings, than some others were left.

Journal Entry of Samuel Harper
Dated July 7, 1930

Word reaches me that Arthur has made the final journey the nature of which he pondered so long. I must make plans for the trip to London to pay my respects. Though I will be too late for the funeral, I can, at least, attend a memorial service planned for Albert Hall on July 13th. But first I must attempt to record my feelings for a dear friend, and a thoroughly kindly and good person.

I pray Arthur's Irish luck did not desert him on the other side, and that there awaited him those he longed so passionately to see — Kingsley, Innis, his mother (Ma'am as he called her) to mention but a few. I have no doubt they were there, and I am likewise certain he is in a happier place than the one he left. It will not be long before I join him.

As I reflect upon the life of this man, who rendered such heroic service to so many for so long, I am at once moved by the feeling of awe at both the astonishing similarity of the belief system at which he arrived as compared to Mormonism, my chosen pathway, and the great chasm separating our views.

We see now only the vestigial remains of an attitude which reached a peak during World War I, nonetheless an ever-growing interest in the occult, in poltergeists, in strange appearances from the world beyond, in psychic communications of all kinds betrays the indestructible interest of all people to know who they are, why they're here and where they go after death. In a science-addicted world all such questions demand an answer definable by the senses. The world seems endlessly able to ignore the fact that things spiritual are discernible only by the spirit. The price of learning this truth, a sincere desire to know its truth, and obedience to the commandments, is one that even a good person like Arthur was unwilling (or unable?) to pay. How less likely are they to do so who, unlike him, are sunken in their fleshly attachments. And as they fail to satisfy this demand for sensory evidence by which means alone they can be convinced, they stumble ever deeper into drugs, alcohol and the Eastern belief systems, reincarnation, etc. I can imagine no worse expectation than the latter. Is it possible to take solace in a system in which one is required to return and return through successive lives to this putrefying world?

But mankind, I fear, will ever seek to define with scientific precision what can only be learned through the spirit, the tuning of the spirit to things spiritual coming only through a Christ-like life, Christ as he was, not as we are told he was by the established clergy.

It was to this kind of world that the shock and horror of World War dawned. And death became the ubiquitous visitor in every household. Seven million young men, the flower of the home islands and the Empire perished in shockingly wanton losses. Wave upon wave of the best and finest, on both sides, marched into the jaws of death without possibility of exemption. The efficiency of modern warfare in consuming human life exceeded the fondest expectations of satan himself. Not less than 25 million men from all the nations died in battle and millions more in the ranks of the civilians died of starvation and disease.

And thus, a world without faith suddenly found itself in desperate need of assurance that life does not end with the grave. It is not surprising in such circumstances that the interest in psychic phenomena reached such a peak. There was ample evidence coming from the battlefields to satisfy the craving.

Thousands of perfectly ordinary men (and therefore assumedly believable) reported seeing the ghostly apparition which came to be called the Angel of Mons, a figure in military garb who stopped the German onslaught by marching across no-man's land between the opposing forces. And tales are heard of legions of phantom cavalry squadrons incessantly advancing before the eyes of men not given to exaggeration, but whose fatigue was so great as to make it quite as likely the bearers of such stories had hallucinated.

Suffice it to say that interest in spiritualism undoubtedly reached a peak during this period when literal millions were surrendering their lives on the battlefield, leaving behind their sorrowing tens of millions. No one has recorded with more genuinely sympathetic emotion the feelings of those whose loved ones were lost in the war. Having lost his son, Kingsley, around whom his life centered, this is not surprising. But as I read, a few years ago, Doyle's books on Spiritualism I was impressed with the methodical way in which Arthur had ordered his belief system and how precisely he was able to state what those beliefs were. But more astonishing even than this is that, with but the most minor (but deadly) exceptions, his understanding of the nature of life beyond the grave was exactly what has been revealed by Mormon prophets.

As he himself had noted, the coincident origins of both Mormonism and Spiritualism in time and geography were interesting. I am quite certain though, it would never have occurred to him that Spiritualism is Satan's response to the restoration of the gospel by Joseph Smith.

As a true Victorian believer in science, Arthur was convinced of truths accepted by all 'enlightened' people, amongst which was Darwin's theory of evolution. And if man evolved from lower organisms, there was no Creation, no Garden of Eden, no fall, no atonement and no Messiah. Also the God of creation is an unknowable God. Modern understanding of psychology as propounded by Freud left no room for a devil. It was thus easy for him to proceed in the new 'Science' of Spiritualism unhampered by any fears that he was deceived by satan. And being a person of ultimate good will, he could not believe the spirits he was contacting could speak well of Christ and yet be evil. Only an essentially unsuspicious person, as surely Arthur was, could fail to recognize this supremely cunning deception — to invoke the name of the Saviour in luring people from the pathway that leads to Heavenly Father and the Saviour's presence.

Being essentially a suspicious person, I was not so trusting either of Science or Satan. Perhaps that is why Arthur was a writer of fiction and I am a detective, a profession in which suspicion is the absolutely indispensible characteristic. Without question, it is why we trod such different paths in reaching our separate philosophical destinations.

I am too familiar with counterfeits not to recognize a good one when I see it. And when Satan makes a counterfeit, it is, to most humans, undetectable. It is clear that the appeal of Spiritualism is generally not to the ungodly. The followers of this philosophy are genuinely seeking truth within their best understanding of Christlike ideals. The Churches have failed them, it's true, but they seek the best part of Christianity without the excess baggage the standard churches insist upon in their dogmas. And therein lies the trap into which the unwary fall including, without doubt, my good friend Arthur Conan Doyle.

By a fallacious belief that man evolved from an ape he concluded there could have been no fall, no transgression requiring atonement. Therefore while admiring Christ, he and they deny his divinity. They thus ignore Christ's direct scriptural warning that none can come to the Father save in His name.

But equally important, they proceed in ignorance of the requirements which existed in the ancient church and which have been restored through Joseph Smith's mission. These require that earthly ordinances are necessary to advancement in the hereafter. True, we can perform these ordinances for the dead and the power of such ordinances can be made available to those beyond the veil when the dead are finally ready spiritually to elect to use them. But the devil's plan is to keep men from discovering the restored gospel. To this end he brought spiritualism into the world with its false consolations for those grieving over the dead. And many, without the truth, accepting satan's false doctrines undoubtedly lose their way and are drawn into satan's net.

The tragedy, of course, is that they die in a condition which frequently determines the level of their potential advancement in the spirit world. All Mormons know there are three levels of advancement in the afterlife, and they seek the highest level wherein Christ dwells — the Celestial Kingdom. Arthur died thinking all can ultimately have access to the Celestial Kingdom. Such is not the case if they refused the gospel in this life.

I pray Heavenly Father will not feel Arthur has refused the truth. I don't believe he has, and I will see that the necessary ordinances are performed on his behalf — a final acknowledgement of a true friend, a kind human being and a benefactor to mankind.

But finally I am most impressed with how central to human experience are both Mormonism, God's gift to the world, and Spiritualism, Satan's counterfeit, which is rapidly being corrupted into a profane interest in all things psychic.

My respect for the adversary increases steadily as I perceive the cunning with which he devises his ruses. For Spiritualism is 90% true, but the false 10% can be, and often is, fatal to the eternal progression of its followers which is Satan's sole aim.

My love for my friend is such I can but hope he comes to perceive the truth of these matters in that kingdom where now he dwells. Like King Arthur for whom he was named, the epitaph Jean has told me she intends to erect over Arthur's grave is apt:

Steel True,
Blade Straight.

Editor's Postscript

The man who returned to New York City on the Carpathia with the rest of the survivors of the Titanic was not the Samuel Harper who had left such a brief time prior thereto. And it was not only the ghastly events associated with Titanic's sinking that wrought the change.

It is apparent from his journals that life had taken on a new focus for my father even had there never occurred the disillusionment all the world felt, the betrayal of the modern belief in science's great potential, by the sinking of the 'unsinkable' ship.

In fact, the blasphemy uttered in so characterizing the Titanic was clear to many, even a few aboard, just as my father had recognized the idolatrous nature of the modern commitment to science. But the sinking was a watershed occurrence in all our lives and serves perfectly well as an event from which to date subsequent developments. The world did indeed enter the modern era with the sinking of the Titanic.

In truth, it can be misleading to ascribe too much of the change in my father's life as having resulted from the trauma of Titanic's passing. True enough, with Futrelle's death no chronicler of father's exploits remained. And, in a sense, father may have felt vaguely responsible for his death — that Jacques was, in a sense, a victim sacrificed on the altar of Samuel Harper's (and, in frankness, Jacques' own) pride. For from that time forward not only was there no chronicle maintained but also none was desired. Others offered to serve as Doyle had and as Futrelle intended to do, but all were rejected.

It was as though he abjured any activity that might be construed as prideful. I think it is safe to say that in adopting his new religion father decided much more should change in his life than abstention from a few minor vices. The destruction in the sinking of his files of past adventures thus came to have both a real and a symbolic meaning. It can, in truth, be said that one important part of Sam Harper, the detective whose fictional exploits entertained the world died on the Titanic.

He maintained his business relationships but only long enough to effect a sale of the business and an orderly transfer of his responsibilities to his clients to the new owners.

But with the business ties severed which had prevented his returning to his homeland, he did not seriously consider taking up, once again, permanent residence in England even though my stepmother was perfectly willing to do so if he so desired. He (and his family) spent frequent holidays there, but America was 'home.' Doyle was mystified, perhaps even hurt, by this transfer of allegiance, but their relationship was never quite the same again after father's conversion. Doyle knew how father's new beliefs caused him to feel about spiritualism and while he still talked like the old comrade of yesteryears, there was little of the fire left in his feelings.

It is apparent that father had learned much as a consequence of the Fenster case that led him to conclude that Europe would surely go to war and that America, just as surely, would join in the fray. He made half-hearted attempts to influence those in power to see that Europe need not go to war, and that, if she did, America need not be drawn into the battle.

But all he had come to understand of the dynamics of European politics had convinced him the Kaiser could not abdicate the leadership of Germany's thrust toward world domination. And just as surely, he knew Britain must resist the establishment of German hegemony over Europe.

He saw this web of conflicting interests in both its Biblical context, that of the fulfillment of prophecy as to what must happen to the children of Israel (the Anglo-Saxons) in the latter days, and in its secular or profane context, that which worldly men call 'Realpolitik' — divorced from any philosophical or religious considerations.

He came to believe that the two must ever be one and yet be separate. Men for their own (they believe) reasons must pursue objectives they regard as materialistically profitable to themselves and their nations, and yet, they must, unknowingly, fulfill prophecy.

To attempt to convince the man pursuing what he regards as practical, advantageous ends that he must start to see his actions within the framework of prophecy and as having overriding ethical and religious consequences that must supersede the practical objectives he pursues is inane and fruitless — rather like trying to convince swine that pearls are valuable.

All unknowing, mankind must act out a role in the great drama, and whether on the side of righteousness or evil, the drama described in Scripture must be played out. Evil men sometimes deliberately achieving evil but still contributing some good unintentionally. Good men sometimes deliberately achieving good, but still contributing some evil unintentionally.

But through all this confusion he saw the necessity for men to examine their lives and to let righteousness enter the only premises over which a man has any control — his own life.

Samuel Harper may have appeared to Doyle and other 'practical men' to have withdrawn from the real world. The most practical of men, my father, saw that 'practical men' will forever have 'practical' reasons for going to war, for victimizing the disadvantaged, for, indeed, causing mankind everywhere to bear the heavy yoke and the bitter consequences occasioned by all the corrupt projects of 'practical men'. Just as 1500 innocent and not-so-innocent people paid the price for the blasphemy of those who came to believe their own lies and thought the Titanic unsinkable.

And so, while he appeared to his friends and former associates to have withdrawn from reality, Samuel Harper, to the end, pursued the only realistic solution to human problems that exists — for mankind to live the Christian ideal, the Gospel of Jesus Christ in all its fullness. In ways as quiet and unostentatious as his former adventures had been flamboyant, he worked to the end. One on one he travailed with the honest in heart he chanced to meet to bring about the change in their lives we all desire but which only can come when we resolve to live our lives better.

He had, finally, done what he hoped to do all his life — to pursue truth and once discerned, however difficult, to act upon it.

But lest it be thought his life had become joyless and arid, it should be emphasized that he regarded his new life as 'most rewarding', employing his own often-used phrase. He applied his talents as a sleuth to the search for the genealogical records of our forebears and he enjoyed the deep satisfaction of seeing the ordinances performed in the temple for our dead by which each of them might be enabled to join our family circle in the Celestial Kingdom. "An opportunity," he often said, "to repay those to whom I owe so much and heretofore have been able to give so little." And he made frequent trips to Salt Lake City where he and Cornelia visited the Temple to participate in the ordinances for the dead. It was as rewarding as it was different from all his prior life had been and he savored this new, subtle nectar, the lovely fragrance of a life in Christ, as a connoisseur of the more rarefied delights only the spiritually awakened can appreciate.

Salt Lake City
April 15, 1975